Frontier Military Series
XXIV

Guarding the Overland Trails

The Eleventh Ohio Cavalry in the Civil War

By

Robert Huhn Jones

THE ARTHUR H. CLARK COMPANY
Spokane, Washington
2005

Also by Robert Huhn Jones:

The Civil War in the Northwest, 1960

The Centennial Years (with Fred A. Shannon), 1967

The Roads to Russia: Lend-Lease to the Soviet Union, 1969

Disrupted Decades: The Civil War and Reconstruction Years, 1973

My Dear Carrie: Civil War Letters of George K. Pardee and Family (ed.), 1994

Fields of Conflict: The Civil war and Reconstruction in America, 1998

LIBRARY OF CONGRESS CATALOG CARD NUMBER 2005007705
ISBN 0-87062-340-0

Library of Congress Cataloging-in-Publication Data

Jones, Robert Huhn, 1927–
Guarding the overland trails : the Eleventh Ohio Cavalry in the Civil War / by Robert Huhn Jones.
p. cm. — (Frontier military series ; 24)
Includes bibliographical references and index.
ISBN 0-87062-340-0 (hardcover : alk. paper)
1. United States. Army. Ohio Cavalry Regiment, 11th (1863-1866) 2. United States—History—Civil War, 1861–1865—Regimental histories. 3. Ohio—History—Civil War, 1861–1865—Regimental histories. 4. Overland Trails—History—19th century. 5. Indians of North America—Wars—1862–1865. 6. Indians of North America—Wars—West (U.S.) 7. West (U.S.)—History—Civil War, 1861-1865—Cavalry operations. 8. United States—History—Civil War, 1861–1865—Cavalry operations. I. Title. II. Series.
E525.611th .J66 2005
973.7'471—dc22
2005007705

for those who followed us:
Rob, Judy, Kevin, Jennifer, Gretchen, and Len
and those who followed them:
Eric, Matt, Esme, Nicholas, Dylan, and Kaio

Table of Contents

Illustrations

Maps

The maps are not cartographically or professionally drawn, but are approximations. They cannot include all the information one might prefer regarding specific locations, but an effort has been made to include as much detail as possible. Except for one map, states and territorial boundaries have been excluded. *Based on maps by author.*

Acknowledgements

I owe a great deal to Hedy J. Jones, Ph.D., my wife, who proved to be an invaluable researcher. Historical societies and libraries across the country will recognize her inquiries that came to them via e-mail. Many thanks to those who cooperated with her, especially historical society and university librarians in Colorado, Kansas, Montana, Nebraska, and Wyoming, who promptly sent copies of articles and other items and who participated in many inter-library loans. Heyward Schrock, Photograph Historian, at the Wyoming State Archives provided valuable advice and assistance. The gracious aid of librarians at the Denver Public Library's Western History Collection was especially valuable. Thanks also to archivists at the Fort Collins Public Library. Most particularly, many thanks to Sandra Lowry, Librarian at the Fort Laramie National Historic Site, who patiently provided files and assisted my wife and I with research. I also owe a large debt to the readers who helped to improve this manuscript, scholars, colleagues, and fellow emeriti Jerome Mushkat and Keith Bryant, Jr.; as well as Bob Clark and Ariane C. Smith at the Arthur H. Clark Company. The remaining shortcomings are mine.

Introduction

By the time the American Civil War erupted, a geographically vast United States reached from ocean to ocean, spanning over 3,100 miles from Boston on the Atlantic to San Francisco on the Pacific. Most of the population was clustered in the thirty-two states east of the 95th parallel (except for Kansas and Texas), or roughly east of the Missouri River. By 1860 two new states had appeared on the Pacific rim, Oregon and California. Extensive barriers of massive and often forbidding mountain ranges, as well as arid deserts and plains, separated these recent additions from the older members of the republic. On a direct line, the distance from Omaha on the Missouri River to the valleys of Oregon or California measured over 1,600 miles, but it took intrepid explorers and brave emigrants many additional miles, winding up, down, and around, to find passages through the awesome obstacles.

Aside from spending weeks at sea, rounding the southern tip of South America or interrupting the voyage by crossing the Isthmus of Panama or Nicaragua, the way west to the Pacific had to be by land. Several trails, none easy going, provided the way. The main route went from Independence, Missouri, or Omaha, Nebraska Territory, through the Platte River valley, vaulted over South Pass, and divided at the fur trade post of Fort Hall. The northern branch wound on to Oregon, the southern to California. This was the Oregon-California Trail. Mormon emigrants, unhappy with often violent discrimination east of the Missouri and mistrustful of the United States government, had colonized the Salt Lake Valley west of South Pass and south of Fort Hall. The government distrusted them in return, suspicious of their loyalty and critical of the Mormon's polygamous religious faith. To the south, but also departing from Independence, ran the Santa Fé Trail, following the Arkansas River in central Kansas, meandering to Santa Fé, New Mexico Territory. Emigrants then followed other trails along the Rio Grande south, turned west to cross Apache Pass, and eventually ended in southern California.

By these routes, travelers by the thousands crossed through the lands of Native Americans, who, by the 1860s, no longer saw them as harmless wanderers, but considered them troublesome and destructive trespassers. As the United States government began providing vital mail service between the far western states and the rest of the Union, it used these same trails. In 1861 California and Oregon were tied to the Union by the telegraph's thin and fragile wire pinned to slender wooden poles that paralled the Oregon Trail. In a time of national crisis, a monstrous Civil War, ordinary communication between the Union's widely-separated parts was essential. Consider also that California since 1849 had produced substantial amounts of gold, with more being found in other far-western areas, and this useful commodity served to help finance a war that cost far more than the government had ever predicted. The links across the mountains, deserts, and prairies became important, both politically and financially, to the Union.

Before the Civil War, units of the regular army struggled to protect these western lifelines, but the Union's pressing need for troops at the war's outset induced the War Department to call most of them east, leaving the great trails and the mail and telegraph, along with freighters, emigrants, and settlers, with very little security. By 1862, with the war in the East moving into its second bloody year and with western tribesmen poised to close the roads, the Union realized that an emergency existed. Volunteer soldiers made up the vast bulk of the army, and it was to them that the government looked for help.

In the spring of 1862, prodded by the War Department and nervous western territorial governors, Major General Henry W. Halleck reached into the military depot at Benton Barracks, St. Louis, and pulled out a battalion of newly-arrived Ohio cavalry. Already equipped, they were handy and could move west rapidly. Halleck surely hoped those inexperienced troopers, fewer than four hundred of them, would be ample. He could spare no others, as he desperately needed soldiers for higher priority tasks such as keeping Missouri in the Union, reclaiming Kentucky, and opening the Mississippi River. At the moment, western trail security, though necessary, seemed less critical.

That explained why in May 1862 an Ohio volunteer cavalry battalion turned up astride the Oregon Trail at Fort Laramie, in today's Wyoming, so far from the battlefields of the Civil War proper, and so very far from home. At the time, they were properly Companies A, B, C, and D of the 6th Ohio Volunteer Cavalry. The rest of the regiment still remained at Camp Dennison, Ohio, lacking horses and other equipment. They would never follow the lead battalion west, but subsequently replaced these companies with new recruits, and fought in the East. The western units, in the summer of 1862, became the First Independent Battalion Ohio Volunteer Cavalry, and a year later, after more Ohio recruiting, added additional companies to become the 11th Ohio Volunteer Cavalry.

The essential task before them from 1862 to 1866 was to guard roughly seven hundred miles of the Oregon Trail, with its mail and telegraph, from near Scotts Bluff to the South Pass. Later in 1862, when the mail coaches moved south to the Overland Trail, from Fort Collins to Bridger's Pass, that additional duty also fell to them, adding another two hundred miles of road. Curiously, the government expected a few Ohioans to protect nine hundred miles of trail, or about three soldiers to the mile, when possible opponents could muster thousands of eager warriors. This was perhaps not so surprising, as superior officers in headquarters remote from the West had virtually no understanding of either the distances and geography or its climatic conditions. They also held misconceptions of the numbers, fighting ability, and legitimate grievances of Native Americans, whom they considered merely uncivilized nuisances.

Native American vexation multiplied as the trickle of emigrants and other travelers became a vigorous flood in the 1850s. Time after time during that tumultuous decade the regular army engaged Native Americans in conflict, generating additional rancor on both sides. Even as most of the regular troops departed in 1861 and 1862, accumulated Native American bitterness accelerated just as the Ohio battalion arrived in their midst. For some months the Ohioans encountered no serious Native American hostility, but they quickly learned how to treat with the few unfriendly tribesmen found among others who seemed peaceful. As important, the Ohioans came to grips with survival in an often hostile climate, unfamiliar terrain, lonely and dangerous tiny postings, and immense distances.

Just over a year after reporting to Fort Laramie, Lieutenant Colonel William O. Collins, the unit's commander, along with a few others, returned to Ohio to enlist additional companies and boost their strength. The new recruits arrived at Fort Laramie in October 1863, after assisting in the pursuit of Confederate General John H. Morgan when he led an ill-fated raid across southern Indiana and Ohio. They also participated in the chase after Confederate guerrilla leader William C. Quantrill and his band following their savage sack of Lawrence, Kansas. These recruits formed Companies E, F, G, and H of the newly designated 11th Ohio. Many had previously served in other Ohio regiments, and while experienced as soldiers, few knew anything about campaigning in the West. Additional recruits arrived in 1864, forming the basis of Companies I and K. These were largely "Galvanized Yankees" enlisted from among Confederate prisoners of war. Many were experienced cavalrymen. By 1865 most of the enlistments of the old first battalion expired, and those who wished returned to Ohio. But a number reenlisted, and filled the ranks of Company L.

Even so, the days of the Civil War volunteer army in the West came to an end, if not as quickly as many wished. Confederates laid down their arms in April and May 1865, allowing eastern armies to begin demobilization. But by then Native Americans across the West had risen up against the white interlopers. This western conflict erupted with unparalleled fury in November 1864, after Colorado volunteers massacred Cheyennes and Arapahos camped at Sand Creek, Colorado Territory, southeast of Denver. United as never before, the Sioux joined their grieving brothers and vented their rage upon all whites from Kansas to Colorado, from the Black Hills to the Arkansas River. Throughout 1865 the overland roads, never safe, completely closed from time to time as warriors disrupted the mail, tore up the telegraph, killed emigrants, and looted their wagons. Western commanders struggled to meet the challenge and begged for reinforcements. The army hurriedly sent more volunteers west, but when the Civil War ended, those who had arrived, most having been bloodied in the eastern war, demanded at the very least their discharge. If it was not forthcoming, they often deserted or mutinied.

Still charged with keeping the roads safe, the mail moving, and the telegraph ticking, western generals planned campaigns to conquer Native Americans who would not be pacified. At the same time, President Andrew Johnson's government, seeking a return to peacetime conditions with sharply reduced appropriations for the military, proceeded swiftly with demobilization, while redoubling efforts to treat for peace with angry tribesmen. Even so, one last expedition, designed to end the continued threat to safe overland travel, took place late in 1865. While most of the Civil War volunteers in the West were gone by the end of the year, not until July 1866 was the 11th Ohio able to return home. They were the final volunteer troops from Ohio, and among the last from any state raised during the Civil War, to be discharged.

Unlike most Civil War volunteers, 11th Ohio troopers fought Native Americans, escorted emigrants and mail, and operated, rebuilt, and restrung the telegraph. They built and rebuilt tiny stations and other posts along the roads, died in combat, and froze to death in in winter storms. For the most part, these Ohioans were strung out along the roads in small detachments, seldom in company strength, and the regiment never served or fought as one. When other volunteer units subsequently appeared on the scene, particularly the 7th Iowa Volunteer Cavalry and detachments of Kansas, Colorado, and United States Volunteers (other "Galvanized Yankees"), they soldiered with them.

The 11th Ohio, along with other volunteer troops struggling to protect overland communication during the Civil

War, became players in a spectacle of military strategy replete with incompetence and confusion, issues of Native American relations, and the vagaries of local and national politics. Army commanders in offices at St. Louis, Washington, D.C., and even at times Fort Leavenworth were far removed from daily operations along the roads. They knew little about the geography or the fickle climate. Nor did they understand western Native American life and concerns. Even in the West many officers could not tell the difference between a Sioux or a Cheyenne, much less one band of any Native American nation from another of the same tribe. This became a frequent cause of trouble.

Although orders from higher headquarters directly affected troopers on duty along the roads, their daily routines and lives were most immediately influenced by storms, blistering heat, numbing cold, supplies received late or never, unrelieved isolation, and the Native Americans. To understand the conditions of their service, one must observe the local conditions and soldierly life, something not experienced by commanders in remote locations. The trials of individuals on the scene, many from the 11th Ohio, provide a window from which to view the daily life of troopers on the roads in the West.

The 11th Ohio, astride two of the major trans-continental lines of communication and supply, is the the focus of this study. More so than other Civil War volunteers who followed them, the Ohioans left lasting impressions. Camp Collins, an important station on the Overland road, became Fort Collins, bearing the name of the original commander of the 11th. It remains today as the city of Fort Collins, Colorado. Casper, Wyoming, was named for Lieutenant Caspar Collins, who died in a bloody fight at what was then Platte Bridge Station. Major General John Pope renamed that place for Colonel Collins's son, but was not responsible for the misspelling of the lieutenant's first name.[1]

Lieutenant Colonel Collins proved to be a most unusual regimental commander when compared with many others. From the first, he made every effort to befriend and understand the Native Americans with whom he interacted. He learned to tell a Sioux from a Cheyenne and, along with his son, mastered a smattering of their languages. He intended to play fair with the tribes, and became upset when they were treated otherwise. Many Native Americans camped in the vicinity of his Fort Laramie headquarters, and so long as Collins was there they remained peaceful. Subsequent commanders, generally less knowledgeable, became uneasy with their proximity and suspicious of their intentions; the Native Americans reciprocated with thinly veiled hostility.

Historian Clyde C. Walton wrote that "the 11th Ohio Volunteer Cavalry [was] one of the most interesting but least publicized regiments of the Civil War." Walton quoted an Ohio official source during their last year on duty as but one example of their operation:

> From March 1 to September 5, 1865, a single company of this Regiment erected five posts, guarded one hundred and fifty miles of Pacific Telegraph line, and its several detachments had thirteen engagements with Indians. [Later,] two companies, on an expedition to Powder and Tongue Rivers, took part in a charge upon . . . an Indian Village, marched twelve hundred miles and were out fifty-eight days.[2]

---

[1]The present spelling, "Casper," apparently was due to a clerical error by the Post Office Department in Washington, D.C., according to historian Agnes Wright Spring. In any event, spelling was not a long suit in the West. For example, Fort Kearny, named after Brevet Major General Stephen Watts Kearny, provided the name for nearby Kearney, Nebraska.

[2]Eugene F. Ware, *The Indian War of 1864* (Lincoln: University of Nebraska Press, 1994), Walton's notes, 448–49. This Bison Book is a reprint of a 1960 edition published by St. Martin's Press, New York. The original edition was published in Topeka, Kansas, by Crane in 1911. The last part of Walton's quote was from *Official Roster of the Soldiers of the State of Ohio in the War of the Rebellion, 1861–1866* (Akron, Ohio: Werner Ptg. & Litho. Co., 1891), vol. 11, 548.

Troopers of the 11th Ohio served on the Oregon and Overland roads, truly the primary lines of communication between the settled parts of the Union east of the Missouri River and the newer states on the Pacific coast. This study, then, does not include all of the existing and often secondary overland routes. The steamboat waterway up the Missouri River to Fort Benton, Dakota Territory, is one such example. Steamboats had made it as far as Fort Benton by 1859, from which place travelers could move overland southwest to the recently discovered gold fields in Montana Territory. From Fort Benton travelers also could move west over the recently opened Mullan Road to Fort Walla Walla, Washington Territory. The Northern Emigrant Route, running northwest across the Dakota Plains and west along the Missouri River to the Milk River and its tributaries terminated at Fort Benton. Except for the Mullan Road (named after its builder, Captain John Mullan, Second Artillery), constructed by the military, the other northern routes had been opened and used by fur traders for decades. While of growing importance for emigration and commerce, these routes were much less heavily traveled than the Oregon-California or Overland roads, were longer, and were not mail or telegraph routes.[3] This study also does not focus on the Santa Fé Trail, except so far as events there impacted affairs on the western extensions of the Platte River road.

While both the Civil War and western history in the nineteenth century have provided fertile fields for historical investigation, few historians have focused on the plight of the overland roads during the Civil War or the impact of the war on the area they crossed. Fortunately there are a few

[3]Some of this story has already been told for the Civil War years in Robert Huhn Jones, *The Civil War in the Northwest: Nebraska, Wisconsin, Iowa, Minnesota and the Dakotas* (Norman: University of Oklahoma Press, 1960). The Mullan Road had a fairly large migration in 1862, the same year steamboats from St. Louis brought 350 emigrants to Fort Benton, Montana Territory.

papers, a number of reminiscences and diaries, as well as official records that bring life to the story of these devoted volunteer soldiers.

The 11th Ohio played a crucial role during the Civil War years on the overland roads. The first battalion sent to Fort Laramie in 1862 had not volunteered to serve out west. It had enlisted to fight Confederates. Those who enlisted in 1863 and 1864, on the other hand, knew their destination when they signed up. If they sought adventure, they found it. They carried on a titanic stuggle of their own just to keep the roads open, while vastly larger armies, in which their brothers fought, bled, and died, labored to preserve the Union in the East. No war correspondents from eastern newspapers appeared to write about the valor or tribulations of the 11th Ohio or the other volunteers who shared their fate. The thunder of the greater war drowned out the no less violent and deadly war in the West along the overland roads.

Maps of Posts and Stations on the Overland Trails

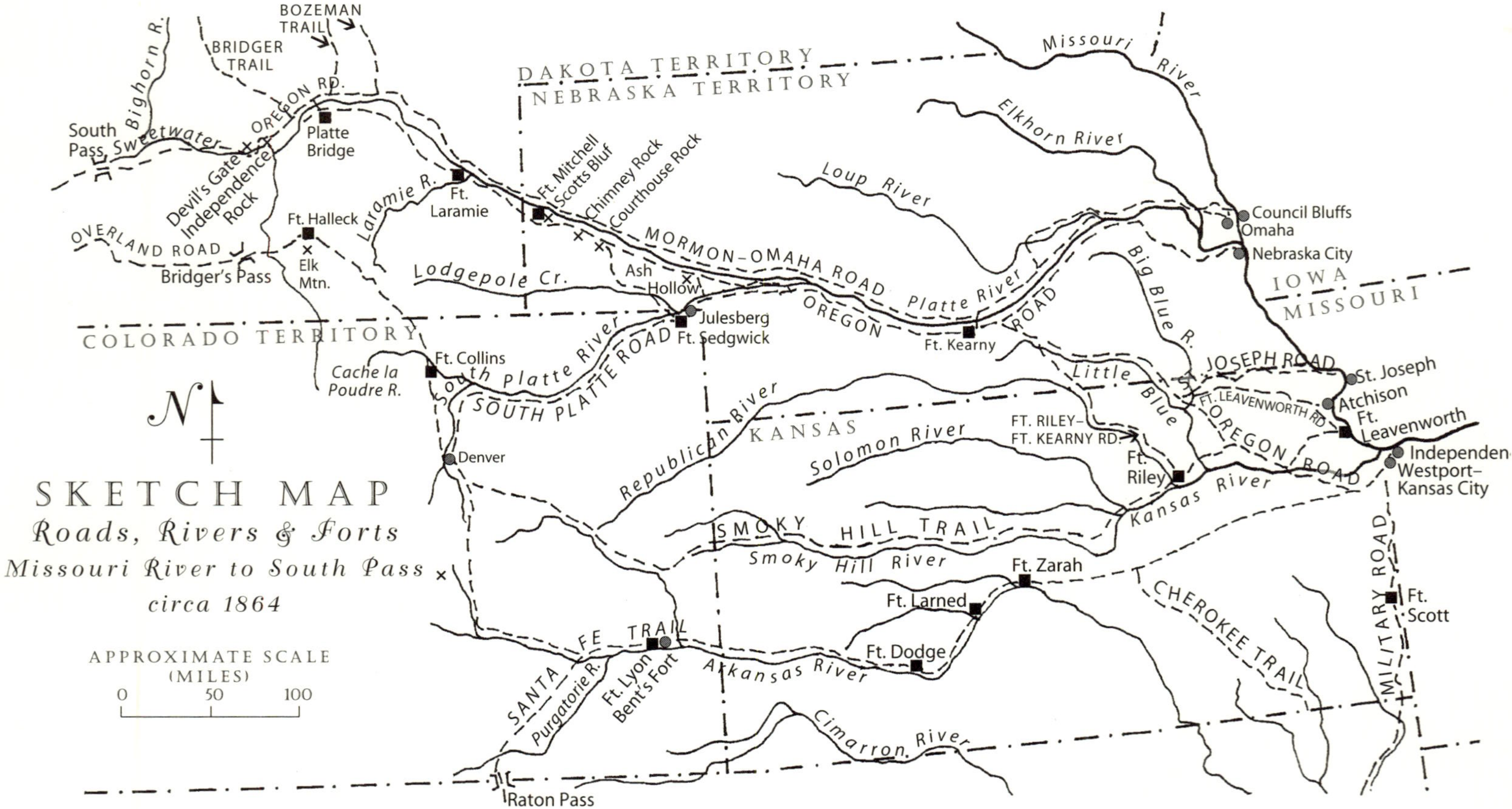
SKETCH MAP
Roads, Rivers & Forts
Missouri River to South Pass
circa 1864
APPROXIMATE SCALE
(MILES)
0
50
100
DAKOTA TERRITORY
NEBRASKA TERRITORY
COLORADO TERRITORY
KANSAS
IOWA
MISSOURI
Missouri River
Elkhorn River
Loup River
Platte River
Big Blue R.
Little Blue
Republican River
Solomon River
Smoky Hill River
Kansas River
Arkansas River
Cimarron River
Purgatorie R.
South Platte River
Cache la Poudre R.
Lodgepole Cr.
Laramie R.
Sweetwater
Bighorn R.
BOZEMAN TRAIL
BRIDGER TRAIL
OREGON RD.
OVERLAND ROAD
MORMON-OMAHA ROAD
OREGON ROAD
SOUTH PLATTE ROAD
JOSEPH ROAD
FT. LEAVENWORTH RD.
FT. RILEY–FT. KEARNY RD.
SMOKY HILL TRAIL
SANTA FE TRAIL
CHEROKEE TRAIL
MILITARY ROAD
South Pass
Devil's Gate
Independence Rock
Platte Bridge
Ft. Halleck
Elk Mtn.
Bridger's Pass
Ft. Laramie
Ft. Mitchell
Scotts Bluf
Chimney Rock
Courthouse Rock
Ash Hollow
Julesberg
Ft. Sedgwick
Ft. Collins
Denver
Ft. Kearny
Council Bluffs
Omaha
Nebraska City
St. Joseph
Atchison
Ft. Leavenworth
Independen
Westport–Kansas City
Ft. Riley
Ft. Zarah
Ft. Larned
Ft. Dodge
Ft. Lyon
Bent's Fort
Ft. Scott
Raton Pass

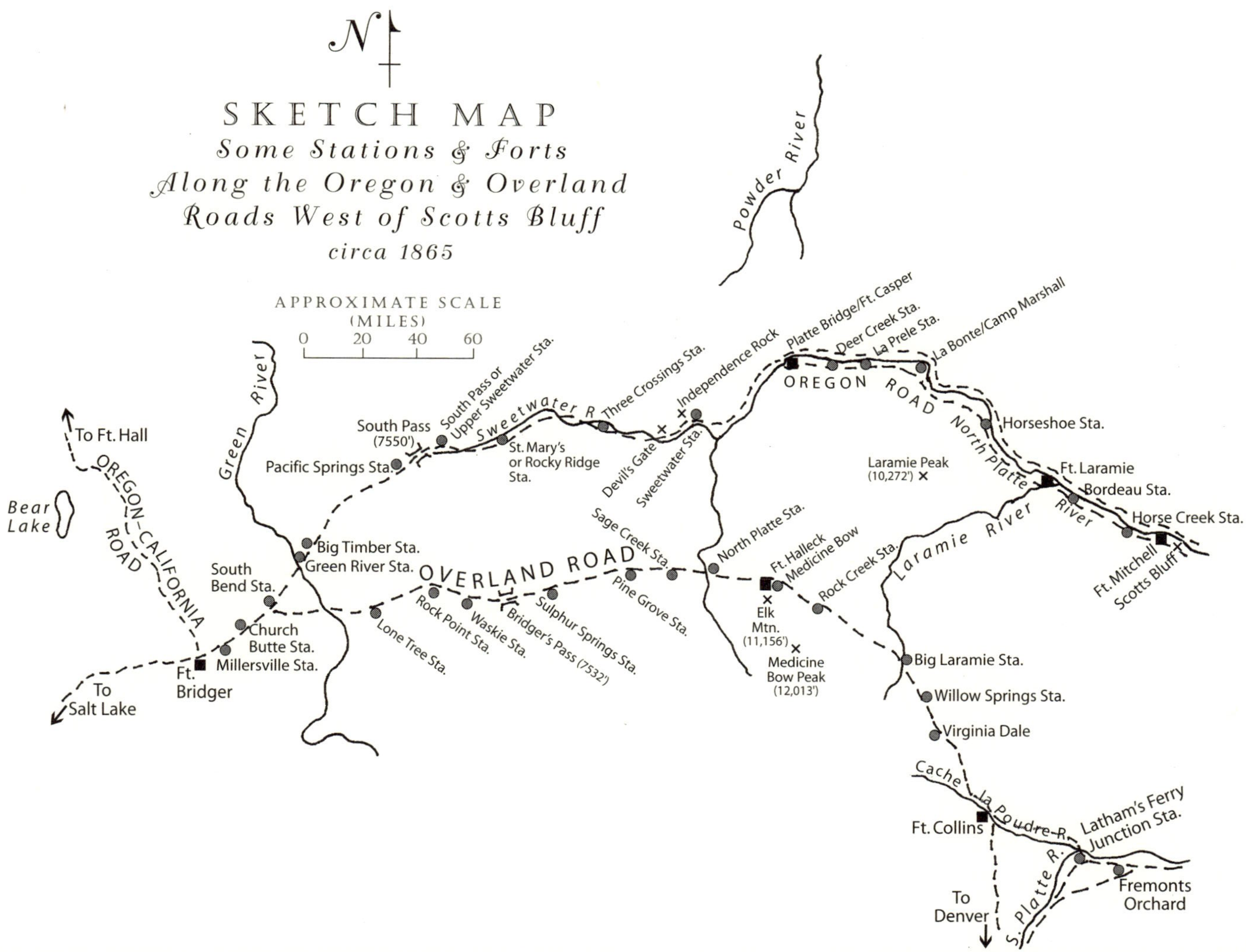
N
SKETCH MAP
Some Stations & Forts
Along the Oregon & Overland
Roads West of Scotts Bluff
circa 1865
APPROXIMATE SCALE
(MILES)
0 20 40 60
Powder River
Green River
To Ft. Hall
OREGON–CALIFORNIA ROAD
Bear Lake
To Salt Lake
Ft. Bridger
Millersville Sta.
Church Butte Sta.
South Bend Sta.
Big Timber Sta.
Green River Sta.
Pacific Springs Sta.
South Pass (7550')
South Pass or Upper Sweetwater Sta.
Sweetwater R.
St. Mary's or Rocky Ridge Sta.
Three Crossings Sta.
Devil's Gate
Sweetwater Sta.
Independence Rock
Platte Bridge/Ft. Casper
Deer Creek Sta.
La Prele Sta.
La Bonte/Camp Marshall
OREGON ROAD
Horseshoe Sta.
North Platte River
Laramie Peak (10,272')
Ft. Laramie
Bordeau Sta.
Horse Creek Sta.
Ft. Mitchell
Scotts Bluff
OVERLAND ROAD
Lone Tree Sta.
Rock Point Sta.
Waskie Sta.
Bridger's Pass (7532')
Sulphur Springs Sta.
Pine Grove Sta.
Sage Creek Sta.
North Platte Sta.
Ft. Halleck
Medicine Bow
Elk Mtn. (11,156')
Medicine Bow Peak (12,013')
Rock Creek Sta.
Laramie River
Big Laramie Sta.
Willow Springs Sta.
Virginia Dale
Cache La Poudre R.
Ft. Collins
Latham's Ferry
Junction Sta.
Fremonts Orchard
To Denver
S. Platte R.

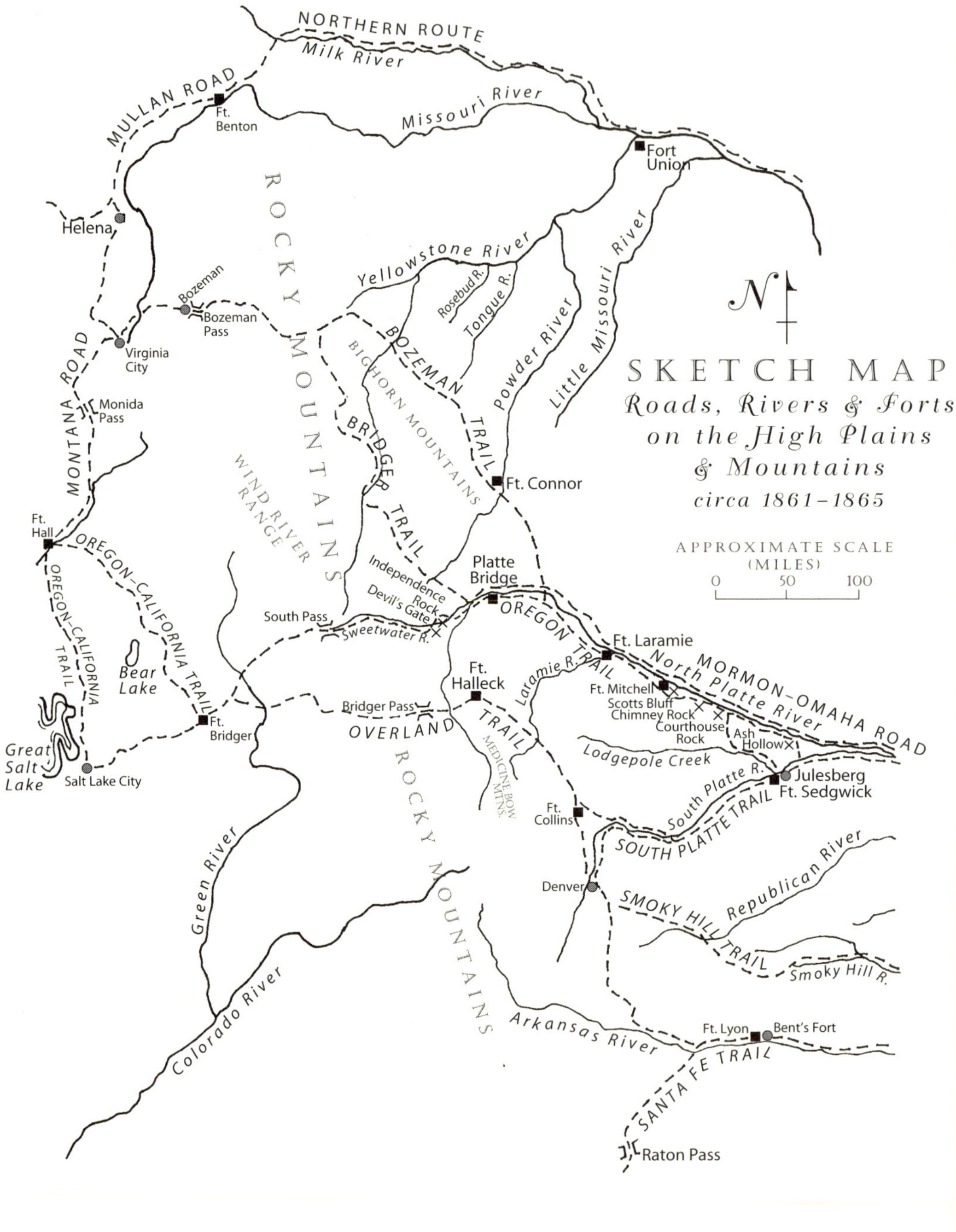
SKETCH MAP
Roads, Rivers & Forts on the High Plains & Mountains
circa 1861–1865
APPROXIMATE SCALE (MILES)
0 50 100
NORTHERN ROUTE
Milk River
MULLAN ROAD
Ft. Benton
Missouri River
Fort Union
Helena
ROCKY MOUNTAINS
Yellowstone River
Rosebud R.
Tongue R.
Powder River
Little Missouri River
Bozeman
Bozeman Pass
Virginia City
MONTANA ROAD
Monida Pass
BIGHORN MOUNTAINS
BOZEMAN TRAIL
BRIDGER TRAIL
Ft. Connor
WIND RIVER RANGE
Ft. Hall
OREGON–CALIFORNIA TRAIL
OREGON–CALIFORNIA TRAIL
Platte Bridge
Independence Rock
Devil's Gate
South Pass
Sweetwater R.
OREGON TRAIL
Ft. Laramie
MORMON–OMAHA ROAD
North Platte River
Bear Lake
Ft. Halleck
Laramie R.
Ft. Mitchell
Scotts Bluff
Chimney Rock
Courthouse Rock
Ash Hollow
Great Salt Lake
Salt Lake City
Ft. Bridger
Bridger Pass
OVERLAND TRAIL
MEDICINE BOW MTNS.
Lodgepole Creek
Julesberg
Ft. Sedgwick
South Platte R.
SOUTH PLATTE TRAIL
Ft. Collins
ROCKY MOUNTAINS
Green River
Denver
SMOKY HILL TRAIL
Republican River
Smoky Hill R.
Colorado River
Arkansas River
Ft. Lyon
Bent's Fort
SANTA FE TRAIL
Raton Pass

N
SKETCH MAP
Little Blue Valley
circa 1864
APPROXIMATE SCALE
(MILES)
0
5
10
Platte River
Valley Station
to Fort Kearny 10 mi.
OREGON ROAD
Summit or Sand Hill Station
Thirty-two Mile Creek
Thirty-two Mile Station
Elm Creek Sta.
Lone Tree Station
Pawnee Cr.
Spring Ranch
Pawnee Ranch
Little Blue River
Liberty Farm Station
Little Blue Station
Oak Grove Station
Kiowa Station
to junction with St. Joseph Road 50 miles

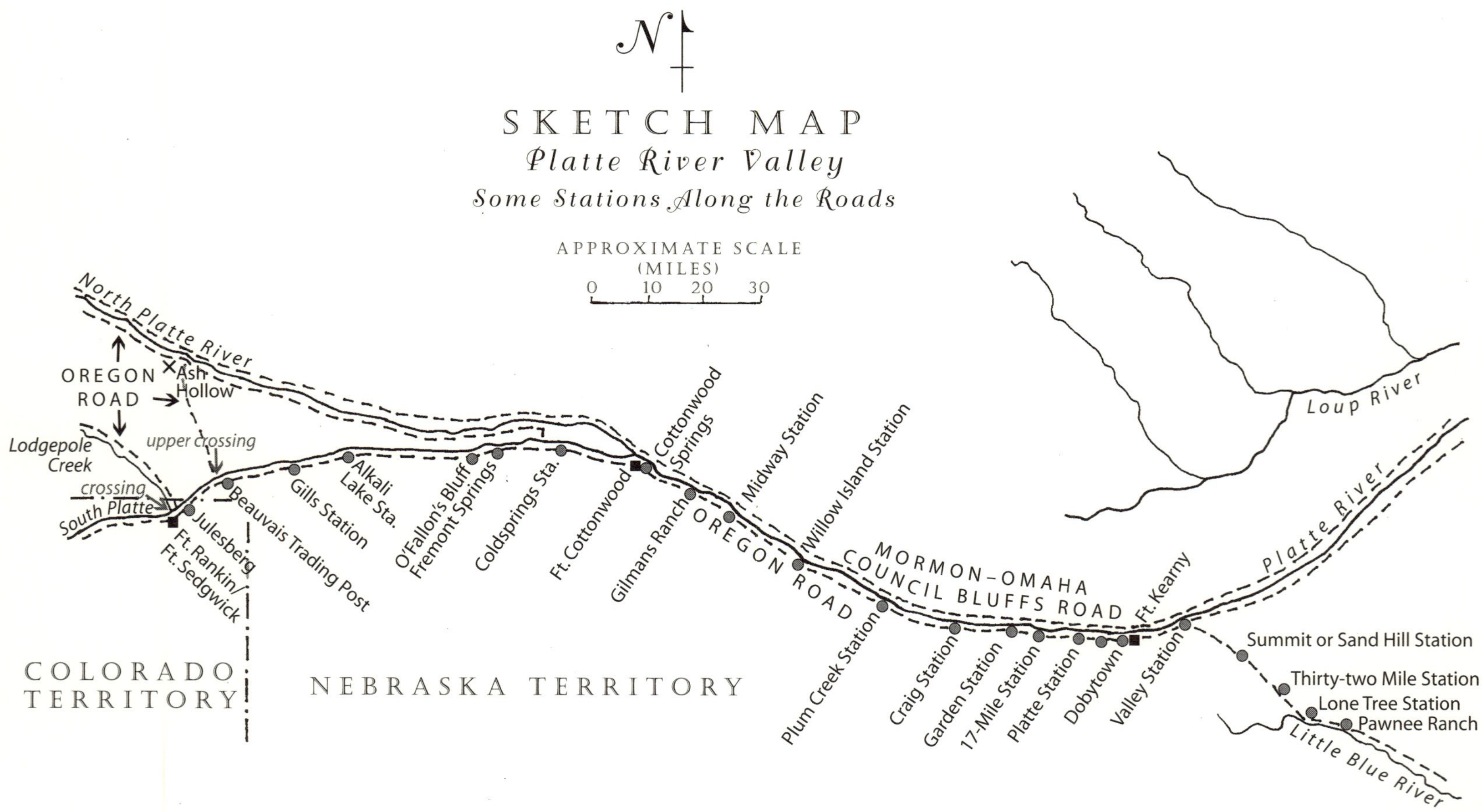
N
SKETCH MAP
Platte River Valley
Some Stations Along the Roads
APPROXIMATE SCALE
(MILES)
0 10 20 30
North Platte River
OREGON ROAD
Ash Hollow
Lodgepole Creek
upper crossing
crossing
South Platte
Julesberg
Ft. Rankin/
Ft. Sedgwick
Beauvais Trading Post
Gills Station
Alkali
Lake Sta.
O'Fallon's Bluff
Fremont Springs
Coldsprings Sta.
Ft. Cottonwood
Cottonwood
Springs
Gilmans Ranch
Midway Station
Willow Island Station
OREGON ROAD
MORMON–OMAHA
COUNCIL BLUFFS ROAD
Plum Creek Station
Craig Station
Garden Station
17-Mile Station
Platte Station
Dobytown
Ft. Kearny
Valley Station
Platte River
Loup River
Summit or Sand Hill Station
Thirty-two Mile Station
Lone Tree Station
Pawnee Ranch
Little Blue River
COLORADO
TERRITORY
NEBRASKA TERRITORY

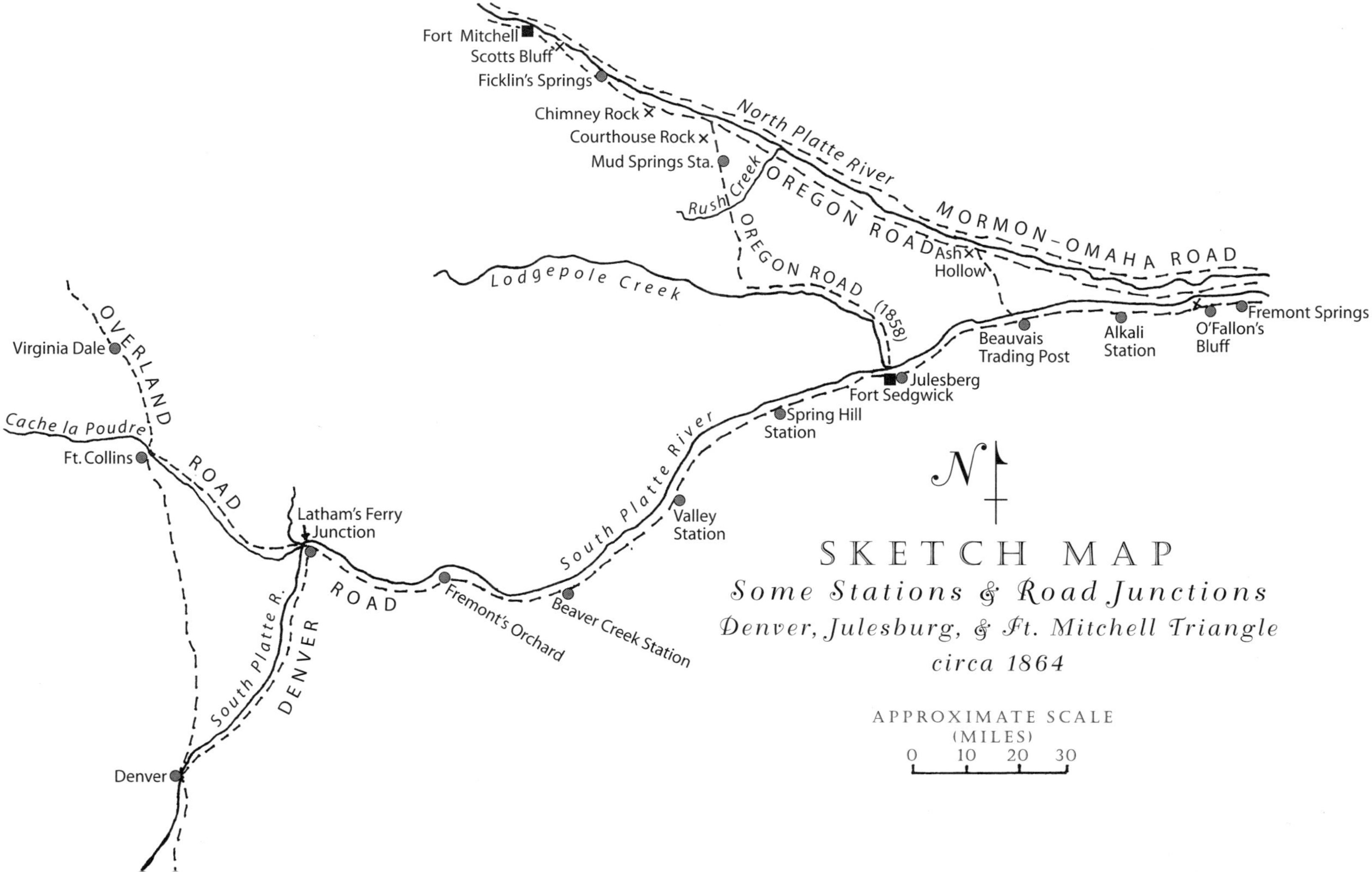

SKETCH MAP
Some Stations & Road Junctions
Denver, Julesburg, & Ft. Mitchell Triangle
circa 1864
APPROXIMATE SCALE
(MILES)
0 10 20 30
Fort Mitchell
Scotts Bluff
Ficklin's Springs
Chimney Rock
Courthouse Rock
Mud Springs Sta.
Rush Creek
North Platte River
OREGON ROAD
MORMON-OMAHA ROAD
Ash Hollow
OREGON ROAD (1858)
Lodgepole Creek
Fremont Springs
O'Fallon's Bluff
Alkali Station
Beauvais Trading Post
Julesberg
Fort Sedgwick
Spring Hill Station
Valley Station
South Platte River
Beaver Creek Station
Fremont's Orchard
Latham's Ferry Junction
DENVER ROAD
South Platte R.
Denver
OVERLAND ROAD
Virginia Dale
Cache la Poudre
Ft. Collins

CHAPTER ONE

The Plains, the People, and the Road

There is a vastness to the area west of the Missouri River as it extends to the awesome snowcapped peaks of the Rocky Mountains. It is an immense country devoid of timber except in the hollow valleys where tentative and shallow streams sometimes exist. A majestic sky visible from horizon to horizon covers and dwarfs everything beneath it. Winters are long, cold, white, and cruel; summers seem brief, hot with green grass at first, then turn ever warmer as moisture disappears and a vast brown trackless plain emerges. This land was once home to massive herds of buffalo, elk, deer, and smaller game and to native people of many nations or tribes, hunters who followed their prey following distinct migratory patterns.

The Native Americans who inhabited this territory knew little, if anything, about developments in the rest of the continent. By the eighteenth century, those living near the Arkansas River to the south knew of the Spanish; those along the Missouri saw or heard of the French and the English. At first those white intruders were few in number and not worrisome. By the middle of the eighteenth century the Native American nation called the Comanches acquired horses and before long became expert in their use. Other nations living on the plains came to fear their prowess, their mobility in war, and their success on the hunt. Comanches also attempted to monopolize trade with the Spanish in the south and the French in the east. The Comanches soon carried on a thriving commerce in deer skins, buffalo hides, dried meat, and captives, largely children, taken from other nations that had the misfortune to resist them. They acquired sugar, corn, horses (both by trade and theft), and ironware from the Spanish, and tobacco, knives, hatchets, and a few muskets from the French.

But the success of Comanches attracted competition. In the early nineteenth century the Sioux moved into the northern plains, to contest not only the Comanches, but also the Arapahos, Kiowas, Crows, and Northern Cheyennes. These people also learned to use horses to become more efficient hunters and warriors. By the 1830s the Sioux ranged from the Missouri basin west to the Continental Divide, and south to the South Platte and Smoky Hill Rivers. Forced south by the Sioux, the Arapahos simultaneously allied with the Southern Cheyennes and made their place on the watersheds of the Platte and North Platte Rivers, though they hunted farther south and east.

By 1800, the Cheyennes had moved out of the beautiful and rugged Black Hills, a portion of the tribe moving north into the Powder River country and others roving the plains as far south as the Arkansas River. They also hunted and traded from the northern Dakotas to northern New Mexico. Reflecting their pastoral heritage from the period before they adopted the horse, they had an extensive knowledge of native plants they used for food and medicine.

Fierce conflicts between the nations claiming hunting and trading rights on the plains proved costly to all. By 1840 the

Comanches, Cheyennes, Sioux, Arapahos, Kiowas, and Plains Apaches made a lasting, mutually advantageous peace. Even so, the peace agreement failed to prevent stealing horses from one another when the opportunity presented itself. But blood still flowed when adherents to the peace treaty found Pawnees, Omahas, Osages, and others daring to invade the plains hunting game, especially the prized buffalo.

Almost like phantoms, a few itinerant but enterprising whites ranged along the fringes of this vibrant Native American plains empire, and after a time they became important to the tribesmen. They were traders, but not Spaniards from the Southwest or the English-Americans who replaced the French to the east. Most were Americans, mountain men, intrepid fur trappers of the Rocky ranges who now faced the problem of diminishing returns of beaver—both the animal itself and the demand for its fur. They turned quickly to other sorts of trading. Before long, the tribesmen supplied them with buffalo hides and deer skins, commodities that replaced beaver pelts, in return for a wide variety of goods. As a result, white trading companies relocated closer to their suppliers, the Bent-St. Vrain post on the upper Arkansas River providing but one example.

The Cheyennes, especially but not exclusively, became increasingly dependent on the trade in buffalo hides. To expedite both commerce and communication, to provide a measure of personal safety, and to relieve their lonely existence, considerable intermarriage took place with the white traders. William Bent married Owl Woman, daughter of an important Cheyenne functionary in 1835, and was accorded membership in the tribe. While this became a more common occurence by mid-century, it was not a new phenomenon. Spanish, French, and English wanderers also had fathered children with Plains women for well over a century. Each society learned much from the other, though each sought to retain its own culture. These contacts produced many racially mixed children, so that when white explorers and soldiers believed they saw whites among the tribesmen they were not mistaken. The Native American nations also intermarried: the Cheyennes and Sioux as well as the Cheyennes and Arapahos counted many such liaisons. Women captured in conflict with other tribes often became the brides of the victors.

By the 1850s living and hunting space on the plains became crowded by tribal standards. The equine population rapidly enlarged, though human increase also played a role. As roving tribesmen usually kept eight to a dozen horses each, a band of twenty hunters might have as many as 240 mounts for which they needed sufficient pasturage around their camps. Security became a problem as tribesmen sought still more horses, and defense against theft compelled constant vigil. From May to October the need for space proved less critical as most bands habitually moved about hunting for game. But from November to April, when the tribes sought shelter from winter storms and biting cold, as well as places where water and forage could sustain their herds, the necessity for greater space loomed large. Many coveted areas along the South Platte River where the front range of the Rockies provided a measure of protection, while others sought out well-timbered stretches along the Arkansas River.

By mid-century larger numbers of white travelers intruded into these busy plains areas. At first it had been only a handful of explorers and emigrants heading west to the Pacific. They found the plains inhospitable and crossed them as quickly as possible. Generally they followed the Platte and North Platte Rivers, then the Sweetwater, and through the South Pass and beyond to Oregon and California. They left the security of Missouri River settlements in May when the plains grass provided forage, but seldom later than early July, when a burning sun parched the plains. Native Americans tolerated this passage since the whites were few and were clearly passing through. Friction was at a minimum, but as the few soon became many, attitudes changed.[1]

Robert Stuart, employed by John Jacob Astor's fur company, first traveled this route from west to east in 1812–13. The way was not much traversed before the 1840s, by which time economic hardship troubled the United States. News that the Oregon country offered attractive and available resources led more eastern citizens, some in considerable need of improving their livelihoods, to take heed. In 1841, with fur trader Thomas Fitzpatrick as their guide, the first organized wagon train left the Missouri River and headed west over what was called the Oregon Trail. Emigration grew nearly every year after that as word came back that opportunity awaited in both Oregon and California.

As the numbers using the route increased, so did discord between the Native Americans and the emigrants. Glaring societal and cultural differences separated them and became the basis for misunderstanding, perceived insults, and growing aggravation. The whites demanded that their government use the military to protect them. In 1829 military escorts for freighters had been used along the Santa Fé Trail from Independence, Missouri, across the Kansas plains, the Arkansas River, and eventually to Santa Fé. A little over a decade later Lieutenant John C. Frémont, reporting on western migration routes, observed that the army was indeed needed in order to keep the Native Americans from disrupting travel. In 1845 Colonel Stephen Watts Kearny took a mil-

[1]Much of this material was suggested by Elliot West's award-winning study, *The Contested Plains: Indians, Goldseekers, and the Rush to Colorado* (Lawrence: The University Press of Kansas, 1998), 64–93.

itary expedition over the Oregon Trail to demonstrate the might of the United States to the Native Americans. He appeared successful, and believed that such a demonstration every few years would be necessary. President James K. Polk, on the other hand, proposed a system of fortifications along the Oregon route from the Missouri River to the Rocky Mountains. Congress agreed in 1846, and by 1848 Fort Kearny arose near the confluence of the Oregon Trail and the Platte River, 316 miles west of Independence. The next year the government bought the American Fur Trade post of Fort Laramie, 351 miles northwest of Fort Kearny, for four thousand dollars. It then established another fort close by the fur trade post of Fort Hall on the Snake River about 620 miles west of Fort Laramie via the South Pass. The army acquired the trading post of Fort Bridger in 1857. Native Americans were surprised by the rapid military invasion of the plains.

Along the Santa Fé Trail to the south, the United States built Fort Atkinson in 1850 to provide some security in that area, but these few posts, hundreds of miles apart, failed to threaten Native Americans. The garrisons were small, mostly infantry, and their officers were usually young and inexperienced in tribal warfare. For the most part the army considered Native Americans no better than ignorant, totally uncivilized aborigines, who in their seeming poverty both begged and stole from them.[2]

The Mormons had founded their new home at Salt Lake in 1846, which increased westward traffic, but with the discovery of gold in California in 1848, the Oregon Trail drew an astonishing expansion of emigration. In 1850 some fifty to fifty-two thousand people, with thousands of animals draw-

[2]Ronald Becher, *Massacre Along the Medicine Road: A Social History of the Indian War of 1864 in Nebraska Territory* (Caldwell, Idaho: Caxton Press, 1999), 5–12; George E. Hyde, *Life of George Bent: Written from his Letters*, Savoie Lottinville, ed. (Norman: University of Oklahoma Press, 1968), 97–98.

ing perhaps ten thousand wagons, trekked west over the road. The Native Americans looked on with wonder and consternation as the flood of whites turned the trail into a mile-wide highway virtually devoid of plains grasses. Timber disappeared from the streamside woodlands and debris, dumped to lighten wagon loads, fouled the land. Whites killed buffalo and carelessly left much of the carcass to decay by the wayside. This waste infuriated tribesmen, especially as buffalo began to avoid the vicinity of the trail, disturbing the integrity of the herds and taking some of their livelihood from them. To make matters worse, the whites brought their diseases and passed them to tribesmen, who lacked immunity. In 1849, cholera, perhaps the worst plague, swept through the Northern Cheyennes and Sioux.

As yet there had been minimal conflict between Native Americans and whites, but certainly antipathy and anger smoldered. Something had to be done. Thomas Fitzpatrick, now holding appointment from the U. S. government as an Indian agent, agreed with his friend, trader William Bent, that a peace conference was needed. They understood that the traditional way of tribal life on the plains was fast coming to an end with the entry of white civilization. Fitzpatrick wanted to hold a great peace conference to reduce conflict among the tribes as well as prevent further strife between Native Americans and whites. The government agreed, and in September 1851, about ten thousand tribesmen, some three hundred soldiers, white civilians, including mountain man Jim Bridger and missionary Jean Pierre De Smet, as well as government agents and interpreters, met in council near Fort Laramie.

Cheyennes, Sioux, Arapahos, Shoshonis, Crows, Assiniboins, Mandans, and others attended, but some tribes did not: Comanches, Kiowas, and Apaches refused to join the conclave. The conferees agreed that each tribe was to have its own place between the Platte and Arkansas Rivers, but all could hunt anywhere on those plains. The United States agreed to hold aggressive whites in check and pay yearly annuities of fifty thousand dollars to the tribes. Some believed this Treaty of 1851, the "Fort Laramie Treaty" or the "Horse Creek Treaty" (where it was actually consumated), presaged a time of peace. Whites could travel unharmed, Native Americans would be protected from them. The treaty was broad and vague, and doubtless meant different things to the tribesmen and whites, but it was at least an honest effort to prevent war. Even so, with cultures so vastly different, understandings so divergent, and outlooks so opposite, this time of peace would soon be tested, and the treaty shortly shattered.

Around the first of August 1854 several thousand Sioux gathered near Fort Laramie to receive annuity goods guarenteed them by the 1851 treaty. Before long, tensions between the Sioux, soldiers from the fort, and immigrants moving along the emigrant road rose. As a wagon train passed camps of Sioux and Cheyennes, an ox strayed into one of them, where it was killed and butchered by a Miniconjou Sioux. The owner of the animal, a Mormon emigrant, reported the incident to the commander at Fort Laramie, a second lieutenant named Hugh Fleming. On August 19, he sent another second lieutenant, John L. Grattan, to arrest the tribesmen responsible. Grattan, fresh out of the military academy, ignorant of tribal ways, and eager to make a name for himself, took with him a detachment to carry out his assigned task. Grattan entered a Brulé camp, drew the men up in line of battle, and demanded the surrender of the culprits who had "stolen" the ox. Miscommunication between the interpreter, who allegedly was drunk, the Brulé chief, and a nervous Grattan led him to order his troops to fire on the Sioux. When their chief fell, furious warriors killed all the white soldiers.

Sioux chiefs and trader James Bordeaux restrained the Sioux from attacking Fort Laramie itself, but, reckoning now that no annuities would be distributed to them, they broke into the warehouse and stripped it of whatever they needed. The Sioux knew the ox was a stray, and to their way of thinking it belonged to no one. Even so, the Sioux had offered to pay for the animal with a number of horses, but Grattan had insisted that those who stole it surrender to him. The commissioner of Indian Affairs subsequently observed that the military was not authorized to arrest or try Native Americans for such an offense, but the Indian agent was not present to make a determination. Also, the Sioux, like other Plains tribes, had no concept of arrest or surrender and believed the whites would kill them as they would enemy warriors. Those at Fort Laramie were fortunate the Sioux held off their attack—only about forty infantrymen were on hand. Some young and impetuous Sioux warriors of various bands nevertheless later raided along the Oregon road. Most of the Sioux who broke into the warehouse broke camp and moved north. The Cheyennes, who had not been directly involved, received the goods due them, but were furious, knowing their Sioux friends had been treated unfairly.[3]

The War Department blamed the "Grattan Massacre" on the Sioux, though some army officers, along with those who helped frame the 1851 treaty, believed Grattan to be at fault. In any event, the army ordered Colonel William S. Harney to punish the tribe responsible. In September 1855 Harney's expedition attacked a Sioux camp near Ash Hollow. He killed over eighty tribesmen and captured seventy women and children. These Sioux had not been present at the Grattan affair, but the army—and Harney—could not distinguish

[3]Becher, *Massacre Along the Medicine Road*, 32–33; George Bird Grinnell, *The Fighting Cheyennes* (Norman: University of Oklahoma Press, 1956), 105, 108; Hyde, *Life of George Bent*, 98–99.

one band of Sioux from another. Even so, the Sioux were frightened enough to surrender seven men who may or may not have participated in the attack on Grattan; these unfortunates were sent to Fort Leavenworth. Harney then went to Fort Laramie, where he met with a number of Sioux, as well as the tiny garrison. While he warned the Sioux to stay away from the Oregon road, he learned the facts of the massacre and assured the Sioux of the need for peace. Several Sioux gave themselves up when Harney asked for the surrender of any responsible for trouble on the trail. They were also sent to Fort Leavenworth. Meanwhile, news of Harney's action at Ash Hollow quickly spread throughout the tribes.[4]

Harney next took his force northeast through Sioux hunting grounds to Fort Pierre in the Dakotas. This march disturbed the Sioux, who met with Harney in November. They made it clear they wanted peace. Convinced they were serious, Harney met in council with them the following March. When they gave up still other tribesmen supposedly responsible for the Grattan affair, Harney freed the culprits on the spot, and the Sioux agreed to abide by the 1851 treaty.[5]

In April 1856 some confusion occurred concerning ownership of four horses that had strayed near Platte Bridge, about 120 miles west-northwest of Fort Laramie on the North Platte River. Army officers attempted to arrest a few Northern Cheyennes who turned over all but one horse. The Cheyennes sought to escape, but two were captured, one killed, and another managed to flee. George Bent, a mixed-blood son of trader William Bent, later explained that "Indians did not understand being arrested. They never took full-grown men prisoners but always killed them." When

[4]Grinnell, *The Fighting Cheyennes*, 108–9; Becher, *Massacre Along the Medicine Road*, 34.

[5]Robert B. Westbrook and P. Richard Metcalf, "William Selby Harney," in Howard L. Lamar, ed., *The Reader's Encyclopedia of the American West* (New York: Harper & Row, 1977), 486.

soldiers tried to arrest Indians they believed the soldiers would disarm and kill them, so when an arrest was attempted "the Indians usually fought for their lives." The brave who fled warned his village, fearing another Grattan episode, and sure enough, the villagers had just departed when the troops arrived. Soldiers plundered and burned the camp; these Northern Cheyennes fled south to join their relatives.[6]

Later in 1856 a war party of young Cheyennes rode toward the Platte to hunt their enemy, the Pawnees. On August 24 they met a mail coach on the road, and some of the party approached to beg for tobacco. The stage driver believed the Cheyennes to be hostile, and fired into them. Wounded by a Cheyenne arrow, he drove on at top speed. The Cheyennes declined to chase him, being more interested in finding Pawnees. When the stage reached Fort Kearny, a troop of the 1st Cavalry went out to find the Cheyennes. They located them in camp on Grand Island, and charged, killing six and capturing a number of horses. When the survivors returned to the tribe with their account, other young warriors, angry at the soldiers, set out to raid along the Platte. As far as they were concerned, the cavalry attack had been unprovoked. By September's end the Oregon road east of Kearny was not safe for travelers, except for large, well-armed trains of wagons.[7]

The United States government decided it would not tolerate the Cheyenne raids along the Oregon road. In an effort to chastize them, white-haired, sixty-year-old Colonel Edwin V. Sumner led an expedition against them in the spring of 1857. He sent out two columns, one up the Arkansas River, another along the Platte. The Cheyennes easily evaded him, although the young braves wanted to fight. Then on July 29,

[6]Grace Raymond Hebard and E. A. Brininstool, *The Bozeman Trail: Historical Accounts of the Blazing of the Overland Routes into the Northwest, and the Fights with Red Cloud's Warriors* (2 vols., Cleveland, Ohio: The Arthur H. Clark Company, 1922), vol. 1, 78; Hyde, *Life of George Bent*, 100.

[7]Hyde, *Life of George Bent*, 101–2; Becher, *Massacre Along the Medicine Road*, 39–40.

Sumner's 1st Cavalry met three hundred Cheyennes who were hunting buffalo on Solomon's Fork of the Kansas River. They had few guns and had never before fought with white soldiers. Cheyenne spiritual leaders told the warriors that bullets from the trooper's guns would fall harmlessly from the gun barrels and not harm them. Confident, the Cheyennes rode out to meet the cavalry, but were surprised when Sumner gave the order for a charge with sabers. As the swords flashed, astonished warriors turned and fled, closely pursued by the cavalrymen. Sumner thought his troopers killed nine Cheyennes, but the Cheyennes admitted only four dead. Sumner had two killed and nine wounded troops, including twenty-four-year-old Lieutenant J. E. B. Stuart, hit in the breast. The Cheyennes fled south to the Arkansas River. On July 31 Sumner came upon the main Cheyenne camp and demolished 171 lodges, but about as many had been removed before the troops arrived. He also destroyed thousands of pounds of buffalo meat.[8]

Sumner hastened to Bent's Fort to prevent the Cheyennes, all of whom he considered hostile, from attacking the trading post to seize its store of annuity goods and obtain guns and ammunition. After he arrived on August 18, he turned the annuity goods over to friendly Arapahos. By then the Cheyennes were situated south of the Arkansas River in Kiowa and Comanche country, and hunted there until fall. After Sumner returned to Leavenworth in September, the Northern Cheyennes returned north of the Platte and their southern cousins moved back north of the Arkansas.[9]

The Kansas-Nebraska Act of 1854 had opened for settlement a large section of the Plains, compelling Pawnees,

[8]LeRoy R. Hafen and Francis Marion Young, *Fort Laramie and the Pageant of the West, 1834–1890* (Lincoln: University of Nebraska Press, 1984), 280–83; Hyde, *Life of George Bent*, 104–5.

[9]Hyde, *Life of George Bent*, 104–5.

Omahas, Yanktons, and Poncas to relocate. Western Sioux, or Lakotas, immediately felt threatened since this meant their enemies would now share their territory. In 1857 western Sioux met at Bear Butte by the Bad Lands and determined to resist additional white intrusion. They turned back a party of topographical engineers, fearing they were surveying for roads through the Black Hills. They held the surveyors in violation of the agreement Harney had made the year before. In 1859, another topographical team made their way through the region, and again upset the Sioux. That led to another treaty made at the Deer Creek Agency in 1859, by which the Sioux, Arapahos, and Northern Cheyennes consented to live on tracts above the North Platte River, but the treaty was rejected by the United States Senate. Nothing was settled with the tribes north of the Platte River.[10]

Argonauts discovered gold in the foothills of the Rocky Mountains in 1858, in the area where Denver would subsequently appear. Thousands of whites from frontier states to the east scrambled westward in search of wealth. Few grew rich from gold, but white farmers and ranchers began to settle the area west of the South Platte River. The rush began in the spring of 1859. As many as 150,000 "Pike's Peakers" flooded in from spring through summer. Many of these argonauts were soon disappointed and returned east, often through tribal heartlands. The Plains tribes found this white fascination with bits of glittering metal difficult to understand, but had no trouble seeing how whites disturbed their hunting grounds between the Platte and Arkansas Rivers. Some gold seekers traveled along the Republican and Smoky Hill Rivers, and the

[10]Becher, *Massacre Along the Medicine Road*, 34–35. The Lakota or western Sioux, comprised of 7 tribes, inhabited the Dakotas west to Montana; the Nakota or middle Sioux, 2 tribes, clustered around the Missouri River and its tributaries; while the Dakota or eastern Sioux, 3 tribes, ranged from the Great Lakes to the eastern edges of the Dakotas. All spoke the Siouxian language, but each had their own accents. All were Sioux to the whites.

Leavenworth and Pike's Peak Express Company sent coaches through the center of tribal buffalo country.[11]

The gold centers expanding in the Colorado Rockies drew supplies from depots along the Missouri River. Freighters branched off from the Oregon road near Julesburg and followed the South Platte to the gold settlements. Others followed the Santa Fé road. To afford some security in the area, the United States bought Bent's Fort in 1859, renamed it Fort Wise and later, Fort Lyon. Bent built another post on the south bank of the Arkansas River slightly west of the former site. The army also built Fort Larned on the Pawnee River in 1859, close to the Arkansas and the Santa Fé road. Larned was about 275 miles from Independence, about 75 miles downstream from Fort Atkinson, while Atkinson was about 150 miles downstream from Fort Wise. In 1853 the army built Fort Riley at the junction of the Republican and Kansas Rivers, about 110 miles west of Fort Leavenworth and about 170 miles southeast of Fort Kearny. Roads connected both places. Fort Riley was also about 35 miles north of the Santa Fé road.[12] To Native Americans, construction of these posts clearly and ominously portended even greater white penetration into country they knew as their own.

The 1851 treaty had provided that whites would stay out of the buffalo range between the North Platte and Arkansas Rivers, but the Colorado gold seekers paid no attention. Infuriated Native Americans, especially Cheyennes and Arapahos, as early as 1858 prevailed upon their adopted brother William Bent to intercede for them. They wanted to stop the white intruders from cutting timber and otherwise effacing their hunting grounds. When Bent protested to the Bureau of Indian Affairs, the Treaty of Fort Wise followed in

[11]Hyde, *Life of George Bent*, 105–7; Grinnell, *The Fighting Cheyennes*, 125.

[12]Location of posts and distances suggested from the map *Western Emigrant Trails: 1820–1870* (Omaha, Nebraska: Western Emigrant Trails Research Center, 1999).

early 1861. By its terms a reservation was created along the Arkansas for the Cheyenne and Arapaho. The federal government proposed to take them off the plains and make them into farmers. This was not what the Cheyenne and Arapaho had in mind at all, and only a few less influential chiefs signed the document. Others would have nothing to do with it, intending to stay on and hunt over the plains as they always had. The Native Americans were even more disgusted with whites than before, and a realistic peace appeared doubtful. Certainly the younger men among the Cheyennes wanted to fight the whites and drive them out, but chiefs and elders held them in check for the time being.[13]

Native Americans on the plains, under great pressure, fixed the blame for their troubles squarely on the whites. White interlopers destroyed forage, cut and burned timber, killed and drove off game, and brought terrible illnesses. Perhaps, they speculated, the drought along the Arkansas in 1849 and across the whole region in 1855 was their fault as well. Whites made agreements they failed to keep. The sheer numbers of whites moving through and across their country and occupying parts of it astonished them. In response, the tribesmen sporadically raided white ranches and wagon trains, took their horses and other stock, and fought back when attacked.

Meanwhile, additional changes came to the Oregon-California Trail. As travel along it brought more emigrants and freighters and as new military posts appeared, improvements to the roadway were made. From the 1840s on, stream crossings were graded and obstacles such as trees and stones were removed. By the 1850s, enterpreneurs provided ferries over the main streams and crude bridges over creeks. In 1862 William Smedley remarked in his diary that the road was

[13]Hyde, *Life of George Bent*, 107–9, 114; Becher, *Massacre Along the Medicine Road*, 42–45.

kept in "excellent repair." The federal government also provided additional funds for the roads. The Thirty-third Congress (1853–55) provided for military roads in every organized territory in the Trans-Mississippi West. "Military roads were launched . . . in Utah, New Mexico, Kansas, and Nebraska." This Congress appropriated $564,000 for these federal wagon roads, and the 1856 Congress provided another $300,000 for improvement of the Oregon route and $250,000 for other roads such as the Santa Fé trail. It is not known how much was actually spent. In 1857 Lieutenant Francis T. Bryan thought no improvements were necessary between forts Kearny and Laramie. That same year the Interior Department took over improvements and contracts for territorial road building, and created the Pacific Wagon Road Office to handle the business. In 1858 contractor Alfred Hebard built a number of bridges east of the Little Blue River, and proclaimed that part of the route was "in excellent condition for . . . the heaviest trains across the plains." Lieutenant Gouverneur K. Warren, after several surveys of routes west from the Missouri River in 1858, reported that the Platte Valley was best adapted to a national route for a Pacific wagon road or railroad from the Missouri River to the Rocky Mountains via either the South Pass (Oregon road) or Bridger's Pass (Overland road).[14]

The Pacific Wagon Road Office functioned poorly in its efforts to promote federal road building in the West. Engineers and surveyors completed their work satisfactorily for the most part, "but the superintendents, as frontiersmen with political influence, proved incapable managers. The confu-

[14]John D. Unruh, Jr., *The Plains Across: The Overland Emigrants and the Trans-Mississippi West* (Urbana: University of Illinois Press, 1993 edition), 268; W. Turrentine Jackson, *Wagon Roads West: A Study of Federal Road Surveys and Construction in the Trans-Mississippi West, 1846–1869* (Lincoln: University of Nebraska Press, 1979), 130, 139, 172–73, 178, 322; William Smedley, *Across the Plains: An 1862 Journey from Omaha to Oregon* (Boulder, Colorado: Johnson Books, 1994), 32.

sion, moreover, tempted the dishonest." Appropriations disappeared into many pockets along the way. Even so, road improvements were made, but at considerable loss to the taxpayers.[15]

By the late 1850s the Oregon-California Trail was in fact a road. Recent writers have more accurately called the stretch across Kansas and Nebraska the Platte River Road. Traffic to Oregon, California, and Utah in the twenty years between 1840 and 1860 rose as some 296,000 emigrants traveled westward. Additionally, thousands of emigrants used portions of the trail to reach Colorado. No wonder many individuals tried to make their fortunes from the travelers. Scores of individuals, sometimes associated as companies, or often only as families or individuals, constructed "road ranches" along the way. They sought to provide supplies of various sorts to those who used the road and in the process make their fortunes. A recent writer called these small depots "convenience stores" of their day.[16]

For a handsome price the stores dispensed meat (frequently buffalo), coffee, butter, eggs, flour, salt, some tinned goods, tobacco, usually bad whiskey, cooking utensils, and other items. They sold hay and corn as forage. They often traded in oxen, taking foot-sore beasts along with a good deal of cash in exchange for fresh ones, allowing the weary animals to regenerate themselves so that they could be resold later. Some ranches had gardens where conditions permitted that sort of husbandry, and supplied fresh produce in season. They also provided shelter from storms. Though travelers often found the ranches useful, many failed to appreciate the quality of their services. "Lodgings for the stagecoach pas-

---

[15]Jackson, *Wagon Roads West*, 325.

[16]Unruh, *The Plains Across*, 120; Becher, *Massacre Along the Medicine Road*, 47; Merrill J. Mattes' excellent study called it *The Great Platte River Road: The Covered Wagon Mainline via Fort Kearny to Fort Laramie* (Lincoln: University of Nebraska Press, 1979).

sengers were so wretched" that few travelers "could have borne the overcrowded sleeping places, the grubbiness, the insect pests, and the abominable food and drink."[17]

Road ranches also supported both the Pony Express and the Overland Mail Company. Some, if spaced at a proper interval, became stations for one or both. Those ranchers then doubled as agents for the lines, drawing pay from the companies for that work. After the transcontinental telegraph, which paralleled the Oregon road, was completed in October 1861, it required repeater stations no farther than thirty-five miles apart. The galvanized iron wire then in use was only a fair conductor of electricity (good copper wire, with superior conductivity, was not then available, nor would it be for another forty years). The telegraph provided instant news reports, especially valuable to the military but also available to travelers. The Overland Mail provided service along the way on a daily schedule from points on the Missouri River to Salt Lake. The coaches also carried the latest newspapers from those terminals: by the 1860s no traveler need be unaware of happenings back east.[18] Not only was the road well marked and fairly well improved, but neither was it lonely with the road ranches and various stations, not to mention increased traffic.

All improvements aside, it remained an uncomfortable road to tour. Summer heat not only burned prairie grass brown, but also blistered bare skin, brought sunstroke, and shortened tempers of men and animals alike. Sudden drenching rainstorms and driven hail, punctuated with terrifying wind, vivid lightning, and rolling thunder harassed

---

[17]Becher, *Massacre Along the Medicine Road*, 47–51; Dee Brown, *Wondrous Times on the Frontier* (New York: HarperPerennial, 1992), 11.

[18]Becher, *Massacre Along the Medicine Road*, 51; William E. Lass, *From Missouri to the Great Salt Lake: An Account of Overland Freighting* (Nebraska State Historical Society, Publications, vol. 26, 1972), 87, 162; Irving R. Merrill, ed., *Bound for Idaho: The 1864 Trail Journal of Julius Merrill* (Moscow: The University of Idaho Press, 1988), 10.

travelers. Winters entailed unendurable cold temperatures and massive, blinding, and blowing snow storms that made travel impossible for weeks. In some summers grasshoppers appeared by the millions, eclipsing the sun and eating anything that grew. Insects, especially mosquitoes, swarmed, bit, and stung man and animal alike. Other hazards included rattlesnakes, whose strike could kill men and stun oxen; prairie fires that raced across the landscape; great powdery clouds of dust from wagons that engulfed those behind the leaders; and water often brackish enough to sicken both men and beasts. At other times beauty abounded. Acres of colorful wildflowers perfumed the plains in the spring; vistas of brightly colored and often impressive stone formations never were far afield; and when snow-capped mountains arose to the west their majesty proved awesome. Wild game of many kinds tempted even novice hunters.

As certainly as the decade of the 1850s improved travel on the Oregon road, it provoked hostility between Native Americans and those whites who used, worked, or lived along it. East of the Missouri during that same decade, political dissension threatened the fabric of the United States.

CHAPTER TWO

From Fort Sumter to Fort Laramie

Native Americans on the western plains knew little about the flourishing civilization of the United States east of the Missouri River. It had tripled its territory between 1800 and 1860. White Americans flooded into the Ohio and Mississippi valleys, vaulted the Mississippi, trickled into Texas, Oregon, and California, and took title to the remainder of the real estate that filled out the continental United States. Its population had expanded as well, from about 5,300,000 in 1800 to 31,450,000 by 1860. Though primarily an agricultural society, immense technological changes challenged that primacy. Factories powered by water or steam blossomed in the valleys of New England, New York, and Pennsylvania. By the 1840s various industrial enterprises sprouted in parts of the old Northwest and South too, but the heaviest concentration remained in the Northeast.

The largely agricultural states of the South and the old Northwest developed differently because of the constraints that climate imposed on their crops and also because of their origins. By the 1840s Americans thought of themselves as a nation of three or four sections: the East, South, West, and perhaps the Far West. By the East, they actually meant the industrial Northeast; the South signified the slave-holding states with their production of cotton, sugar, tobacco, and rice for world markets; and the West, the old Northwest Territory (Ohio, Indiana, Illinois, Michigan, Wisconsin, and then Missouri and Iowa), composed largely of farmers but with a growing industrial and urban population. The remote Far West included California, Oregon, and the territorial spoils of the Mexican War. Out there roamed Native Americans, some white traders, trappers, miners, herders, and a few farmers. Especially to Eastern and Southern Americans, anything west of the Mississippi River seemed very distant.

Each section had different problems, aspirations, and needs, and while they shared many similar values and traditions, they often divided sharply on political affairs. Each section looked to the federal government for legislation to assist their own economic growth, but often what might have benefited one would have harmed another. Distinct moral and social philosophies also separated the sections.

As industrialization at home and abroad energized cotton production in the South and placed a new premium on slave labor, it also fueled the market for provisions in the Northeast as its industrial workforce grew. The complementary economy of the Northeast (factories and urbanism) and the Northwest (foodstuffs) linked the two sections economically. Transportation, first canals and then rails, cemented the two sections. This new North boasted twenty thousand miles of rail by 1860, while the South had less than half that, with few connections to the North. Railroads became a booming new industry, and its financial rewards went primarily to the North.

Very few of the almost 4 million immigrants that arrived in the United States between 1840 and 1860 were located in the South. They had neither the funds nor experience to grow Southern staples, nor any desire to compete with slave labor.

As of 1860 the northern population increased to nearly 19,500,000, more than two and a half times the white population of the South. Another 4 million slaves labored largely for Southerners. By the 1850s the nation's sections were only two, excluding the Far West.

A vibrant optimism characterized both Northerners and Southerners alike in the two decades before 1860. They considered their free, democratic society (slaves excluded) far superior to the musty monarchies of the old world, and a model for the rest of the world. They sought to perfect their superior society as reformers of all sorts appeared with schemes to better it. In the North many thought Southern slavery morally wrong, but they ignored it so long as their economic progress remained unimpeded.

The North's antislavery movement evolved slowly before 1850, but after mid-century increasingly vocal abolitionist agitators commanded attention. Southerners vigorously reacted with every defense of their slave system they could muster. In the 1850s Northerners and Southerners conducted this volatile struggle in the arena of national politics. Many Northerners and most Southerners believed the expansion of the institution of slavery was necessary for it to remain economically viable. Largely opposed to slavery, Northerners sought especially to block that expansion into the western territories.

In 1848 the discovery of gold in California precipitated the national crisis. Within a year a sudden influx of argonauts and others sent its population to nearly 100,000, absolutely overwhelming California's temporary military government, a byproduct of the Mexican War. After months of heated debate, California vaulted into statehood by virtue of the Compromise of 1850, legislation designed to end the controversy over the extension of slavery into the territories.

But the dispute would not end. The antagonists regrouped, and for the remainder of the decade each struggled strenuously for control of the nation, literally tearing it in two in the process. This disruptive contest involved Congress and the Supreme Court; it destroyed political parties and spawned others; and it claimed lives. To make matters worse, the nation slid into recesssion in 1857 as credit and financial institutions collapsed, especially affecting Westerners.

While the Northern and Southern sections conducted their perilous conflict, few paid any attention to news from the Far West of renegade Sioux killing whites at Spirit Lake, Iowa, in 1857. Perhaps forty whites perished in that action and subsequent raids. Pawnees went on the warpath in eastern Nebraska, then Sioux and Cheyenne tribesmen went after them. Frightened frontier dwellers from Iowa to Nebraska clamored for military protection, but their voices went unheard. A military expedition sent to Utah to chastize allegedly lawless and rebellious Mormons (and perhaps to distract the nation from its sectional controversies) ended with no actual confrontation in 1858, proving only that the army was in many ways incapable of fighting a war on that frontier.

In November 1860 Abraham Lincoln of Illinois won election as president of the United States. Both as a Northerner and head of the new Republican Party that was dedicated to ending the spread of slavery into the territories, he was anethema to Southerners. Southerners had split the Democratic Party in two during the presidential campaign rather than accept the leadership of the Northern wing, controlled by Stephen A. Douglas, also from Illinois. They ran John C. Breckinridge. In hopes of bringing compromise to the political arena, a Constitutional Union Party ran John Bell. Lincoln won just under 40 percent of the popular vote.

Considering their slave system no longer safe with a Northerner in charge, Southerners chose to secede from the Union. Lame duck Democratic president James Buchanan failed to stop them. Seven southern slave states left the Union by February 1, and created the Confederate States of America. In the Union, Lincoln was inaugurated March 4, 1861. When, in the first days of April, he called for Fort Sumter in the harbor of Charleston, South Carolina, to be defended, civil war erupted. On April 12, 1861, Confederates fired on the fort. Four more southern states then seceded.

Across the nation, both north and south, the bombardment of Fort Sumter and the onset of civil war brought feverish reaction in every state. In Columbus, the capital of Ohio, Whitelaw Reid, a young newspaperman, reported that the city "was wild with the excitement of the call to arms." On April 14, Fort Sumter surrendered to the Confederates; the next day President Lincoln called for seventy-five thousand militia to supress the insurrection; on April 16 Reid wrote that agitation in the state capital "was even more intense; troops were arriving . . . the very air came laden with the clamor of war."[1] Even before the shelling of Fort Sumter stopped, Ohioans raised two regiments to defend the Union.

Other state governments vigorously responded to the Union's cause as well. Wisconsin's legislature passed a war act on April 13 that gave the governor broad authority to raise troops and $100,000 to use for that purpose. On April 15, New York appropriated $3 million to raise thirty thousand militia for two years' service. Two days later Rhode Island voted $500,000. Other legislatures not then in session were convened as quickly as possible. By the end of April New Jersey and Pennsylvania enacted emergency measures, and by

[1]Robert H. Jones, "Whitelaw Reid," in Kenneth W. Wheeler, ed., *For the Union: Ohio Leaders in the Civil War* (Columbus: Ohio State University Press, 1968), 122.

Lieutenant Colonel William O. Collins. *Courtesy of the Local History Archive, City of Fort Collins Public Library, Fort Collins, Colorado.*

the end of May Massachusetts provided a $10 million war fund. Individuals and financial institutions hurried to make credit or cash available to the states. The Cincinnati City Council, for example, offered Ohio $225,000.

More ominious news followed virtually each day. Virginia seceded on April 17; on April 19 the 6th Massachusetts Volunteer Infantry came under attack by a Baltimore, Maryland, mob while on its way to Washington, D.C.; and on the same day Lincoln proclaimed a sea blockade of Confederate ports. With others, Ohio state senator William O. Collins voted for a bill to appropriate $1 million for war purposes and strongly supported additional war measures. On April 23, a number of luminaries, including Senator Douglas of Illinois, spoke from the statehouse steps in Columbus vigorously proclaiming forceful resistance to the rebellion. There was no way Collins could avoid being swept up by the excitement, and soon he was part of a new military force.

Elsewhere, others responded the same way. Samuel R. Curtis, mayor of Keokuk and a United States congressman from Iowa, assumed command of the 2nd Iowa Volunteers in June. In that same state, Grenville M. Dodge became colonel of the 4th Iowa Volunteers in July. In Kansas that month, James G. Blunt became a lieutenant colonel of the 3rd Kansas Volunteers, and Robert B. Mitchell a colonel of the 2nd Kansas. California appointed Patrick E. Connor colonel of the 3rd California Volunteers. All of these men would have a future connection with Collins.

Like thousands of others, Ohio senator Collins felt compelled to become involved. Tall, with a dark beard and sharp brown eyes, he was fifty-one years old. Though born in Connecticut, he graduated from Cincinnati Law School at age twenty-four. He practiced law in Hillsboro, Ohio, and served as a prosecutor for Highland County. Late in 1843, Collins married his second wife—his first having died young—Catherine Wever. Son Caspar arrived in September 1844. Not only a lawyer but also a businessman, Collins became both a president and director of railroads. He also held a federal appointment as collector of Internal Revenue for the Sixth Congressional District of Ohio. In addition, Collins participated in local educational and agricultural enterprises. These activities served to make Collins well-known and respected by constituents, business leaders, and politicians in Ohio.[2]

A patriot, Collins knew he had to support both the Union and Ohio, even risk his life on the battlefield. But in Collins's own southern Ohio counties, especially Highland and Ross, support for the Union cause was lukewarm. In those areas,

---

[2]Agnes Wright Spring, *Caspar Collins* (Lincoln: University of Nebraska Press, 1969), 35; Elsie Johnson Ayres, *The Hills of Highland* (Springfield, Ohio: H. K. Skinner & Son, 1971), 447.

Lincoln's victory had been only a plurality, not a majority. Elsewhere in southern Ohio, Congressman Clement L. Vallandigham of Dayton, then a brigadier general in the state militia, actively opposed the war. He remained at home when four local companies marched off to defend the Union.[3] National news continued to worsen. On May 7 Tennessee seceded, and on the 20th North Carolina followed. Collins thought if he could raise a regiment in southern Ohio it might infuse that part of the state with enthusiasm for the Union cause.

Raising a cavalry regiment appealed to him. Beside the good effect a southern Ohio cavalry regiment would have on public opinion, he believed mounted troopers were needed. A calvary unit would also provide a market for horses at a time when forage was inexpensive, and best of all, Highland County could benefit since it had the necessary facilities to receive men and horses. He used his influence with friends, including Ohio's Adjutant General and Governor William Dennison. He wanted to start this project immediately.[4] Authorization to recruit the 7th Ohio Volunteer Cavalry materialized by the end of September.

Meanwhile other Ohioans, among them George B. McClellan and Rutherford B. Hayes, had moved into the rugged hills of western Virginia leading a small number of Ohio regiments. They secured the area for the Union by the middle of July. But on July 21, disaster befell other Union forces in Virginia at the first battle of Bull Run. Then, out west on August 10, another calamity befell the Union at Wilson's Creek, Missouri. By September 3, Confederates brushed aside Kentucky's fragile neutrality by invading that state, only to be countered by newly minted Brigadier General Ulysses S. Grant, who three days later occupied Paduc-

[3]Frank L. Klement, "Clement L. Vallandigham," in Wheeler, ed., *For the Union*, 9–10.

[4]*William Oliver Collins Family Papers, 1862–1865*, in the Western History Collection, Denver Public Library, items 39, 40.

ah, Kentucky, at the junction of the Tennessee and Ohio Rivers.

On October 1 the impatient Collins finally managed to establish a camp at the Highland County Fairgrounds at Hillsboro to receive recruits. Men came not only from Highland County, but also from the neighboring counties of Brown, Miami, and Ross. Getting them organized and equipped proved slow. On October 15 Collins asked U.S. Senator John Sherman for help. Back in March, when Senator Salmon P. Chase had been tapped for Lincoln's cabinet, the Ohio legislature chose Representative Sherman to fill the Senate vacancy. But after Fort Sumter, Sherman became a colonel of volunteers, and only reluctantly acceded to Lincoln's suggestion that he would be more useful if he remained in the Senate. Sherman used his considerable influence to encourage Ohioans to enlist in the Union cause, and with his connections in Washington, expedited equipment and supplies for Ohio volunteers.[5]

Collins's work paid off. On October 25, Governor Dennison asked the quartermaster to "furnish a complete outfit of quartermaster stores including horses" for "the Seventh Cavalry, Ohio Volunteers" either "at Hillsboro or Camp Dennison as the Colonel, Wm. O. Collins may direct." Collins chose to receive the material at Hillsboro, where only the 7th was being raised, rather than at Camp Dennison, where many other Ohio units rendezvoused. His equipment could too easily be siphoned off there, as he well knew. The uniforms and arms, including cavalry sabers and Enfield rifles, came first, then horses and other supplies, including Navy Colt revolvers.[6]

---

[5] *Collins Family Papers*, item 41; Jeannette P. Nichols, "John Sherman," in Wheeler, ed., *For the Union*, 377, 382–83.

[6] *Collins Family Papers*, item 61, and file folder 15; Whitelaw Reid, *Ohio in the War: Her Statesmen, her Generals, and Soldiers* (2 vols., Cincinnati, Ohio: Moore, Wilstach, & Baldwin, Publishers, 1868), vol. 2, 819.

Then, suddenly, about the first of December, the War Department halted cavalry recruiting. It ordered incomplete units mustered out unless they could be consolidated with others. Its ranks not yet full, the 7th consolidated with the 6th Ohio Volunteer Cavalry and joined them at Camp Dennison. His commission as colonel not yet received, Collins became a lieutenant colonel under Colonel William R. Lloyd. Because they were fully equipped and had their horses, Collins's men became the First Battalion, Companies A, B, C, and D of the 6th. Other than uniforms, the remainder of the 6th had no equipment. Lieutenant Colonel Collins received his commission on January 28.[7]

Collins discovered to his chagrin that the army moved very slowly. Along with his troopers, he disliked being bogged down at Camp Dennison. His battalion had been equipped for three months, and there was no way of knowing when the remainder of the 6th would be outfitted. Impatient with Colonel Lloyd, Collins tried everything he knew to get his battalion into action, including discussing the matter with Governor Dennison. Finally, on February 19, 1862, Dennison provided him with a letter of introduction to Brigadier General Randolph B. Marcy, inspector general of the Army, in Washington, D.C. Dennison asked Marcy to provide Collins "an early interview" with Major General George B. McClellan and Secretary of War Edwin M. Stanton, another Ohioan. Dennison proposed to get Collins's battalion into action "soon." He also noted the remainder of the 6th, the other two battalions, were not yet equipped.[8]

Whether due to the pressure from Dennison or Collins's persuasion, or because cavalry was urgently needed in Missouri, Major General Henry W. Halleck, commanding in the West, ordered Collins's battalion of the 6th to join fifteen

[7] *Collins Family Papers*, file folder 15; Reid, *Ohio in the War*, vol. 2, 819.
[8] *Collins Family Papers*, item 63.

thousand other troops gathered at Benton Barracks, at St. Louis. Collins kissed his wife goodbye and collected his tall, reddish-haired seventeen-year-old son, Caspar, who went west with him. Once the battalion reached Benton Barracks by rail, it was almost immediately ordered "to Nebraska City." Halleck directed the battalion "to be fitted out for Fort Laramie, to serve for protection of the Overland Mail Route."[9]

Stunned by their assignment in the West, the young men in Collins's battalion had no idea where Fort Laramie was. Some thought New Mexico, others Arizona. But Captain Peter W. Van Winkle of Company D soon set them straight. As a youth he had journeyed to California in 1849 via the Panama route—one of the forty-niners—and returned east over the California-Oregon Trail. Not only had he carved his name on Independence Rock, but he also had laid over for several days at Fort Laramie. Van Winkle told the men the place was 650 miles west of Fort Leavenworth on the North Platte River, smack in the middle of Indian country. This news sorely disappointed the troopers, who felt they had enlisted to fight Confederates in the South, not Indians in the wilderness of the Far West.[10]

Regardless of how the Ohioans reacted, Halleck faced a dilemma that needed a quick solution. Very few troops had garrisoned the posts along the Oregon road before war broke out, and most of those either had been or were being transferred to the East. That movement left the frontier and the

---

[9] *War of the Rebellion: A Compilation of the Official Records of the Union and Confederate Armies* (130 volumes, Washington, D.C.: Government Printing Office, 1880–1901), series I, vol. 8, p. 668 [hereafter referred to as *O.R.*]. Reid, *Ohio in the War*, II, 819; Spring, *Caspar Collins*, 36. It was not until about May 1, 1862, that the remainder of the 6th, with another battalion added to replace Collins's troops, finally received horses: *O.R.* I, 12, pt. 1, p. 9, and III, 1, p. 806. They fought in the east.

[10] Agnes Wright Spring, ed., "An Army Wife Comes West," *The Colorado Magazine*, vol. 31, no. 4 (October 1954): 242.

road west, with the telegraph and the mail, without adequate protection. On the one hand, the War Department desperately sought troops to serve in the East; on the other hand, Lincoln and his advisors claimed they "fully appreciated" how vital western political allegiance was to the Union, not to mention how valuable western gold and silver were to war finance. So emigrant routes and mail and telegraph lines had to be kept open. If the regulars departed, then volunteers had to replace them on the "Indian frontier." Halleck had found a battalion of Ohio volunteers already mounted: enough, he thought, for the job at hand.[11]

There seldom would be enough troops on the Oregon road to keep the lines of communication clear. Obviously, the demand for fighting men to pursue the Civil War necessarily proved to be vastly more important to the survival of the Union than any real or perceived threat of Native Americans to a far western communications link. Also, the War Department, the Interior Department, and other Washington leaders believed a few dozen troops on the western plains could easily control thousands of ragged, uncivilized Native Americans. Congress tightly controlled army purse strings before the Civil War, and not only was there little money to provide for more than tiny western garrisons, but the belief also persisted that such were not very necessary anyway. The departure of regular troops ordered east after Fort Sumter only made matters worse. Late in 1861 the commander at Fort Kearny reported he did not have enough manpower to protect army property at the fort from dishonest civilians as well as passing emigrants who shamelessly looted the post. Fortunately, the Native Americans remained quiet in 1861, but that situation would soon change.[12]

---

[11]Robert M. Utley, *Frontiersmen in Blue: The United States Army and the Indian, 1848–1865* (New York: The Macmillan Company, 1967), 215–16; *O.R.*, I, vol. 3, pp. 123, 129, 141–42, 222–23, vol. 8, p. 631.

[12]Becher, *Massacre Along the Medicine Road*, 62.

In February 1862 malcontent Sioux murdered several whites just east of Fort Kearny. Next, Sioux and Cheyenne west of Fort Laramie, unhappy over the depleted buffalo herds and angry that annuities distributed to them included no powder and lead—which they saw as a violation of the 1851 treaty—turned to raiding along the Oregon road. By April 1862, they had closed the route west of Laramie.[13]

Even as these events unfolded, Collins's battalion left St. Louis on April 4 for Fort Leavenworth, Kansas, the first stop on their way to Fort Laramie. That same day, the Overland Mail Company reported that sixty head of stock disappeared east of Fort Bridger. Raiding tribesmen torched mail stations all along the Oregon road from Fort Bridger to the North Platte River, destroying mail coaches and their cargo and killing several employees. Mail accumulated at some points, and at others mauraders sliced open the bags and left their contents strewn about.[14]

The journey of the 6th Ohio up the Missouri River to Fort Leavenworth aboard the river steamers *Robert Campbell* and *Sam. Gaty* proved exciting. Confederate guerrillas fired on the boats, and the Ohioans enthusiastically returned it. For the first time, the men used their Enfields against an enemy. This doubtless impressed young Caspar Collins, and certainly kept the troopers alert for the week it took to reach Leavenworth. The battalion remained at the fort for another two weeks until the army provided mules, wagons, and commissary stores for the long overland journey along the Oregon road to Fort Laramie.[15]

While at Leavenworth, Colonel Collins hired a couple of experienced frontiersmen to assist him. He needed them primarily for their knowledge of the Native Americans he

[13]Ibid., 65.

[14]LeRoy R. Hafen, *The Overland Mail, 1849–1869* (Cleveland, Ohio: The Arthur H. Clark Company, 1926), 242–45; Reid, *Ohio in the War*, vol. 2, 819.

[15]Reid, *Ohio in the War*, vol. 2, 819.

almost certainly would encounter, to act as interpreters and provide much needed advice to these green troops who did not know the country. The scouts could find agreeable campgrounds, pasture, and water; they could hunt to supplement rations. The army paid five dollars a day for the capable Jim Bridger to accompany Collins. He also hired Leo Pallady (or Pallardy, or Palladie), another man of the plains and mountains, as a general aide and helper.[16]

On Saturday, April 26, 1862, Collins's battalion of the 6th Ohio Volunteer Cavalry departed Fort Leavenworth and began its trek west to Fort Laramie. The 9th Wisconsin Volunteer Artillery travelled along with the Ohioans, although they had been ordered to Denver. The Wisconsin men would leave the Ohioans when the road forked just west of Julesburg. The order of march put the cavalry in front, followed by the artillery, the wagon train with supplies, then an ambulance and a few troopers as rear guard.[17]

In a letter to his wife, Collins described the daily routine. A bugler announced reveille as darkness began to weaken sometime after 4:00 A.M., allowing the troopers to dress and secure their bedding. Roll call followed at 4:30, sick call at 5:00. "Cooking and eating breakfast, feeding horses, saddling, striking tents, packing and loading tents, cooking utensils, and baggage of all sorts into wagons keep all busy." Colonel Collins then mounted up about 5:45 and checked "each company to see their progress and urge along the tardy, and all being in rank, mounted at six, the advance is sounded." After about an hour's travel, they rested for fifteen minutes, halted again at 10:00 or 11:00 to find "good grass" to feed and water the horses. The wagon train, slower moving than the cavalry, moved on without stopping. Collins, probably

[16]J. Cecil Alter, *Jim Bridger* (Norman: University of Oklahoma Press, 1962), 297; Ware, *The Indian War*, 463.

[17]*O.R.*, I, 8, pp. 664–65; 22, pt. 1, pp. 891, 893–94; Spring, *Caspar Collins*, 36–37.

with Bridger and Pallady (though he fails to mention them), or at least one of them, rode ahead during the day to select the stopping places and locate the evening camp.[18]

The column usually halted for the night between 2:00 and 5:00 P.M., sometimes later, depending on location, weather, or other circumstances. Occasionally they travelled as many as thirty miles a day, once thirty-six, but with an average of over twenty. Reaching a suitable campground, they pitched tents, unloaded necessary baggage, took care of the horses, cooked supper, and held roll call. Horses were brought inside camp lines and fed with corn when available. Guards were set, countersigns given, and tired men turned in. Collins provided his men with a long seine to net fish when they followed a river. A detail of eight or ten troopers could bring in "several" bushels of fish after a "few hours [*sic*] work" nearly every day. In addition, Pallady proved a proficient hunter and from time to time supplied the headquarters with game. Otherwise, the government diet of salt meat and hard biscuits, without vegetables, was monotonous and unpleasant; Collins believed he detected "symptoms of scurvy," especially west of Fort Kearny where fishing was poor.[19]

Collins claimed he usually slept only five hours a night while on the march, spending much of the time reading or going out to challenge the guards, to keep them alert. "Our bed," he wrote, "is an India rubber blanket on the ground in the tent and a buffalo robe laid upon it hair side up." Over that, a "blanket or two." Other officers had "cots or mattresses." Collins neglected to report how his men fared at night, other than in tents. Son Caspar and Pallady shared his accomodations. Collins told his wife that he wore a "broad-brimmed drab hat, . . . a flannel shirt over a muslin one, a dark blue woolen blouse, sky blue regulation pantaloon, cavalry

[18] *Collins Family Papers*, item 31.

[19] Ibid.; Spring, *Caspar Collins*, 36–37.

boots reaching to the knees, and spurs." Along with "buckskin guantlets, a belt with a revolver, cartridge box, cap box, etc., attached" he looked the picture of a western cavalry officer. He wore no saber, nor did his troopers, as they were "packed away during the march."[20]

Collins wrote very little about his officers or his men. Major John O'Ferrall, a physician in civilian life, was his second in command. Four captains, Thomas J. Mackey, Thomas M. Shipley, Hamer Hayes, and Peter W. Van Winkle, headed the four companies. Four first lieutenants and four second lieutenants completed the commissioned roster. The battalion included about 350 enlisted men on the march to Fort Laramie. From time to time they were battered by storms: rain, hail, and even snow; they encountered often dangerous streams, swollen by snowmelt from the mountains and augmented by hard rain, which turned the dusty road to mud. The Ohioans faced an unexpected springtime weather mix, very changeable and often threatening, unlike the milder springs they knew back home. Frost and snow were not unusual in April along the Oregon road. Some of the men and livestock suffered; exposure brought illness, and several men died along the way. They were buried at Fort Kearny. Collins noted "the ambulances are tolerably full."[21]

Fort Kearny, south of the Platte River, was just west of two branches of the Oregon road, the northerly one that ran east to Omaha and the southerly road that the Ohio battalion followed, which came up to the Platte from Fort Leavenworth, St. Joseph, and Independence. The first major depot west of Leavenworth, Kearny included a large storehouse, post office, telegraph station, and barracks. The buildings, of both adobe and wood, stood around a relatively small parade ground. No earthworks or stockade surrounded the post.

[20]*Collins Family Papers*, item 31.

[21]Reid, *Ohio in the War*, vol. 2, 818–19; Spring, *Caspar Collins*, 43; *Collins Family Papers*, item 31.

This is almost certainly a photo of Private Wayman St. Clair, Co. G, 11th Ohio Cavalry, mounted with pistol in hand and Spencer Carbine at his side. Photo provides a glimpse of the dress and equipment of the Ohio cavalrymen in the West. *Photo courtesy of Wyoming State Archives.*

Usually garrisoned by regular troops, their ranks were much depleted when the Ohioans arrived. Two miles west of Kearny, the settlement of Dobytown sprouted, where entrepreneurs sold goods and liquor at inflated prices to plains travelers, traders, stage and freight drivers, and soldiers. They also provided gambling and "soiled doves" or "scarlet women" for entertainment.[22]

[22]Ware, *Indian War of 1864*, 438–39. Dobytown's real name was Kearny City, but Dobytown was more descriptive and people called it that. Just to the north of it was Central City, which quickly disappeared except for Dirty Woman Ranch, a brothel. See Becher, *Massacre Along the Medicine Road*, 244. Dee Brown, in *Wondrous Times on the Frontier*, 10, lists a dozen synonyms for frontier prostitutes, including "Calico Cats." See also Albert Watkins, "History of Fort Kearny," *Collections of the Nebraska State Historical Society*, vol. 16 (Lincoln, Nebraska: The State Historical Society, 1911), 227–67.

Collins wrote little about the many stations and ranches that dotted the Oregon road west of Fort Kearny. They appeared at irregular intervals from six to twenty miles apart, all the way to Julesburg. He only mentioned their construction, more remarkable to him than their businesses or their numbers. "The houses, stations, stables, ranches, and all other buildings with very few exceptions . . . are built of turf cut brick fashion and laid up regularly like cut stone or brick. The roof is usually poles covered with turf, . . . warm in winter and cool in summer. It is called 'adobe'—pronounced 'doby.'"[23]

In mid-May the Ohioans met a delegation of about two hundred Sioux. Collins knew they were "greatly alarmed at our presence and think we come to make war on them and take their land." Collins noted that "more than half" of them were "women and children. . . . They arranged themselves in two circles before my tent, men in front and women and children behind." Collins courteously listened to the chief, as Bridger or Pallady interpreted, then calmly replied. He took "great pains," he said, to let the Sioux know his intentions were not only friendly, but also "to reassure them that if they are peaceful we will protect them." His "conciliatory remarks were received with evident satisfaction," Collins wrote. To further cement relations, he ordered his troopers to feed the Sioux, and donate to them all the old clothes they could spare. Though Collins had been warned by "traders" that the Sioux would beg and steal, this group behaved well. They asked for papers "stating that they are trustworthy Indians who do not lie or steal," but Collins neglected to note if he supplied such. To make a point of friendship, one brave "even returned two of our horses that had strayed." On a light note, Collins mentioned the only "damage they did to us was to sell some of the men buffalo robes" crawling with lice.[24]

---

[23]*Collins Family Papers*, item 31; Becher, *Massacre Along the Medicine Road*, 244–49.
[24]*Collins Family Papers*, item 31.

Perhaps advised by Bridger and Pallady, Collins made the right move by feeding and donating to the Sioux. White traders and travelers often accused the Sioux of begging, but this was a different matter to the tribesmen. They expected a "reciprocal system of gift exchange as a form of hospitality." Whites often misunderstood this notion as begging or theft, especially when the Sioux took livestock, for instance, when gifts were not forthcoming. To them, gifts were "presents in exchange for resources." When Sioux appropriated livestock "as compensation for their material losses," such as game taken from their territory by travelers, they implied "no immorality." Yet to whites such was theft, and friendly Sioux appeared "vicious and duplicitous."[25] By his actions, these Sioux saw Collins as a friend, a perception Collins would assiduously attempt to maintain.

The battalion continued on, past many stations and road ranches, passing slower moving wagon trains headed either to or coming from Laramie or Denver. Just after Julesburg, along the South Platte River, the road forked, with the Oregon road taking a ford across that stream, then angling northwest to pick up the North Platte again, while the Denver road followed southwest along the South Platte. The 9th Wisconsin left the column for Denver, as the 6th Ohio crossed the river and took the road north. At the Mud Springs telegraph station, eight miles east of the landmark known as Courthouse Rock, about forty-six miles from Scotts Bluff, the 6th joined Company G, 8th Kansas Volunteer Infantry, and escorted it to Fort Laramie. The Kansans were "no trouble," Collins said.[26] The units moved on, passing other famous landmarks such as Chimney Rock and Scotts Bluff. Fewer road ranches and stations dotted the road after Julesburg, and other traffic thinned as well.

---

[25]Michael L. Tate, "From Cooperation to Conflict: Sioux Relations with the Overland Emigrants, 1845–1865," *Overland Journal* 18, no. 4 (Winter 2000/2001): 21–22.

[26]Spring, *Caspar Collins*, 106–7; *O.R.*, I, 22, pt. 1, p. 893.

On May 30, a violent thunderstorm with cold, driving rain soaked the 348 men of the 6th Ohio and the Kansans who marched with them as they finally arrived at Fort Laramie. Young Caspar, though, kept dry by riding in the ambulance. The 6th pitched its tents in the rain just outside the fort. Collins reported to Colonel Edmund B. Alexander, commander of the post. The garrison at Laramie included two companies of the 10th United States Infantry and two skeleton companies of the 4th United States Cavalry. Collins and Alexander conferred by telegraph with Brigadier General James Craig, who since April 16 commanded "all troops in the vicinity of the Overland mail Route" from the Missouri River to "the western boundary of the district." Craig delighted Alexander by ordering him to take the 10th Infantry to Fort Kearny; Collins, as ranking officer, took command of Laramie and its garrison of four companies of the 6th Ohio, the two small companies of the 4th United States Cavalry, and the company of Kansas Infantry.[27]

The march from Fort Leavenworth, about 670 miles in twenty-six days, took its toll on both men and animals. "The men are getting ragged," Collins wrote to his wife from Laramie, and need needles, "buttons, thread, darning needles, and woolen yarn." He added that "many" of his mules were "unfit to haul." But little rest would be in store for either the troopers or the mules.[28]

In the winter of 1862 Bannock, Shoshoni, Sioux, and Northern Cheyenne tribesmen harassed stage stations along the Oregon road from Fort Bridger east across the Continental Divide and along the Sweetwater River to Platte Bridge

[27] *Collins Family Papers*, items 30, 32; *O.R.*, I, 13, p. 362; David B. Robrock, "The Eleventh Ohio Volunteer Cavalry on the Central Plains, 1862–1866," *Arizona and the West* 25, no. 1 (Spring, 1983): 24.

[28] *Collins Family Papers*, item 32. Rest would have been welcome: the 6th had gained over 3,400 feet elevation since leaving Leavenworth; Laramie was 4,200 feet above sea level.

station on the North Platte, about 130 miles north of Fort Laramie. On April 4, about the time the Ohioans left St. Louis for Fort Leavenworth, the Overland Mail Company reported that "marauders" burned their stations "between Fort Bridger and the North Platte, destroyed mail and coaches . . . and killed several men." Another report April 17 chronicled similar trouble along the Sweetwater. By the end of April, mail and passenger stages no longer ran on the Oregon road, and the telegraph was cut, making communication with California impossible. Colonel Alexander knew that his small detachments could not handle the problem.[29]

The Oregon road also served as a lifeline for the Mormons in the Salt Lake settlements. They reacted to its closure when their leader, Bringham Young, sent Colonel Robert T. Burton and a detachment of twenty mounted men to escort a mail and passenger train bound east over the road on April 24. The convoy passed through the danger zone to the North Platte River bridge safely, at which point the armed escort returned to Salt Lake. Unharmed, the Mormon train continued east. Burton and his Mormon militia made the round trip in thirty days, the extent of their rations.[30]

On April 28, four days after Burton left to escort the Mormon train east, the War Department authorized Young to raise a company of cavalry for ninety days of service. They had orders to protect the telegraph and overland mail "in or about Independence Rock," on the Sweetwater River about forty-eight miles west of Platte Bridge on the Oregon road, and were to remain in service until troops from the East could take over from them. Mustered in by April 29, Captain Lot Smith took command. They struck out May 1, with ten baggage and supply wagons for support. They reached Independence Rock

[29]Hafen, *Overland Mail*, 242–46; Becher, *Massacre Along the Medicine Road*, 65.

[30]Ray C. Colton, *The Civil War in the Western Territories: Arizona, Colorado, New Mexico, and Utah* (Norman: The University of Oklahoma Press, 1959), 161.

about May 20, ten days before Collins and the Ohioans arrived at Fort Laramie. As they followed the road east they passed many mail stations, "one every ten miles," that "lay in heaps of blackened ashes," many still smoking. "Wagon-loads of United States mail were scattered and destroyed by the Indians."[31] Lot's Mormon company remained on station until the Ohioans made contact with them.

When Collins's battalion reached Fort Laramie on May 30, they found a military post that in many ways resembled a village. Most of the living quarters for officers and men were located around a large parade ground. Some buildings were built of logs, others of lumber, and a few of adobe. The structures included houses for officers, barracks for enlisted men, stables, a hospital, a bakery, a jail, a telegraph office, and a sutler's store and house. Other edifices existed as well. Emigrant wagon trains camped nearby, as did Native American traders. No earthworks or stockade existed; it was not a fortified post. It was the largest military station west of Fort Leavenworth.[32] Forty-five miles west, the slopes of Laramie Peak (10,272 feet above sea level and 6,072 feet above the fort) provided timber for the post's sawmill. But most of the 6th Ohio remained at Laramie only a few days before they saddled up again and took the Oregon road north and west.

---

[31]E. B. Long, *The Saints and the Union: Utah Territory during the Civil War* (Urbana: The University of Illinois Press, 1981), 84–89; *O.R.*, III, 2, p. 27; Roy P. Basler, ed., *The Collected Works of Abraham Lincoln* (8 vols., New Brunswick: Rutgers University Press, 1953–55), vol. 5, p. 200n.

[32]*Collins Family Papers*, item 21. Caspar drew a large landscape picture of the fort, which is reproduced, among other places, in Spring, ed., "An Army Wife Comes West," 254.

CHAPTER THREE

On the Overland Roads, 1862

While Collins was leading the Ohio battalion to St. Louis and up the trail to Fort Laramie, and as Lot Smith's Mormon company climbed over the South Pass to the vicinity of Independence Rock, the war in the East thundered on. The intrepid Grant took forts Henry and Donelson in Tennessee in February. Bringing to the world the important notice of ironclad warships and the vulnerability of wooden navies, the Union *Monitor* fought the Confederate *Merrimac* to a draw March 9. On the 17th McClellan sent his Union army south to begin his ill-fated Peninsular Campaign. West of the Mississippi, Brigadier General Samuel R. Curtis chastized Confederates at Pea Ridge, in Arkansas, on March 7. Three weeks later, on March 28, Colorado troops helped save New Mexico for the Union at Glorietta Pass. Grant's army managed to pull victory from disaster at Shiloh, Tennessee, on April 7, while Brigadier General John Pope opened the upper Mississippi by taking Island Number 10 about the same time. And then on April 25, New Orleans fell to daring Flag Officer David G. Farragut. In May the news from McClellan's campaign in Virginia was not good; Confederate General Thomas J. Jackson raided in the Shenandoah Valley; and as May turned to June an overly cautious Major General Halleck crept from Shiloh to Corinth in northern Mississippi.

Although the attention of government officials in the nation's capital clearly focused on these and related events, some remained worried about the loyalty of Mormons in Utah and how motivated they would be to protect the roads to California and Oregon, not to mention the mail and telegraph. Opting not to rely on the Mormons, the War Department, rather than dispatch more troops from the East where it seemed every man was needed, chose to send California troops east to Utah in May. In this way they could keep a wary eye on Brigham Young and his disciples and police the Oregon road east of Salt Lake to the South Pass. But the Mormons would have to keep order until the Californians arrived. Colonel Patrick Edward Connor started the 3rd California Volunteer Infantry and five companies of the 2nd California Cavalry eastward three months later, with instructions to make his headquarters in Salt Lake. They would not be on station until October.[1]

The Ohioans knew of the fighting taking place back east. The telegraph line that passed by Fort Laramie brought nearly instantaneous war news and instructions from their commanders. On June 4, 1862, with only five days' rest after the long march from Fort Leavenworth, Collins received orders to saddle up and follow the Oregon road to the South Pass, stationing detachments of his battalion along the way as he thought necessary. When he met Lot Smith's Mormon unit, he could use them temporarily if he chose. Collins left a detachment of Company A at Laramie, and moved out with the other three companies and portions of the 4th U. S. Cavalry, whose veterans who knew the way.[2]

The column moved rapidly along the road, through gener-

---

[1]Colton, *Civil War in the Western Territories*, 164; *O.R.*, I, 50, pt. 2, pp. 5–6; James F. Varley, *Brigham and the Brigadier* (Tucson, Ariz.: Westernlore Press, 1989), 25–34.

[2]Spring, *Caspar Collins*, 37; *Collins Family Papers*, item 1; Alvin M. Josephy, Jr., *The Civil War in the American West* (New York: Alfred A. Knopf, 1991), 248.

ally arid, rolling country. Some of the hills were thickly carpeted with spring flowers, contrasting with the high, snow-capped mountains visible in the distant north and west. The Ohioans arrived at Deer Creek station, eighty-nine miles from Fort Laramie, two days later. There they met an emigrant wagon train waiting for an escort. Collins assigned Lieutenant Oliver S. Glenn and thirty men that duty, and rode on, leaving orders for the slow-moving train and escort to join him at South Pass. Glenn and the train traveled only about twenty-two miles from Deer Creek when an estimated five hundred Indians appeared on the opposite bank of the North Platte River. Glenn dispatched a messenger to Collins, who quickly sent sixty more men back to Glenn's aid. By the time reinforcements arrived, the Indians had disappeared. The river, "a roaring torrent from mountain snowmelt," would have been difficult for troopers to cross in pursuit and easy for tribesmen to defend if they chose.[3]

By June 16, Collins and his troopers arrived at Sweetwater station, 164 miles west of Fort Laramie. A bridge spanned the Sweetwater River at that time, opposite the landmark Independence Rock, upon which many who had passed before had cut their names, including Captain Van Winkle. There Collins met Lot Smith's Mormon detachment, which would join the Ohioans march to South Pass. The troopers had faced hard rain and hail the previous day, and while that abated, the wind still howled. Bridger sought shelter away from the wind, but young Caspar and Pallady shot at targets near Independence Rock. Caspar wrote that food was abundant on the march, with plenty of fish, a cattle herd to supply fresh

---

[3]Spring, *Caspar Collins*, 38; *Collins Family Papers*, item 1; Hebard and Brininstool, *The Bozeman Trail*, vol. 1, 78. Spring identifies the river twenty-two miles west of Deer Creek as the Sweetwater, but that is geographically impossible. It had to be the North Platte. Most of the distances given in the text above are computed from Gregory M. Franzwa, *Maps of the Oregon Trail* (St. Louis: The Patrice Press, 1990).

beef, and syrup, sugar, and coffee among the quartermaster stores. They baked fresh pan bread. Bridger and Pallady dined with Caspar and his father. Pallady had brought in an antelope the day before, the "finest flesh ever tasted, resembles venison a little" but better, Caspar wrote. Along the way they often saw bears, and "a great many immigrants," including Mormon provision trains.[4]

Lot Smith later told Brigham Young of his meeting with Collins. "Col. Collins is decidely against killing Indians indiscriminately, and will not take any general measures, save on the defensive, until he can ascertain satisfactorily by whom the depredations have been committed, and then not resort to killing until he is satisfied that peaceable measures have failed." Collins had learned, perhaps from Bridger and Pallady, that there were differences between tribes and even bands of the same tribe, something others in the army usually ignored and could have profited from. It marked Collins as a more sophisticated leader than many other army officers.[5]

Collins's cavalry moved on west, dropping off along the way detachments of ten to twenty men at each of the four major stagecoach stations, located about twenty to thirty-five miles apart, beginning with Sweetwater Station. East to west, the other stations were Three Crossings, St. Mary's or Rocky Ridge, and South Pass or Upper Crossings. These were "home stations," bigger than others along the way, and included a building where stage passengers could find food and lodging, a telegraph office, a corral, and a barn to house supplies and hay. All were much in need of repair, another job for the Ohioans stationed there. Over the summer the troops also built barracks and stables. The farthest station was over

---

[4]*Collins Family Papers*, item 1. The bridge across the Sweetwater is mentioned by William Smedley in his diary. Smedley was with a couple of partners in a lone wagon and crossed the bridge a few days after Collins. See Smedley, *Across the Plains*, 27.

[5]Long, *The Saints and the Union*, 87.

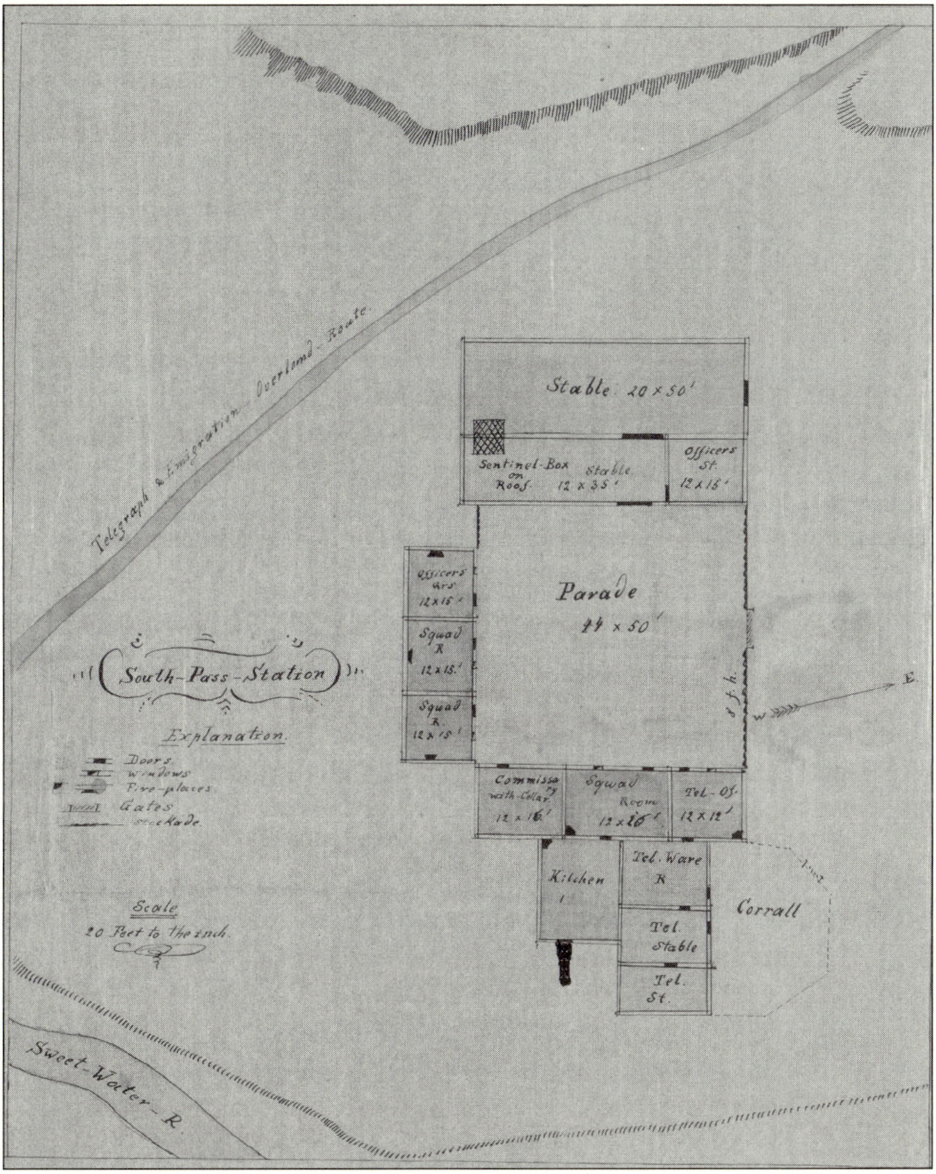

South Pass Station

Sketch by Second Lt. Caspar Collins, Company G, 11th Ohio Volunteer Cavalry. Collins was mustered into service June 30, 1863, and was killed in action at Platte Bridge, Dakota Territory on June 26, 1865. *All Collins sketches are courtesy of the Caspar Collins Collection, Archives and Special Collections Department, Colorado State University Library.*

South Pass Station
Drawing by Private Charles F. Moellman, bugler, Company G, 11th Ohio Volunteer Cavalry. Moellman was mustered into service July 17, 1863, and mustered out on may 2, 1866, at Omaha, Nebraska Territory. Note the telegraph line in each drawing. *All Moellman drawings are courtesy of the American Heritage Center, University of Wyoming.*

330 miles from Fort Laramie; supply wagons took twenty days to make the trip.[6]

On June 27 Collins ordered the Mormon company to return to Fort Bridger to protect the Oregon road from Green River, west of South Pass, through Fort Bridger to Salt Lake. That was quite a task for them, but one that echoed the directive previously given by General Craig. Collins believed his Ohioans could handle the job east of South Pass; he arrived at Upper Crossing, close to South Pass, on June 29.[7]

Meanwhile, Craig arrived at Fort Laramie on June 26, though he had the option of making his headquarters at either Laramie or Kearny. Craig's superiors told him that it was "of

[6]Josephy, *Civil War in the American West*, 249; David B. Robrock, "The Eleventh Ohio Volunteer Cavalry on the Central Plains, 1862–1866," *Arizona and the West* 25, no. 1 (Spring 1983): 26.

[7]Long, *The Saints and the Union*, 87; Colton, *The Civil War in the Western Territories*, 162. Collins's troopers gained another 3,300 feet of elevation from Fort Laramie. Elevation of the South Pass was 7,550 feet above sea level.

the utmost importance that the overland mail should be uninterrupted" and was ordered to "insure ample protection to . . . [the] mail company and their property against Indians or other depredators." When he reached Fort Laramie he learned of Collins's troop dispositions by telegraph. He immediately provided that information to his commander, Brigadier General James G. Blunt, who headed the military Department of Kansas, which then included the Oregon road as far as South Pass. Craig told Blunt that "Indians" daily commited depredations on the road between Green River and Salt Lake, but though this was outside Blunt's department, Craig nevertheless used the Mormon troops there, knowing "they are not sufficient." The Ohioans, he telegraphed, "are now distributed on 300 miles of line, and it would be dangerous" to send any of them to assist. Craig admitted he had no answers, as "the California troops" would not arrive "for some weeks to come." Blunt did not respond. Craig incidentally also assigned First Lieutenant Wesley Love, Company B, Ohio battalion, to his staff.[8]

Near South Pass, Collins established what his son called "a permanent camp." Caspar thought it a "pleasant" place, but there was no timber close by, and "emigrants have chased off nearly all the game, and their oxen have eaten nearly all the grass." A messenger had come into camp the previous day with news that Lieutenant Glenn, still escorting the slow-moving provision train that was to rendezvous with the Ohioans at South Pass, had been attacked by Indians. This time Collins put one hundred men in the saddle and again sped to Glenn's rescue. By the time Collins arrived on the

[8] *O.R.*, I, 53, Supplement, p. 520; I, 13, pp. 362, 451; *Collins Family Papers*, item 1. James G. Blunt, a physician, was a Kansas antislavery activist who rose quickly from lieutenant colonel to brigadier general in Kansas volunteer service. Later, Blunt would be promoted to major general after victories over Confederate forces in Missouri, Arkansas, and Indian Territory.

scene, the attackers had fled, after managing to kill two emigrants and narrowly missing Glenn. Caspar noted "nearly every tribe of Indians in this country are at war with one another," and speculated that the attackers were Sioux who had unsuccessfully raided the Snakes, enemies of theirs west of the divide, and hit the emigrant train on their way back to their village—not at all an uncommon tactic of young warriors.[9]

The trail between Independence Rock west to the South Pass proved a busy one just at that time. William Smedley, an adventurer bound for Oregon, camped for the night of July 2 with "about fifty soldiers," doubtless Ohioans, who had passed him earlier in the day. He believed the soldiers were an escort for the "Governor of Utah." On July 4 Smedley passed the graves of the two emigrants killed "six days before," no doubt those Caspar mentioned. On July 5 Smedley found "a deserted stage coach and the wreck of a trader's wagon which had been plundered by the Indians a few days previous." On July 6, he crossed the South Pass, camping that evening at Pacific Springs, just west of the divide. The next day he heard that during the night the Indians stole "some stock from the soldiers, quartered nearby for the protection of emigrants."[10]

While in camp near the South Pass, young Caspar provided his mother with literary snapshots of his surroundings, but transmitted no news of military activity. He wrote that "the Colonel" (his father) finally issued the stores they brought from Fort Leavenworth. The gastronomic delicacies he listed included "pickled cucumbers and onions, French mustard, Worcestershire sauce and pepper, green tea," and a jar of strawberry preserves "that we intend to eat on the 4th of

[9] *Collins Family Papers*, item 2. The "Snakes" were Shoshoni, traditional enemies of both the Sioux and Cheyenne.

[10] Smedley, *Across the Plains*, 28–31. The new governor of Utah was Stephen S. Harding. Smedley, by the way, made it to Oregon safely.

July." For comfort, they had two tents, a small one "with a fly to sit under in warm weather," and a larger regulation Sibley tent. They took their meals in the Sibley tent, and Caspar noted, "Mr. Pallady sleeps there." But Jim Bridger and his father slept "in the little tent." He failed to specify where he slept.[11]

"These old mountaineers," Caspar continued, "nearly all wear big white hats with beaver around it," a comfortable buckskin coat "trimmed with beaver fur," and "buffalo breeches" as they sat astride a Mexican saddle, moccasins on their feet but with "spurs . . . two inches long which jingle as they ride." Their bridles had "maybe ten dollars [*sic*] worth of silver ornaments on," they rode Indian ponies, and were armed with "a heavy rifle, a navy revolver, a hatchet and bowie knife." They carried a "rawhide lasso tied on one side of the saddle" as well. Caspar painted a romantic picture of Bridger and Pallady.[12]

Unlike Caspar, Craig found his situation far from poetic. At Fort Laramie on July 1, Craig telegraphed Blunt that some 160 head "of animals" were stolen from emigrants two days earlier at Ice Springs, between Three Crossings station and St. Mary's station along the Sweetwater River. Craig asked for more troops:

> I cannot cover 500 miles of road with the small force now here. The Indians do and can get in between my detachment[s]. . . . The road is in danger daily from Platte Bridge to Salt Lake Valley. Two men were murdered [recently] . . . at Rocky Ridge [just west of St. Mary's station]. . . . The telegraph line is down west of this post.[13]

---

[11] *Collins Family Papers*, item 2.

[12] Ibid. Caspar filled his letters with sketches right in with his text. However, spurs on moccasins is questionable: he may not have meant it that way. Examples of Caspar's letters and sketches can be found reproduced in Alex Service, *The Life and Letters of Caspar W. Collins* (Casper, Wyo.: The City of Casper, 2000), illustrations 11–15.

[13] *O.R.*, I, 13, p. 459. Smedley said the loss was 135 horses, and the military could not do anything about it because the telegraph was down and they couldn't get authorization to make a search. Smedley, *Across the Plains*, 27–28.

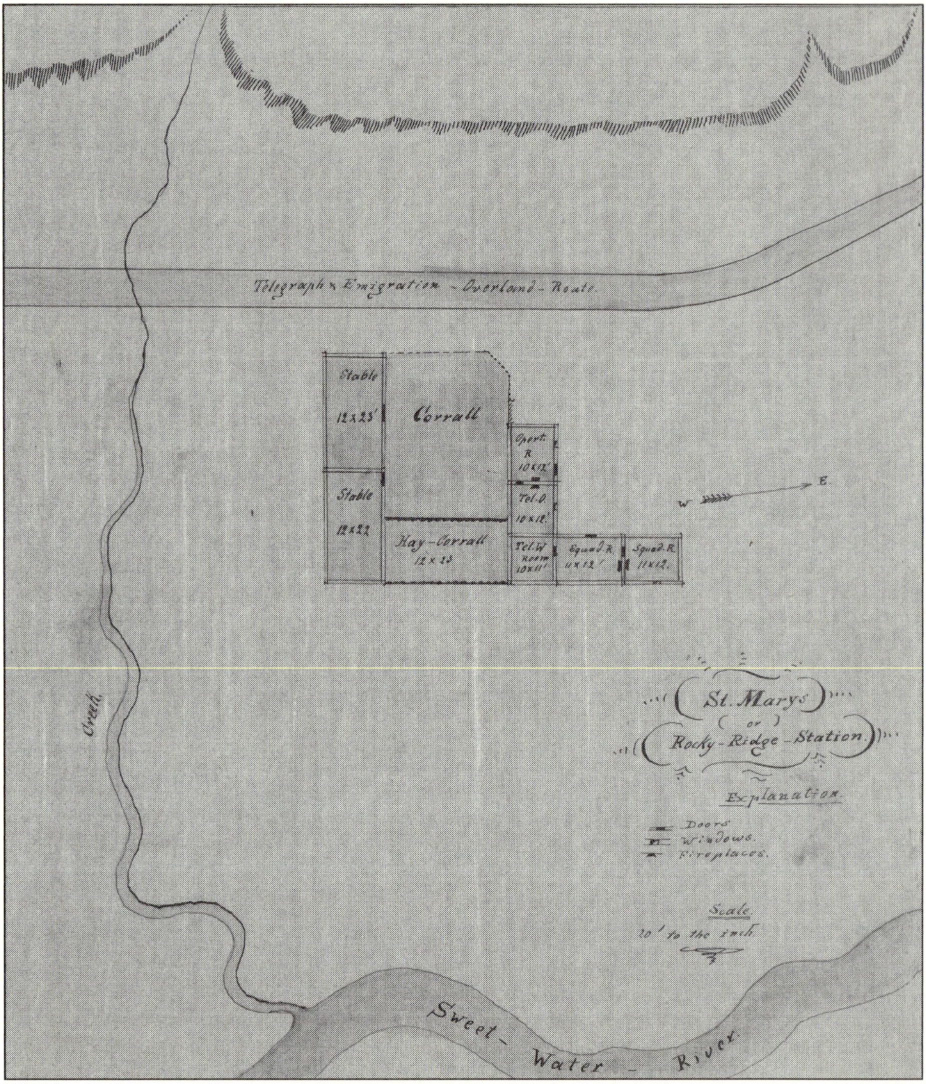

St. Mary's Station
Sketch by Second Lieutenant Caspar Collins.

St. Mary's Station
Drawing by Private
Charles F. Moellman.

On July 2 Collins took a scouting party of perhaps a dozen men and rafted up a section of the Sweetwater looking for a ford. Shortly after he left, five young men of the Ohio battalion, most all from Company D, drew a week's rations, borrowed extra revolvers, and deserted. They told the others that Collins had ordered them to follow the south side of the river until they could cross it and join him. They became the first of a small number who deserted from time to time. Captain Smith and a squad of Mormon troops trailed them to Fort Bridger, then lost them.[14] Later on, some other deserters also willingly traded military duty for dreams of wealth in the gold fields of Montana.

On July 6 Caspar wrote his mother again. They were still camped near South Pass, but he now found life "very dull." Two companies had left the day before "to guard the road below here," leaving only one company and a few men from

[14]Spring, *Caspar Collins*, 38–39. Spring claims one of these men was from Co. E, but there was no such company then.

Three Crossings Station
Drawing by Private Charles F. Moellman.

others who were ill "or whose horses can't travel." Quite a few troopers bought ponies to use in order to save their "regular horses," so Caspar did, too. It was "a very pretty and gentle one." He assured his mother they had plenty of "very good" rations and antelope meat, as well as "desicated [*sic*] potatoes" that "look like corn meal when they come out of the package, but are just like any other potatoes when cooked." He marvelled that the mountains were still white with snow and there was even a "large snow bank within 300 yards" in July "when the weather is as warm as back home." Almost as a footnote, Caspar mentioned that Lieutenant Carman Vanada returned from Utah, after escorting federal judges there.[15]

On July 10 Craig reported to Blunt that the Post Office

[15] *Collins Family Papers*, item 3. Escort duty like Vanada's was common for the Ohio battalion; to Caspar it doubtless appeared more exciting than remaining in camp. Also, cavalry horses were scarce on the frontier, and men sought to rest them as often as possible. The larger cavalry horses required more subsistence than lighter western ponies.

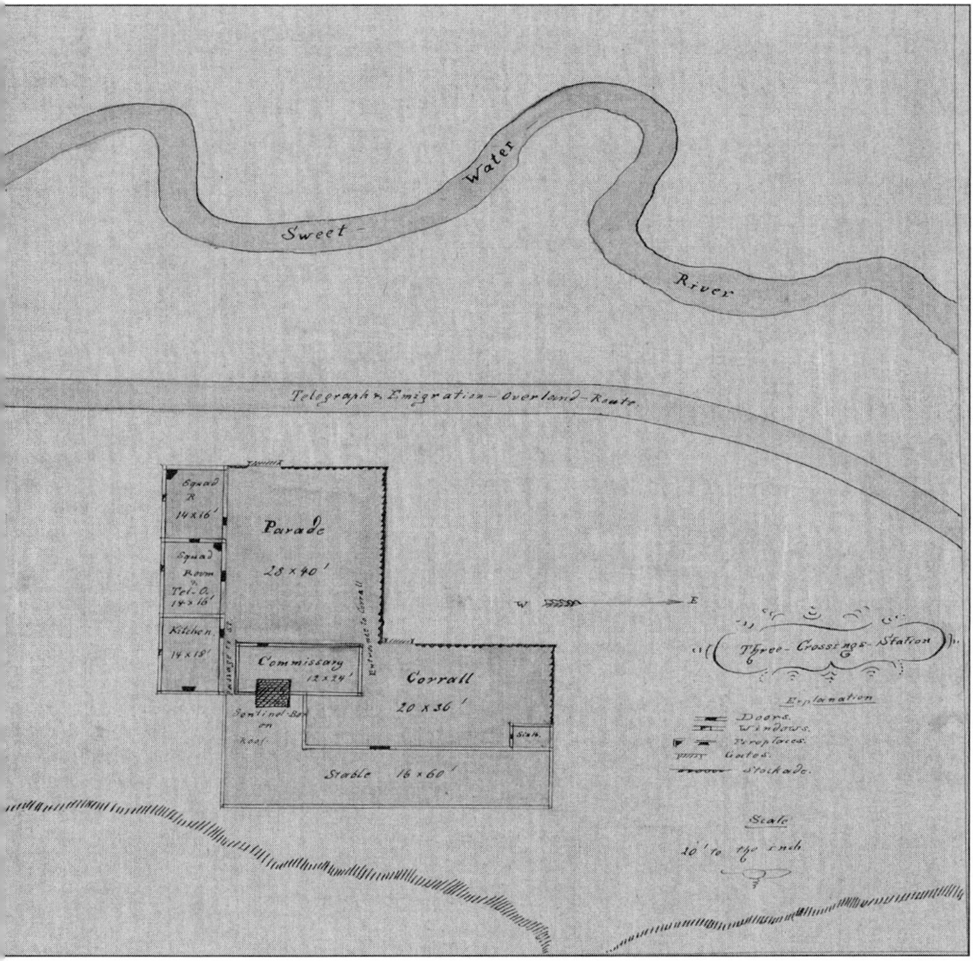

THREE CROSSINGS STATION
Sketch by Second Lieutenant Caspar Collins.

Department ordered the mail company to remove their stages and stock from the Oregon road "to a route 100 miles south," the old Cherokee or Overland Trail, thought to be a less hazardous route. He could furnish escorts "for the property and men," but he quite properly worried that emigrant trains and the telegraph on the Oregon road would be left unprotected if the troops went south to guard the mail. Craig also claimed that "white men are leading the Indians." The next day Craig told Blunt his orders were to protect the overland mail "along the telegraph line." But now the mail was moved away, the telegraph remained where it was, and he was not sure how to monitor both. With the few troops he had, "the Sixth Ohio Cavalry about 300 strong and two skeleton companies of the [United States] Fourth Regiment Cavalry, about 60 men," how could he guard the many additional miles between Bridger and Fort Laramie? The Indians were bold, even robbing a mail station within two hours after a detachment of Collins's troops passed by. Congress required the mail to run daily from the Missouri River to California, and twice a week to Salt Lake City and Denver. Again Craig requested reinforcements so he could do his job. He also needed hay and grain for the cavalry horses for the winter.[16]

The Ohioans reacted to their challenging new orders swiftly. Major O'Ferrall gathered troops from Company D at Platte Bridge and Fort Laramie, rode west to Sweetwater station where he met much of Company A and employees of the Overland Mail Company with their coaches and stock, and escorted them south to the new mail route. (No sooner had they gotten underway when Indians attacked and burned the Three Crossings station, thirty-five miles west of Sweetwater, and ran off the stock.) By July 20 O'Ferrall and

[16] *O.R.*, I, 13, pp. 466, 468–69. At least some of the "white men" probably were Native American mixed-bloods.

the Ohioans camped at the foot of Elk Mountain, unaware of the trouble behind them. They set to work to build a fort to anchor this central portion of the new mail route. The Overland road followed the South Platte to the Cache la Poudre River about sixty miles north of Denver, then arched across the Laramie plains past the north base of Elk Mountain, then west through Bridger Pass to Fort Bridger, where it joined the Oregon road. By the end of August the new post was largely in place and received the name Fort Halleck, after Major General Henry W. Halleck, recently promoted by Lincoln to general-in-chief. When fully completed, Fort Halleck would have quarters for two companies, along with officer's quarters, headquarters, storehouses, a hospital, bakeshop, stables, and a sutler's store. Fort Halleck would be on a center line from where the Cache la Poudre River met the South Platte, to Bridger Pass, about 175 miles. Fort Bridger was still about 150 miles from the pass; the 6th would have to patrol at least as far as the pass.[17]

That August Collins's battalion of Ohioans was officially detached from the 6th Ohio Volunteer Cavalry, and became the First Independent Battalion of Ohio Volunteer Cavalry, at least so far as Ohio authorities were concerned. Official army reports continued to call them the 6th, which should have been confusing because after Collins left Ohio, the remainder of the 6th, at Camp Dennison, recruited a battalion to replace Collins. They received their horses and equipment and went to fight Confederates in the East. The change mattered little to Collins and his men, who were quite busy building Fort Halleck on the Overland road, repairing and enlarging the little posts on the Oregon road

[17]Ibid., I, 13, p. 592; Spring, *Caspar Collins*, 130; *Collins Family Papers*, item 5; Robrock, "Eleventh Ohio," 26–27; John D. McDermott, *Frontier Crossroads: The History of Fort Caspar and the Upper Platte Crossing* (Casper, Wyoming: The City of Casper, 1997), 30. Other names mentioned for Fort Halleck were those of Secretary of War Edwin Stanton, the late Colonel (and former Senator) Edward D. Baker, and Lincoln.

between Platte Bridge and the South Pass, and dealing with emigrants as well as marauding tribesmen who delighted in cutting the telegraph.[18]

Early in August Collins, along with Caspar, Lieutenant Glenn, Bridger, Pallady, and twenty-two troopers, plus teamsters and their wagons, left the Upper Crossing station on an exploratory trip to the Wind River country in the north. Gone over ten days, they braved a couple days of rain and "two heavy frosts"; ate deer, antelope, sage hens, ducks, pheasants, jack rabbits, and trout; and saw exciting new scenery but no Indians. While they were gone, raiders on the Oregon road killed a teamster and took his mule herd. In a pursuit led by Captain Hamer Hayes of Company B, the soldiers managed to recover "almost all the mules."[19]

Meanwhile an event took place in Minnesota that disturbed Native Americans throughout the West, and both directly and indirectly affected the Ohio battalion. On August 17 the Sioux in Minnesota went on the warpath and ravaged the Minnesota frontier, killing hundreds of white settlers. Hastily assembled Minnesota volunteers ended the brief but bloody war in mid-September. This Sioux outburst frightened Minnesota's neighbors, particularly in Wisconsin, Iowa, and Dakota and Nebraska territories. Word quickly spread to Sioux cousins and friends throughout the northwest. Hundreds of frightened white settlers fled outlying areas for safer ground, abandoning towns and farms not only in Minnesota, but also in Dakota and Nebraska. The news streaked across telegraph wires, alerting the entire northwestern frontier.[20]

The news troubled Craig, too, as an even larger picture appeared to him. On August 23, he telegraphed Secretary of War Edward M. Stanton that "Indians, from Minnesota to

[18]Ware, *Indian War*, 488; Reid, *Ohio in the War*, vol. 2, 819; *O.R.*, I, 13, p. 811.
[19]*Collins Family Papers*, item 4.
[20]Jones, *The Civil War in the Northwest*, especially Chapter 2.

Pike's Peak, and from Salt Lake to near Fort Kearny" were on the warpath. He had far too few troops to handle the situation. If nothing else, he wanted authority "to raise 100 mounted men in the mountains and re-enlist the Utah troops for a limited time." He urged Stanton to answer by telegraph, for "we have no mails at this post." Relocation of the postal route had left Fort Laramie without mail delivery. This time Craig received the authorizations he sought from Stanton. Craig told Halleck that "he was satisfied rebel agents have been at work among the Indians. Many emigrants" en route to the Montana mines "were from border slave states," where it was "too hot" for them to remain. Presumably these were "rebel" sympathizers, although no evidence of a Confederate conspiracy in the Northwest existed.[21]

If permission to raise more troops pleased Craig, it was short-lived. He complained to Blunt on August 30 that he could not "re-enlist the Mormon troops" nor could he find the mountain men he had requested. He still desperately needed more manpower, so now he asked if he could raise "two companies in Colorado." He reviewed his troop placements and noted that they were poorly supplied, their horses worn out, and were short of ammunition. "Indians have murdered many immigrants west of the continental divide between Fort Hall and the Salmon River," along the road to the Montana mines immediately west of his district, and were about to pounce on his "scattered detachments on the telegraph line." He added that he would "carefully avoid doing anything that would inaugurate a war with the Indians," since if he tried to strike them, it "would insure the destruction of the emigrants, the telegraph and mail lines," and he had too few soldiers to prevent it.[22]

---

[21]Craig corresponded with Stanton because he couldn't reach Blunt, his department commander, as Blunt was "in the field." *O.R.*, I, 13, pp. 592, 600, and also III, 2, pp. 449, 453. Stanton's reply in Series III bears the correct date.

[22]*O.R.*, I, 13, pp. 607–8.

On August 31 young Caspar Collins, finally on his way back to Fort Laramie, wrote his mother again from Independence Rock. He told about an excursion to Green River, west of the Continental Divide, that took six days. They found plenty of game along the way. He mentioned that they planned to visit the new Fort Halleck with General Craig after they returned to Laramie. He noted again that their horses "are pretty well ridden down," after all the use they had. Caspar commented on the "large Mormon train" that "passed here yesterday, 80 wagons with 5, 6, and 7 yoke of Oxen. All [the emigrants] were from Denmark and Sweden and few could speak English." They were "travel worn, the greater part having walked on foot all the way from Omaha."[23]

As Caspar and a detachment of the 6th Ohio made their way back to Laramie, passing many westward-bound wagon trains, Craig tended to business. From his headquarters at the fort, Craig protested an order to send Company G, 8th Kansas Infantry, back to Fort Leavenworth: with too few troops already, and no others in sight, he could hardly do anything else. It was Halleck, responding from Washington, who told him to "retain the Kansas company." About the same time, the governor of Nebraska complained to Secretary of War Stanton that "a powerful band of Indians returning from Minnesota" was infesting northern Nebraska. There, "settlers by the hundreds" were "fleeing. Instant action demanded." He asked Stanton for money to subsist and pay Nebraska militia, as the territory was "without credit or cent of money." The governor claimed his militia could handle the situation if only he could pay them. Stanton referred him to Major General John Pope, who, after his defeat at Second Bull Run, had been hastily reassigned to command the new Department of the Northwest, headquartered in St. Paul, Minnesota. Pope, whose new job was to handle the Sioux uprising there, would

[23] *Collins Family Papers*, item 5.

"take proper measures to protect" Nebraska Territory too, so Stanton assumed. At least Stanton put no demands on Craig for any of his soldiers. Both of these instances illustrated an urgent need for more troops than existed on the frontier, and at a time when the federal government almost totally focused on the terrible war in the east.[24]

After he returned to Fort Laramie, Caspar wrote his mother a little about life on that post. "They make soldiers wear white gloves at this post and they cut around very fashionably." Many of the regulars of the 4th U.S. Cavalry were married, he wrote, "and have their wives and families with them." In addition, "there are five women allowed to a company, who are furnished with transportation and rations, and wash and mend, etc. Their pay is kept out of the soldiers' wages and given to them on pay day." At Fort Laramie they lived in small two-room houses, and these housekeepers were "nearly all Irish and Germans." Caspar also thought "any of the noncommissioned officers" among the regulars "are better than a great many commissioned officers of volunteers." For themselves, the Ohioans drilled five days a week, and each evening officers and men attended classes related to military procedures. They enthusiastically practiced target shooting. Those individuals chosen for the artillery (howitzer) detachment became proficient.[25]

On about September 20 a party of Cheyenne Indians visited Fort Laramie, on their way to the Powder River country in the north. "They had expected to find some game along the way, but found little" and "were hungry," Caspar wrote. They "seated themselves on the parade ground" in the center of the fort's buildings, with the "chiefs in a small semi-circle, old men and medicine men in two small semi-circles at each side

[24] *O.R.*, I, 13, 614, 616, 621–22.

[25] *Collins Family Papers*, item 7; Spring, *Caspar Collins*, 40. It is not clear what Caspar meant by "better," perhaps he meant better behaved or perhaps more experienced, or both.

a little back, warriors behind them," back of them "the boys, and in the background the women and other children." Caspar estimated the group included about ninety warriors and three hundred women and children. "Some of the men had guns, but most had bows and arrows." Caspar failed to relate the subsequent details, but doubtless Collins reassured them of his peaceful intentions, as he had the Sioux previously, and certainly fed them.[26]

In the last week of September Collins took a party from Laramie to Fort Halleck, both to explore an alternate route there and to inspect the new post, just as Caspar had earlier said they would. It took the command six days to make the 125-mile trip. "For the first few days, we had nothing to eat but fat pork, etc., but at last we killed two antelope" and other game. Besides his father, the party included General Craig, Lieutenant Glenn, a wagon master, a few troopers, teamsters, and a cook. "The whole country" between forts Laramie and Halleck "is covered with lakes, both large and small, which are covered with ducks. We came through a pass in the mountains, the sides of which were . . . three or four hundred feet high and perpendicular." They spent two nights in rain and sleet without tents "and had a rather disagreeable time."[27]

They found Elk Mountain, immediately south of Fort Halleck, "covered with new-fallen snow." The area proved rich in game, many elk, deer, and bears. Lieutenant Thomas P. Clark commanded the post, and a surgeon and quartermaster of the 4th United States Cavalry were on hand, in addition to the Ohioans. An abundance of wood was nearby; three small streams ran through the post; the stables had been completed but not the barracks. "This is the windiest place I ever saw," wrote Caspar, "a hurricane blowing the

[26] *Collins Family Papers*, item 6.

[27] Hebard and Brininstool, *The Bozeman Trail*, vol. 1, 95–96. They quoted Caspar's letter, in which he mistakenly calls General Craig "Captain."

whole time." But "it is a beautiful place" with the "tall mountains rising so abruptly" behind it.[28] Caspar made no reference to the Overland road or the mail coaches that used it.

Taking a different route, just over a hundred miles in seven days, the party arrived back at Fort Laramie on October 7. According to Caspar, the party had "a very pleasant trip through the mountains." They "killed a great many antelope" on the way. They also "had some pretty hard freezes and one snowstorm that melted as it fell." He thought they traveled through "some of the grandest scenery you ever saw. . . . Immense piles of rock, covered with pines, and beautiful valleys of grass that is up to your waist," and many clear springs. He wrote a good deal about Jim Bridger, clearly impressed by his stories. He found Bridger "totally uneducated, but he speaks English, Spanish, and French equally well, besides nearly a dozen Indian tongues." Caspar was not particularly happy to return to Fort Laramie: "I always dread it," because life on the post was so boring. "Everyday is the same except the changes of weather." Still, it was reasonably warm at the fort, "but in the mountains it is as cold as it is with us [in Ohio] in November."[29]

They returned to Fort Laramie with a wagonload of game "we distributed among the officers and others." A wife of one of the regulars who ran "the boarding house" served them stuffed sage hens, which they had donated. Caspar mentioned that "we" eat some meals at the boarding house, but he liked the work of their own cook better. He "is a miner and has been in Mexico for several years. He cooks all kinds of outlandish dishes one of which he calls a *borro*, a Mexican dish, which takes all night to cook." Caspar thought it a "kind of a baked chowder and is excellent."[30]

---

[28]Ibid., 96. At 11,156 feet above sea level, Elk Mountain towered almost 2,900 feet above Fort Halleck: a majestic setting.

[29]Ibid., 97–98; Spring, *Caspar Collins*, 143–44.

[30]*Collins Family Papers*, item 9.

Collins took his son, who liked more excitement than Fort Laramie provided, with him and went back into the field. About the same time, Major General Samuel R. Curtis took over for Blunt, though Craig retained his command. A detatchment of Company C, 6th Ohio (as the official returns continued to call them), remained at Fort Laramie with Companies F and H of the 4th U.S. Cavalry and Company G of the 8th Kansas infantry. Company A, along with the rest of C, 6th Ohio, stayed at Fort Halleck, while Companies B and D, 6th Ohio, were strung out on the telegraph line.[31]

The only significant problem for the Ohioans that fall was an attack on Upper Crossing station November 24. According to the report, "several hundred" Indians descended upon the place, whereupon the tiny garrison alerted their compatriots at the other stations by telegraph. When reinforcements arrived, some from as far away as Platte Bridge, the hostiles were gone. They were thought to be Snake Indians, from west of the divide, looking to take what they could. An investigation showed that no guard was out, but barking dogs set off the alarm. A private from Company B fired at the attackers from atop a haystack, but an arrow killed him. The next day, eight Indians appeared who carefully stayed out of gunshot range, fired a few shots at the post, then rode off. During the night attackers had loosened several posts of the corral, and had the dogs not complained, the garrison would have lost their horses. Ohioans believed they killed three of their adversaries.[32]

This episode illustrated a typical attempt by the Indians to steal horses, as valuable a commodity to them as to the caval-

---

[31]*O.R.*, I, 13, pp. 666, 696, 811. Curtis graduated from West Point in 1831, but soon resigned to practice as a civil engineer. He studied law; served in the Mexican War; and became a congressman from Iowa, where he became involved with Pacific railroads. He resigned his seat in Congress to participate in the Civil War, and subsequently was promoted to major general for his victory at Pea Ridge. Failing to end fractional strife in Missouri, he was reassigned to the Department of Kansas.

[32]Spring, *Caspar Collins*, 45. Spring claims Private Joseph Good, Company B, was the first battle casualty of the Ohio Battalion, but Ohio records list the victim as Private Bazil Glaize: *Official Roster*, vol. 11, 553.

ry. It was exactly the sort of adventure the small garrisons would have to contend with for some time, as the Overland Mail Company and other travelers on the road could tell them. It also demonstrated why the Ohioans would constantly have to be on guard, and that their duty was in fact quite dangerous, if lonely. Fortunately, there were few disturbances for the rest of the year.

Meanwhile, those California troops that Craig had worried about in June finally arrived in Utah in October. Colonel Connor set up headquarters at Camp Douglas, later Fort Douglas, just east of Salt Lake City. Not only was Connor a strict disciplinarian with his Californians, but also an unsympathetic, intolerant watchdog over the Mormon community. Connor quickly demonstrated the energy that characterized him. Shoshoni and Bannock tribesmen had captured an emigrant boy whose parents had been massacred. Connor sent Major Edward McGarry and sixty 2nd California cavalrymen to the camp of Chief Bear Hunter in Cache Valley, northern Utah. A sharp engagement on November 23 resulted in the death of three tribesmen and the wounding of another. None of McGarry's soldiers were hurt, and Bear Hunter surrendered the boy. A few days later, on December 4, McGarry led the cavalry again to recover stolen livestock. Most of the raiders escaped with the livestock, but four were captured and held as hostages. When the livestock were not returned, the captives were killed and the cavalry returned to Camp Douglas.[33]

[33]Long, *Saints and the Union*, 96–98; Colton, *Civil War in the Western Territories*, 163. Colonel Partick Edward Connor, a 42-year-old Irishman, came to the United States as a child with his parents. He enlisted in the regular army at age nineteen, served in the Seminole War, then in Kansas and Iowa. Discharged as a private in 1844, he went to Texas, enlisted with Texas volunteers in 1846, and fought the Mexican War as a first lieutenant. Accepted in United States service later in 1846, he served under General John E. Wool. Slightly wounded in the battle of Buena Vista, he was discharged as a captain in May 1847. He next went to California, and in 1854 married another native of County Kerry, Johanna. A rancher with business interests as well, the pair lived in Stockton. Because of his military experience, Connor became colonel of the Third California Volunteer Infantry in September 1861. See Long, *The Saints and the Union.*

With his 3rd California Volunteer Infantry and five companies of the 2nd California Volunteer Cavalry—about seven hundred all together—Connor developed a different strategy of protecting the overland roads than Collins and his Ohioans. Connor preferred not to act on the defensive, but chose to attack Native Americans whom he believed troublesome. By carrying the fight to them Connor won a reputation among frontiersmen and the military as a man of action whose power would make tribesmen submissive and so insure peace.

In November 1862 the military administration of the overland roads and their troops changed once more. Curtis commanded a new Department of the Missouri and divided subordinate responsibility within the department with the creation of twelve new military districts. Eight of the districts concerned the states of Missouri and Arkansas, where the primary problems concerned Confederate and bushwacker activities, which consumed much of the Department's attention. Craig headed the District of Nebraska Territory, and before the end of the month his headquarters were relocated from Fort Laramie to Omaha. Colonel John M. Chivington headed the District of Colorado Territory, which included the road along the South Platte to Denver. Curtis made it clear that the districts were a matter of convenience, and that "commanders in the field will not hesitate to cross lines and cooperate with adjacent commands" when necessary.[34]

Curtis's report for December 31, 1862, puts Company A, 6th Ohio, at Fort Halleck, along with Company B, 9th Kansas Cavalry; at Fort Kearny, the 10th United States, Companies D and K; at Fort Laramie, Company C, 6th Ohio, along with Company G, 8th Kansas Infantry, and Companies F and H of the 4th United States; and along the telegraph line, Compa-

[34]*O.R.*, I, 13, p. 777; 53, Supplement, p. 543. Chivington was colonel of the 1st Colorado Volunteer Cavalry.

nies B and D, 6th Ohio with Colonel Collins. At Camp Collins, near the mouth of the Cache la Poudre, where the Overland road began its turn northwest to pass by Fort Halleck, Colorado Volunteers, under Chivington's command, provided the garrison. Connor, headquartered at Camp Douglas by Salt Lake, commanded the District of Utah, administered not by Curtis from Missouri but by Brigadier General George Wright, from the Department of the Pacific at San Francisco. At Camp Douglas, Connor, on December 31, had four companies of the 3rd California Infantry and four companies of the 2nd California Cavalry. At Fort Bridger one company of the 3rd California Infantry was stationed to patrol the Oregon and Overland routes in their area. Three companies of the 3rd were stationed in Nevada, along with one of the 2nd, for the California road.[35]

The Ohio battalion, while having the principle responsibility for important segments of the Oregon and Overland roads, welcomed other arrivals to share some of their duties as well as the loneliness of the isolated outposts.

---

[35] *O.R.*, I, 22, pp. 891, 893; 50, pt. 2, pp. 272–73.

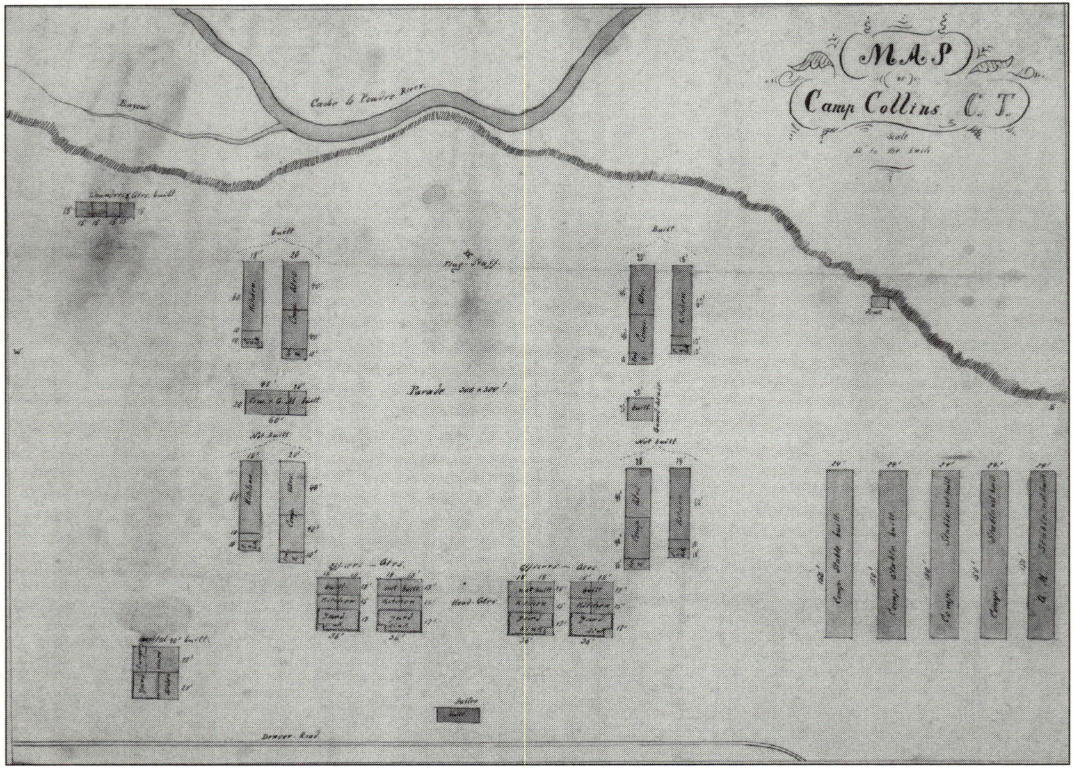

Camp Collins

Sketch by Second Lieutenant Caspar Collins.

CHAPTER FOUR

The 11th Ohio: Morgan, Quantrill, and Fort Laramie

Every winter along the Oregon and Overland roads was harsh, but for the Ohioans it was beyond anything they had known. It grew so cold at Fort Laramie that the mercury in their thermometers froze each night between January 3 and 5, 1863. They could only estimate that it may have been fifty to sixty degrees below zero. Some Ohio boys put whiskey in a tin cup, and it froze solid in twenty minutes. They tossed it about as if it were a frozen snowball.[1]

As the Ohioans hunkered down trying to keep warm in this severe weather, west of the Continental Divide the California troops in Utah fought in it. Mormon settlers in the Cache Valley had been continually harassed by Shoshoni and Bannock tribesmen led by chiefs Bear Hunter, Pocatello, and Sagwich. The Native Americans had also murdered several miners in December, and they continued to cause trouble on the Overland Mail route. In late January 1863, Connor took three hundred of his California cavalry and infantry, a couple of howitzers, and a supply train through the bitter cold and deep snow to the Indian village.

---

[1]Spring, *Caspar Collins*, 46; Robrock, "The Eleventh Ohio," 27; but see also Reid, *Ohio in the War*, vol. 1, 821, who places this incident in 1864. The evidence supports 1863.

Connor ordered the camp surrounded, and at 6 A.M. on January 29, the Californians attacked. By 10 A.M. accurate rifle fire from the soldiers routed the warriors, though chiefs Pocatello and Sagwich escaped with perhaps 50 to 100 men. Chief Bear Hunter and over 200 tribesmen died, including some women and children. So too did 14 troopers. Another 54 were wounded (of whom 6 later died). Connor's Californians captured 160 women and children and 175 horses. In the village the soldiers found firearms, ammunition, meat, wheat, and many items described as emigrant plunder. Connor supplied his prisoners, whom he released, with some provisions and destroyed over seventy lodges with their contents. In a very hard march through bitter cold and snow, the expedition returned to Camp Douglas. A number of the Californians suffered frostbite. But the winter victory completely broke the power of the Shoshoni and Bannocks along the Oregon road, and won Connor promotion to brigadier general.[2]

The Shoshoni and Bannocks might have been quiet after Connor's conquest, but the Utes busily raided along the Overland road. Captain Asaph Allen, 9th Kansas Volunteer Cavalry, then commanding at Fort Halleck, reported trouble at the mail station at Pass Creek on February 19. The Utes stole Overland Mail stock and destroyed harnesses. Allen sent one of his lieutenants with a small detachment—he had only twenty horses at Fort Halleck—to investigate. The lieutenant, Henry Brandley, subsequently suffered an arm wound, but killed his attacker. Five days later, Allen sent a sergeant and thirty-five men in pursuit of tribesmen reportedly active some twenty miles west. While the soldiers recovered some stolen stock and chased the Utes through a snowstorm, the raiders escaped. Even so, Allen felt the stage

[2]Colton, *Civil War in the Western Territories*, 164–66; Varley, *Brigham and the Brigadier*, 87–113.

line was secure "for the present," but he expected the Utes would "favor it with a call in the spring." He detached men "up the road to the different stations" to protect the mails.[3]

The trouble with the Utes near Fort Halleck prompted Collins to try to reinforce the company of the 9th Kansas. Lieutenant Thomas P. Clarke and forty-three men of Ohio's Company C, with supply wagons, left Fort Laramie for Fort Halleck on Monday, February 23. Collins himself, with six men, followed the next morning and overtook Clarke's detachment Wednesday. On Saturday a violent snowstorm enveloped them and cut visibility to less than ten yards. Thirty men pushed on to Fort Halleck, but ten others, including Collins, stopped to try to build a fire. Unsuccessful, they followed the others as best they could. A few miles from Halleck, a trooper fell from his horse, too cold to hold the saddle any longer. Another private appeared to be near death. Collins managed to get the man into the fort, and sent help back for the fallen trooper. The rescuers retrieved the man, but he soon died. The soldier whom Collins carried in subsequently recovered. A corporal with the first group to make the fort also died, and Collins himself was unable to move his legs for a time. The wagon crew managed to corral their wagons, and used blankets and provisions to survive. When the storm abated, they came in with their horses and mules, but the wagons were stuck in the snow and left behind.[4]

Back at Fort Laramie, the garrison celebrated Washington's birthday the day before Collins led the reinforcements south to Halleck. Ohioans of companies A and C and the men of the 4th U.S. Cavalry held a "ball," even though there were only eleven "white ladies, including soldier's wives" present. Caspar reported this event to his mother. It was a far cry from the death and cold at Fort Halleck.[5]

---

[3]*O.R.*, I, 22, pt. 1, p. 234.

[4]Ibid., pt. 2, p. 1456; Spring, *Caspar Collins*, 46–47.

[5]*Collins Family Papers*, item 12.

February passed quietly on the Oregon road, but on March 13 marauders stole thirty-three horses from Platte Bridge, including Captain Van Winkle's mount. Six days later a party of Arapahos returned eighteen of those animals, claiming to have liberated them from Shoshonis. On April 7 raiders struck the Platte Bridge herd again, but the garrison recovered most of them. On April 3 a small war party of as many as twenty tribesmen attacked Sweetwater station. Collins reported they were "driven off," with the loss of one fatally wounded trooper. The twenty-six troopers then at Sweetwater apparently outnumbered the raiders, and Collins noted that "no property [was] destroyed except some wagon harness."[6] Along all the roads west, troops remained on alert as commanders feared increased raids with the advent of spring. On April 13 General Connor reported to Washington that he expected accelerated Indian attacks, and claimed that unless he was immediately provided with more cavalry, "the Indians, urged on by the Mormons"—whom he patently distrusted—"will break up the overland mail and make the emigrant route impassable." Connor based much of his worry on two attacks made on Eight Mile station in western Utah, one in March and the other in May.[7] Connor became still another frontier commander asking for reinforcements that would never come. In this case, the anticipated trouble failed to materialize.

On May 13 Halleck removed Curtis from his command and replaced him with Major General John M. Schofield, at Lincoln's request. The president disapproved of the way Curtis handled political affairs in Missouri; it had nothing to do with affairs on the overland roads. Adequate protection of the overland roads, the mail, and the telegraph still concerned Halleck. He asked Schofield if he could "raise any troops in

---

[6]*O.R.*, I, 22, pt. 2, p. 198; McDermott, *Frontier Crossroads*, 31.

[7]Ibid., 215; Hafen, *Overland Mail*, 250.

Northern Missouri, Kansas, Nebraska, or Colorado to guard emigrant trains" and communications. Colorado governor John Evans also pressured Schofield. "Indians have given notice we must fight or leave. Have just had a report of a big secret conference between Sioux, Arapahos, and Cheyennes, about 100 miles north. May want our forces strengthened in a few days." Evans exaggerated the response of Cheyennes, who in his view failed to recognize the terms of the treaty of 1861. George Bent, half-blood son of long-time trader William Bent, said of that situation "the whites . . . claimed that the paper was a 'solemn obligation' and that if the Indians did not hold to the agreement it was a pretty good sign that the tribe was hostile and was plotting an uprising." Evans had been told by his emissary that the Cheyennes "did not care about peace any longer."[8]

Governor Evans of Colorado was a very ambitious man whose activities as governor directly affected the overland roads and their guardians. The fifty-year-old Evans had made a fortune speculating in real estate and railroads in Illinois and Iowa before accepting his appointment in Colorado Territory. He knew Colorado was rich in mineral resources, and that he might quite possibly increase his wealth. When Colorado achieved statehood, he wanted to be politically powerful there, because he could then run for the United States Senate as a prominent Republican. He envisioned Denver, Colorado's capital, as an important point on a Pacific railroad. That might serve to increase his fortune as well since he was an incorporator and director of the Union Pacific Railroad. For these dreams to come true, however, he

[8] *O.R.*, I, 22, pp. 277, 290–92, 294; Basler, ed., *Collected Works of Abraham Lincoln*, VII, 78, 100; Hyde, *George Bent*, 118–19. Schofield, age thirty-two at the time, graduated from West Point and followed a regular army career. He became a brigadier general in late 1861, having fought at Wilson's Creek and then commanded the Army of the Frontier in Missouri. Later, he would command part of Sherman's army in the Atlanta campaign, and then was with George H. Thomas at Nashville.

needed to be noticed in Washington at a time when whatever happened in Colorado was eclipsed by the urgent demands of the Civil War. Would not an Indian war that threatened Colorado and the West bring him that sort of notice?[9]

George Bent, another participant in the overland roads saga, came into the picture by 1863. His father, William, operated an important trading post on the Arkansas River in southeastern Colorado, along the Santa Fé road. George's mother was Owl Woman, a daughter of White Thunder, a very important Southern Cheyenne divine and the keeper of the Medicine Arrows. William saw to it that George, along with his brother Charles, were schooled in Westport, now Kansas City, from 1853 to 1857. In the latter year, George went on to study at an academy in St. Louis. With a light complexion, he easily could have been thought to be a white man when soldiers noticed him among his tribesmen. While he was at the academy in St. Louis, the Civil War broke out.

Along with many other students at his academy, George, at age seventeen, enlisted in a Confederate cavalry unit. He took part in the battles of Wilson's Creek and Pea Ridge, then participated in Major General Earl Van Dorn's campaigns in Arkansas and Mississippi. Captured at Corinth on October 4, 1862, he was taken to St. Louis along with other prisoners. His brother Robert and friends of his father prevailed on the Union commander to grant him a parole. It was just as well, for George had had quite enough of "the white man's methods of making war." He went home to his father.

[9]David Howard Bain, *Empire Express: Building the First Transcontinental Railroad* (New York: Viking Penguin, 1999), 184–85. The Union Pacific Railroad had a curious connection with events on the overland roads. Major General Samuel R. Curtis, while serving as a congressman from Iowa, not only introduced a Pacific Railroad bill in 1862 but chaired the House Committee on Pacific Railroads. Major General Grenville M. Dodge, who commanded the overland road scene in February 1865, was a stockholder in the Union Pacific, and after the war, its construction engineer. Add Evans to the mix. They all served on the frontier and each had some influence on the course of events there; they all knew or knew of each other; and they knew little about the Native Americans, seeing them only as obstacles to be overcome.

George and his brother Charles, who had shared his fate, were not safe at the trading post. Whites in the area were Unionists who thought the boys were renegades who ought to be slain on sight. At their father's urging, the two young men went to live with their mother's people. Although they had spent nearly a decade gaining an education among whites, they quickly absorbed the ways of the Cheyennes on the plains. They hunted buffalo and visited other Cheyennes, Arapahos, and Sioux. Some of the younger tribesmen George knew made up war parties and raided the Pawnees on the Platte and the Utes in the mountains. His first fight as a Cheyenne came against a party of Delaware hunters in central Kansas.

Among the things George learned as a Cheyenne was the tribe's reaction to the Treaty of Fort Wise, negotiated in February 1861. In that treaty a few Cheyenne and Arapahoe chiefs gave up all their land for a small reservation on the Arkansas River below Bent's Fort. George discovered that "the few chiefs who signed the treaty did not know what they were agreeing to," and since most chiefs were not represented at Fort Wise, the Cheyenne would never recognize it. This was the very treaty that Governor Evans claimed the Cheyennes ignored, giving him justification for labeling them as "hostile."

George also learned that it was "about half true" that Confederates plotted to have the tribes make "a combined attack on the frontier settlements and the overland roads." He also heard that his father had warned the Cheyenne to have nothing to do with the Confederates, and that the Cheyenne chiefs followed that advice. But news of the Sioux war in Minnesota in 1862 had made the Cheyennes very uneasy about any white man's intentions.[10]

---

[10]Hyde, *George Bent*, vii–ix, 110–20. George's sojourn among the whites and especially his education marked him as unusual among his fellow tribesmen. He witnessed the conflicts along the overland roads and wrote about them from the Cheyenne viewpoint.

While Evans looked for an Indian war and George Bent took to the ways of his Cheyenne brothers, Schofield reported his military dispositions along the overland roads on June 30, 1863. Companies A and C of the 6th Ohio, under Major Thomas L. Mackey, were at Fort Laramie, Company A having returned from Fort Halleck. Only two companies of the 6th Ohio now made up Laramie's garrison; the company of the 8th Kansas Infantry and the two small companies of the 4th United States Cavalry were gone. The 9th Kansas Cavalry, Company B, remained at Halleck, while 6th Ohio Companies B and D, with Collins, garrisoned the telegraph line north and west of Laramie to the South Pass. Companies B and C of the 2nd Nebraska Cavalry replaced the regulars at Fort Kearny. Company M of the 1st Colorado Cavalry occupied Camp Collins, Colorado, about a hundred miles southeast of Halleck on the Overland road, originally built by a detachment of the 6th Ohio and named after their colonel. Also, Major Edward W. Wynkoop took four companies of the 1st Colorado to General Connor's aid on the overland mail route, going as far west as Fort Bridger. This last was necessary, Schofield claimed, because of continued attacks on the mail.[11]

Back east, Congress had passed a new Conscription Act in March 1863, which led a number of Ohioans to respond favorably to calls for volunteers and avoid the stigma of being drafted. That spring, Ohio sought men to fill up their regiments. On May 30, this poster appeared across the state:

FRONTIER CAVALRY SERVICE!

Lieut. Col. Wm. O. Collins is authorized by the War Department to recruit an additional Battalion of Cavalry to add to his present command now in the Rocky Mountain Indian Service, Head-Quarters at Fort Laramie, in the newly-formed Territory of Idahoe. This service is full of novelty and adventure, and offers a

[11] *O.R.*, I, 22, pt. 2, pp. 325, 346–47, 368–69; Hafen, *Overland Mail*, 251.

rare chance to *live* young men who would like to see the center of the Rocky Mountain country, which is now assuming great importance, from the discovery of new gold mines, the expected commencement of the Pacific Railroad, etc., etc.

The First Independent Battalion Ohio Volunteer Cavalry (formerly the First Battalion Sixth Ohio Cavalry), with which the new battalion will be connected, has been more than a year in the Mountains, and the constant health of the men, as well as the testimony of all who know the country, shows it to be the most healthy portion of North America. The remarkable purity of the atmosphere renders it especially beneficial to those having a tendency to pulmonary complaints, and the effect upon all, is to invigorate the constitution and prolong life.

The best of arms and equipments are promised, and will be ready when needed.

The subscriber has been authorized to raise a Company for this battalion, in the Counties of

....

though recruits offering themselves from any part of the country will be received.

His recruiting Head-Quarters will be at

....

and he invites active and enterprising young men, who prefer choosing their own service to being drafted, to enlist with him. Recruits will be entitled to the usual bounty of $100, and one month's pay in advance.

As this is the most pleasant season for crossing the Plains, it is desirable to fill the Company at once and be ready to move. Any full Company can start immediately, without waiting for the completion of the Battalion.

Leaving the men of the 6th Ohio in the capable hands of Major Mackey, Colonel Collins took son Caspar and a few others with him and returned to Ohio in May to recruit this new battalion at Camps Dennison and Chase in Ohio. The entire regiment now became the Eleventh Ohio Volunteer Cavalry, no longer the 1st Independent Battalion as Ohio called them, nor the 6th Ohio as the *Official Records* persisted in designating them. Caspar also enlisted and secured a commission as a second lieutenant of a new Company G, based on his year of experience on location in the west. The new recruits boosted Collins's strength to over eight hundred officers and men, more than doubling their number.[12]

While Lieutenant Colonel Collins (who remained a lieutenant colonel, never a full colonel, despite his command of a regiment, not just a battalion) recruited in Ohio that July, the month was not quiet on the western roads. Ute tribesmen terrorized the mail route. On July 7 Captain Allen, 9th Kansas, leading seventy men from Fort Halleck, overtook about 250 Utes in the mountains thirty miles west of the fort, skirmished with them for two hours, and left twenty Utes dead on the field and many others wounded, with his loss reported as one dead and six wounded. The warriors had taken twenty-two head of stock from the mail company, which were not recovered. Major Wynkoop and his four companies of the 1st Colorado had orders to recover the stock, but there is no record that they were able to do so. Subsequently, on July 8 and 9, Utes struck other mail stations.[13]

On July 11 "a large number of Cheyenne and Arapaho braves" appeared at Camp Collins, hoping to capitalize on the war against the Utes, their traditional enemies. They wanted to follow Wynkoop's command into the field and exact a little vengeance of their own. Wynkoop received stern orders not to

[12]Reid, *Ohio in the War*, vol. 2, 820; Spring, *Caspar Collins*, 50–51; Robrock, "The Eleventh Ohio," 28–29. Poster reproduced in Alfred James Mokler, *Fort Caspar (Platte Bridge Station)* (Casper, Wyo.: The Prairie Publishing Company, 1939), p. v. Co. F mustered in at Camp Chase, June 26, Cos. E, G, and H at Camp Dennison, July 8, 20, and 31 respectively. Also in May, Collins contracted to buy carbines from Ben Kitteridge and Company of Cincinnati at his and the troopers' expense (at twenty-three dollars each). Collins had complained that the single-shot Enfield rifles were not suited for cavalrymen, especially on the frontier (they were almost useless on horseback). Fort Laramie National Historic Site Library, file MCOR-69, *Military Correspondence*, 47; Service, *Life and Letters of Caspar Collins*, notes 51–53. It was not unusual during the Civil War for Union units to buy their own guns; see William B. Edwards, *Civil War Guns: The Complete Story of Federal and Confederate Small Arms* (Harrisburg, Penn.: The Stackpole Company, 1962), 148–50.

[13]*O.R.*, I, 22, pt. 2, pp. 363, 369–70, 443–44.

allow the Cheyenne and Arapaho to participate. But when the Colorado troops arrived to cooperate with the one company of the 9th Kansas, the Utes disappeared and their raids east of Fort Bridger abated. In fact, the Ute threat to the Overland Mail route ended. With the Shoshoni neutralized by Connor, the troops now had just the powerful Arapaho, Sioux, and Northern Cheyenne to worry them.[14]

Back east in Ohio, Collins assembled new companies that July, while the Union basked in remarkably good news. Major General George G. Meade engineered a great victory on the field of Gettysburg, Pennsylvania, July 1–3, while Grant successfully ended the campaign against Vicksburg, Mississippi, on July 4. These two stunning Union triumphs came just before Confederate Brigadier General John Hunt Morgan led 2,100 raiders eastward through southern Indiana and Ohio July 9 to 18. They burned bridges; destroyed canal boats, depots, and railroad tracks; stole money; and generally looted along the way. Morgan was surprised at the amount of resistance he encountered. It seemed as if the entire population in Indiana and Ohio considered his raiders their enemy. It had been different with his forays through Kentucky and Tennessee, where he found many sympathetic to his cause, and where many others simply remained neutral. Morgan's day and night march exhausted his horses, so his men requisitioned nearly every horse along his route. Ohio turned out militia to impede Morgan's advance, blocked roads with felled trees, removed roadbeds from bridges, and constantly sniped at Morgan's column from ambush. By the time Morgan reached the Ohio River, his troops were fatigued. But Morgan was confident. Once across the river and into western Virginia they would return to the safety of southern territory.

It was not to be. Regular Union infantry and artillery defended the ford, and unknown to Morgan, his pursuers

[14]*O.R.*, I, 22, pt. 2, pp. 370–71; Hafen, *Overland Mail*, 252; McDermott, *Frontier Crossroads*, p, 31.

were close behind him. Morgan chose not to force a night crossing, which proved a mistake. Union forces surprised his raiders with an aggressive attack as dawn broke. In addition, gunboats braved difficult river conditions to seal off the river. In the end, Morgan's troopers scattered and were captured, but Morgan eluded his opponents until July 26.[15]

On July 13 Ohio governor David Tod called up 20,000 militia. A few days later, Lieutenant Colonel George W. Neff, commander at Camp Dennison, reported that he had 1,900 recruits in camp, 700 armed, among whom were four new companies of the 11th Ohio. They engaged in scouting and gathering information, and joined in the effort to contain and capture Morgan's raiders.[16]

The new Company H, 11th Ohio, though not yet officially mustered into federal service, participated in the campaign against Morgan until his main force surrendered July 18. It joined Brigadier General Edward H. Hobson's cavalry in a grueling forced march in pursuit of the raiders. It moved "both night and day, never halting over three hours to rest" and feed the horses. "The day's march was never under thirty-three miles . . . and the last day's march was fifty-one miles. The weather was intensly hot and the animals suffered much from heat, dust, and want of water." Captain Jacob S. Shuman's Company H lost four horses killed and three abandoned as worn out. After the July 18 surrender, a portion of Company H boarded the steamer *Ida May* and returned to Cincinnati, arriving there July 24. Shuman and his men returned to Camp Dennison with a week to spare, in time to be mustered in before the new battalion headed west.[17]

---

[15]James A. Ramage, *Rebel Raider: The Life of General John Hunt Morgan* (Lexington, Ky.: The University Press of Kentucky, 1986), see 170–82, passim.

[16]*O.R.*, I, 23, pt. 1, pp. 737, 748–50, 754, 757–58.

[17]*O.R.*, I, 52, pt. 1, pp. 70–71. They began with eighty cavalrymen, but what with the rigors of the chase, many dropped out or returned to Camp Dennison some other way. Only thirty-four returned on the steamboat.

Before the Morgan raid, slow progress obtaining new recruits in Ohio "discouraged" Governor Tod. But Morgan's raid across southern Ohio greatly stimulated enlistment, and Collins's 11th Ohio reaped the benefit. Some joined up out of renewed patriotism or to escape the draft. It also provided a way for Ohioans who sympathized in some way with the Confederacy to serve in the West, where they would not have to fight against Southern relatives or friends. Western adventure attracted still others, including a few who saw enlistment as a free ride to the vicinity of western gold fields. As it turned out, Confederate prisoners of war, even some from Morgan's outfit, escaped prison camps by enlisting in the 11th. Thus Collins had little difficulty filling a battalion of four companies, E, F, G, and H, and even had authorization for two more companies, which would materialize later. The new recruits provided sorely needed reinforcement for protection of the overland roads.[18]

Benjamin M. Connor, alias Ben Munroe, alias Ben Arnold (the name he used the rest of his life), was one of the new recruits in Company E. As Benjamin Connor he had previously enlisted in Company C, 39th Ohio Volunteer Infantry, in July 1861. He received a discharge ten months later after an attack of measles, which led to chronic bronchitis. The following August he enlisted again, same company, same regiment. Three months later he deserted near Grand Junction, Tennessee. Next, in July 1863, this time as Ben Munroe, he joined the 11th Ohio.[19]

Twenty-four-year-old Hervey Johnson of Highland County, Ohio, also enlisted in the 11th that July. When he joined Company G, he received the $100 federal bounty, $25 down, the

[18]*O.R.*, I, 23, pt. 1, p. 701; pt. 2, p. 584. In 1864 three new companies would be formed.

[19]Lewis F. Crawford, ed., *Rekindling Camp Fires: The Exploits of Ben Arnold* (*Connor*) (Bismarck, North Dakota: Capital Book Company, 1926), 1–15, passim. Connor, a.k.a. Arnold, wrote an account of his experiences at age seventy-seven, fifty-seven years after enlisting in the 11th Ohio.

remainder on discharge. Johnson participated in the Morgan affair with his unit. Young Johnson found it hard to adapt to military discipline and consequently came to dislike the officers. Charles F. Moellmann, a friend of Johnson, enlisted in the same company a week later and became the company's bugler. Moellmann, something of an artist, made about sixty shetches in pencil, crayon, and watercolor of life on the plains, including nearly every post and station he visited.[20] Both Arnold and Johnson provided considerable insight into the different problems and daily duty of the newly-created 11th Ohio.

On August 1 Collins took his four new companies, none completely equipped yet, by train to St. Louis. Recruit Hervey Johnson thought Benton Barracks, which was inhabited by several thousand soldiers, many of them "paroled prisoners," a very large camp. They boarded the steamer *Sioux City* and arrived at Fort Leavenworth on August 13. Johnson's letters home included his complaints about the service from the first, including his dislike of officers. The officers ate well on the boat, he told his sister, though he did not; otherwise the boat ride was fine. Some of the other recruits went west by rail to St. Joseph, Missouri, were ferried across the river, and arrived at Leavenworth the same day as their compatriots.[21]

Brigadier General Thomas Ewing, Jr., a brother-in-law of soon-to-be-famous Major General William Tecumseh Sherman, reported about a week later that five companies of the 11th Ohio were busily outfitting at Fort Leavenworth for their trip to Fort Laramie, but were as yet without arms. Another company at Leavenworth City was receiving horse equipment. Ewing took three hundred men from the 11th Ohio and issued arms to them, as he needed troops quickly for a special mission.[22]

---

[20]William E. Unrau, ed., *Tending the Talking Wire: A Buck Soldier's View of Indian Country, 1863–1866* (Salt Lake City: University of Utah Press, 1979), 13, 17, 27–31.

[21]Ibid., pp, 32–33; Crawford, ed., *Rekindling Camp Fires*, 17.

[22]*O.R.*, I, 22, pt. 1, pp. 582–83. Actually three, not five, companies were at Fort Leavenworth.

Though some of the Ohioans in the 11th may not have been aware of it, hostility between Kansas Jayhawkers and Missouri Border Ruffians had disturbed the borderland between those two states since the 1850s, and affairs worsened with the outbreak of the Civil War. Guerrilla chieftan William C. Quantrill, who fancied himself a Confederate, now sought revenge for the accidental deaths of five wives and sisters of his followers who had been arrested by Union troops. With a band of over three hundred, Quantrill attacked Lawrence, Kansas, at dawn on August 21. He ordered his men to kill every man and burn down every house in town. They very nearly did so, killing over 180 men and boys and incinerating about a quarter of the town. They also robbed the stores and banks. Furious, General Ewing promptly organized a vigorous pursuit.

Suddenly, as Ben Arnold remembered it, "these young fellows, for the most part boys from eighteen to twenty-one" who "were anxious to get on the road to the wild and romantic regions about which so many stories had been told," were handed weapons, provided with horses, and went off to hunt Quantrill. "The men were new recruits for the most part, unused to horse-back riding and . . . active campaigning." They moved fast, "had no time for rest or sleep." They departed Fort Leavenworth about 1:00 P.M. on August 21, in sultry August weather. They rode about a hundred miles in the first twenty-four hours, and both horses and men suffered from the heat. Four men of the 11th Ohio suffered sunstroke, including Lieutenant David S. Dick of Company E, "who fell dead on dismounting to rest," reported General Ewing, with whom Dick had been riding. Dick had been in service just about a month. The 11th remained with the pursuit for several days before returning to Leavenworth. Quantrill escaped.[23]

[23]Ibid.; Crawford, ed., *Rekindling Camp Fires*, 18–20.

After returning from their breathless adventure, the 11th remained at Fort Leavenworth until September 2, when it departed for Fort Laramie. The first leg of the journey, to Fort Kearny, passed uneventfully. Private Arnold recalled the troops "followed the Little Blue to its head . . . thence over a sandy prairie divide for perhaps thirty miles to the Platte Valley, then up the valley about fifteen miles to Fort Kearny." He noted "the trail was rutted and worn by thousands of livestock and wheeled vehicles" that had gone before. Along the way, they usually tried to camp by water, but so many had previously done so that grass was scarce and they had to camp several miles from water and fuel. While they were at Fort Leavenworth, Private Johnson reported that a couple of Kansas boys enlisted in Company G, and at Fort Kearny another couple of young men joined up. These last two were Ohioans from Highland County who promptly quit their jobs as ox team drivers. They had been en route to Denver from Omaha and were surprised to find Ohio troops so far west.[24]

While the 11th remained at Fort Kearny for a few days, Jim Bridger appeared to accompany it to Fort Laramie. The Ohioans spent some time and money in Dobytown and met some of the emigrants camped there. Arnold remembered many were from border states, some escaping the draft, some Southern sympathizers, and some "disappointed emigrants returning home . . . to the 'States.'" While in a saloon Arnold overheard four members of Company E plan to instigate a mutiny when the 11th reached Julesburg, then rob stages on the Denver road, head southeast to Kansas, and eventually join Quantrill. The information frightened Arnold, who hated to be an "informer against my comrades," but at the same time did not want to be an accessory to their actions either.[25]

---

[24]Crawford, ed., *Rekindling Camp Fires*, 21–24; Unrau, *Tending the Talking Wire*, 36, 45.

[25]Crawford, ed., *Rekindling Camp Fires*, 27–32, 40–41.

The morning after Arnold heard of the planned mutiny, the 11th departed from Kearny and headed west. He observed the troublemakers still at work making plans, but did nothing until the next evening. He reported the situation to his captain, Levi G. Marshall. Marshall claimed he noticed some unrest among the men, but had not known a reason for it. The following morning Marshall arrested the four plotters. Disarmed, they were forced to walk the rest of the way to Fort Laramie at the rear of the wagon train and in its clouds of dust, under mounted guard. "No greater punishment," Arnold remarked, "can be meted out to a cavalryman than to disarm him and make him walk." There was no mutiny.[26]

The rest of the journey was uneventful. The recruits of the 11th passed all the landmarks along the road: Courthouse Rock, Chimney Rock, Scotts Bluff. They marched near Ash Hollow, where General Harney had chastized the Sioux in 1855 in response to the Grattan Massacre. They camped along the Laramie River when they arrived on October 10, 1863. The Laramie River was "a mountain stream, clear, cold, and sparkling, alive with trout." Arnold observed that the fort took its water from that stream, using "large tank wagons" drawn by six mule teams. The older buildings of the fort were constructed of logs, but the "barracks and stables were made from lumber" provided by a little sawmill "now running at the foot of Laramie peak." The men had a few days' rest before being assigned "to different posts along the 'wire' road."[27]

Private Johnson saw things differently on the trek to Laramie. The Oregon road proved too sandy for his taste, and the march wearied him. He thought at one point he had yellow jaundice and had no appetite except for fresh fish, but he felt better by the time he reached Fort Laramie. He mentioned that several men had deserted "from this battalion since

[26]Ibid., 42–45.

[27]Ibid., 52–61.

it left St. Louis, and one company lost nearly half," an exaggeration. His company, G, lost "one at [Camp] Dennison, one at cincinnati, one at St. Louis, two at Leavenworth and two on the march two discharged at Leavenworth making nine in all." Johnson wrote that he was arrested when he "mouthed off" to the corporal of the guard and officers overheard him. He had to sleep in the guard tent, then walk twenty-two miles the next day and sleep in the guard tent that night. "If I ever felt like deserting twas when I had to walk all that time." He found army discipline too strict and arbitrary to suit him. They even refused to let him be late to a formation! But his quarters in the barracks were quite comfortable.[28]

Johnson described his daily routine at Fort Laramie. The bugle sounded reveille at dawn,

> then twenty minutes after roll is called every man must . . . fall out in ranks. . . . [then] the men are marched off to the stable . . . nearly a quarter of a mile. there every man has to begin on the right side of his horse and curry till the sergeant says, change. Then they curry on the other side

until they are called to attention, standing alongside their horse. A sergeant and a lieutenant conducted an inspection, after which the troopers were marched back to the barracks.

> then at half past six, the bugle sounds the breakfast call . . . At nine the guards are mounted . . . At half past ten we are marched to the stables again to water the horses. . . . At twelve dinner call is sounded. . . . at half past one drill call, at half past two recall from drill. at five water call again, then inspection and march back to quarters. at six supper call,

roll call at sundown, roll call again at 9:00, at 9:15 "the bugle sounds 'lights out,' then every man must be in bed and the lights and fire out."[29]

While the new recruits of the 11th Ohio marched to Fort

---

[28]Unrau, *Tending the Talking Wire*, 54–58. When quoting Johnson captialization and sentence structure, etc., are his. [29]Ibid., 63.

Laramie, their part of the frontier was quiet. On September 14, Major Scott J. Anthony, 1st Colorado, reported to his superior, Colonel John M. Chivington, that Kiowa and Arapaho chieftans told him that Sioux and Cheyenne "runners have been down among the Indian tribes on the Arkansas . . . trying to get the Indians of the plains all united for a general attack upon both the Platte and Arkansas routes" that fall, and all the tribes refused "except the Cheyennes." They agreed with the Sioux to make war on the "Platte route very soon." His informants told him there would be trouble "up there, but not here." Anthony thought depredations in the south would happen too, however, regardless of what the chiefs said. George Bent, on the other hand, claimed to have been in the Cheyenne camps "at this time and knew that this . . . story [Anthony heard] was a lie from beginning to end." Bent admitted the Sioux had sent a war pipe, but maintained that the Cheyennes and Arapahos firmly refused it. In spite of Anthony's uneasiness, no uprising materialized.[30]

Collins spent most of the remainder of the fall training the new recruits. Johnson was one of forty-eight men chosen from various companies to operate the four mountain howitzers they brought with them: they called it the Mountain Battery. Arnold, along with thirty troopers, was sent to Rawhide Buttes, over thirty miles north, to pasture the cavalry horses since "the grass was much better there than at the fort." Arnold's detachment managed to make a comfortable camp in "an old fur trading outpost." Johnson despised the Indians living around Fort Laramie. He wrote, "of all specimens of humanity that I ever saw, the Indians around here are the most low-lived, dirty, sneaking, and impudent." Arnold, on the other hand, learned that the local tribesmen "were hostile only toward emigrants, not to traders."[31]

---

[30] *O.R.*, I, 22, pt. 2, p. 533; Hyde, *Life of George Bent*, 118–21.

[31] Unrau, *Tending the Talking Wire*, 59, 61; Crawford, ed., *Rekindling Camp Fires*, 61.

On November 14, 1863, Catherine, Colonel Collins's wife, arrived at Fort Laramie. She had traveled by train as far as she could and took the stagecoach from Atchison, then army wagon and ambulance from the stage line to Laramie. At the time Mrs. Collins traveled it was the weather, not tribesmen, that made the journey uncomfortable. She joined Mrs. Van Winkle and Mrs. Love, wives of other battalion officers, who, along with their young children, had preceded her by over a year.[32] It was not unusual then for wives of officers, and even non-commissioned officers, to join their husbands when accomodations sufficed.

About the time Catherine Collins arrived, Arnold was recalled from the Rawhide Butte camp and, once back at Laramie, became part of a detachment of thirty ordered to Platte Bridge station. While at Laramie, he saw the four men—"two Sullivans, Grey, and Crawford"—who had plotted the mutiny "shackeld in ball and chain, chopping wood and policing the post. They had been court-martialed, found guilty, and sentenced to three months hard labor with pay suspended."[33]

Once Arnold arrived at Platte Bridge, he, along with another soldier, was "detailed" to take the "horse herd" ten miles south to better grazing land. The two men constructed "a dugout with an open fireplace and chimney of stone and sod." They had plenty of army rations, except for meat, but they found that "black-tail deer were plentiful" and they also took "sage grouse" and rabbits to supplement their government rations. They had monotonous duty and saw no tribesmen or anyone else "all the remainder of the winter." Johnson

[32]*Collins Family Papers*, items 17, 18; Spring, "An Army Wife Comes West," 249n. 14. The wives of Peter Van Winkle, captain of Company D, and Wesley Love, then captain of Company B, had brought along Van Winkle's two daughters, ages twelve and six, and Love's "little son." Other wives known to be on hand were those of Dr. T. M. Smith and Sergeant Richard J. Wright of Company D.

[33]Crawford, ed., *Rekindling Camp Fires*, 62.

remained at Fort Laramie. He liked the "Soldiers Reading Room" that Collins furnished at his own expense. There were four large tables with benches, and on them "are found all the principal newspapers, and magazines published in the United States, besides telegraph dispatches, which are coming in every day." On the walls hung maps, and there was a library "of three or four hundred volumes." Compared to Arnold, Johnson spent a comfortable winter.[34]

Also that November Collins corresponded with Joseph Henry of the Smithsonian Insitiution. Collins had made weather observations of the Laramie area that he sent to Henry; Spencer Baird, also of the Smithsonian, asked Collins to collect various natural history objects for them, something Collins was delighted to do. Further correspondence with Baird resulted in a Smithsonian decision to send field representatives to Laramie in the spring.[35]

By the end of October, Company B, 9th Kansas, had been ordered to Fort Leavenworth from Fort Halleck, so Collins had to garrison that post. Major Mackey took Companies C and F there, while the rest—Companies A, B, D, E, G, and H, minus detachments on the Oregon road north and west of Laramie—wintered at the fort. Company B, 1st Colorado, occupied Camp Collins on the Overland road that the mail coaches traveled. To the east along the Oregon road, the 7th Iowa Volunteer Cavalry arrived to garrison Fort Kearny, Cottonwood Springs, and other stations. In December General Schofield remarked that the "Indians in those Territories, though occasionally manifesting a hostile disposition, have thus far remained quiet."[36]

That December Catherine Collins wrote some observations she thought of interest to her daughter back in Ohio. She said she "saw a wagon with a stovepipe through the

---

[34]Ibid., 63; Unrau, *Tending the Talking Wire*, 70.
[35]*Collins Family Papers*, items 72–74.
[36]*O.R.*, I 22, pt. 2, pp. 17, 528, 764.

cover. The team was a large pair of oxen and the driver was covered up with capes, with a pair of moccasins on his feet." It had to be rare to see a wagon moving that time of year, equipped with a heater! She went on to describe Native American women. Their heads are uncovered, she said, with "black straight hair [that] hangs down over their cheeks and necks," and many who had parted their hair "have the seam painted a bright vermillion." They wore "tunic" dresses, "made of calico, blue drilling or even bed ticking with a leather belt." Also they wore "moccasins, leggings of blue or red cloth and over all a buffalo robe worn like a cloak." Occasionally the cloak "is ornamented with beads and painting but it is usually plain and very dirty. The fur side is turned in." She also noticed many old women, "but no gray hairs. Perhaps," she thought, "going with their hair uncovered may prevent the hair from turning gray or falling off." Of the young men she wrote, they "look quite gay with their painted faces and beaded leggings, and" she "saw one who cut quite a dash."[37]

The men of the 11th appeared to like Catherine, who nursed them, taught them, listened to them, wrote letters for them, and proved a good hostess. Naturally, she also nursed her husband, who in December had "bilious colic" or "mountain fever," characterized, among other things, by "violent pain in the face." She thought he worked too hard and should rest more.[38]

Apparently the colonel's illness yielded to his wife's ministrations, for when Christmas 1863 rolled around, the day was filled with parties. First came a dinner for about seventy-five officers and non-commissioned men and five of the women, hosted by Company D. The bill of fare included roasts of beef and pork, cold ham, mince pie, ice cream, coffee and tea,

---

[37] *Collins Family Papers*, item 19.

[38] Ibid.; Spring, *Caspar Collins*, 155.

and a large cake. The cake, complete with flower decorations and "Co D 11 OVC" inscribed on it, must have awed the Van Winkle children. Next, the colonel and his lady walked over to William G. Bullock's house (Bullock was the sutler's agent), along with about ten officers and most of the women, for egg nog, more cake, and a song fest. Mrs. Collins found Bullock's house and furnishings most agreeable. Following that, they moved on to another large supper, at which the colonel gave a toast. Finally returning to their quarters in "Old Bedlam," the Collinses listened to a serenade by the post band. Fort Laramie's garrison led as active a social life as possible.[39] The New Year would bring not only another frigid winter, but also a return to battle against a thoroughly aroused enemy.

---

[39]Spring, ed., "An Army Wife Comes West," 252–55.

CHAPTER FIVE

Toward a Bigger War: Winter–Spring 1864

January 1864 brought another extremely frigid winter to the 11th Ohio on the Oregon and Overland roads. On New Year's Day 1864, the Christmas festivities at Fort Laramie continued when Company A hosted an elaborate dinner. The menu, wrote Private Johnson, included various meats, "eggs, chickens, Oysters sardines, lobsters, green corn . . . nuts rasins, candies" as well as libations such as "catawba, sherry, champagne" wines and "bourbon, old rye, stews, toddies, gin slings, punch" and others. Johnson said the repast cost Company A about $650. "All the officers of the fort were there with their wives, that is those that have them here; and most of them came away drunk, from the Colonel down." Johnson, though, stood guard duty in eighteen-degree cold. But about an hour before midnight Colonel Collins visited the guard house and brought the men some hot punch—hot "stew" Johnson called it—"and gave us all a drink around."[1]

The men of the 11th Ohio lived in reasonably warm barracks at Fort Laramie. Fifteen– to twenty-six–horse teams brought firewood to the post daily, but it was so cold that they used the fuel rapidly: the wood pile "grows daily less," Johnson commented. Conditions were quite different for

---

[1]*Collins Family Papers*, item 20; Unrau, *Tending the Talking Wire*, 78.

Sketch of Fort Laramie, 1863, by Second Lieutenant Caspar W. Collins and described in detail in a letter of January 16, 1864, to his mother in Ohio. This sketch has been reproduced in numerous publications. This copy appeared in a Fort Collins, Colorado, newspaper, the clipping located in the Fort Collins Public Library Archives. The Laramie River is in the foreground, the parade ground at left with the flagpole. Lieutanant Collins's mother, on her horse *Honest John*, is to the right of the flagpole followed by a greyhound and two pointers, dogs she claimed often followed her. The building with two trees in front, just above Mrs. Collins, is "Old Bedlam," originally Batchelor Officer's Quarters, but home to Colonel Collins and his wife in 1863–64. This reproduction of the drawing does not include other buildings in Lieutenant Collins's sketch that are out of this picture to the left; and Collins's sketch itself did not include quartermaster and commissary buildings and stables, which were farther to the right.

those staffing the outposts. On January 3 Collins telegraphed Schofield at St. Louis that temperatures reached twenty-nine below zero. The mails could not get get through. He had not been able to communicate with Fort Halleck for five weeks, "parties turned back by deep snow." His "detachments

everywhere snowed in. Men and stock suffer greatly." Collins had sent "Lieutenants [Oliver S.] Glenn and [Rufus E.] Talpey" with a "train and beef herd" to Fort Halleck, but they "could not get through Sabille Cañon. It is the third party that has failed." He asked Colonel Chivington in Denver to try to reach them. The next day he told Chivington he could only inspect the troops at Fort Laramie; he had no communication with detachments along the Sweetwater "except by telegraph." The "thermometer 43 below zero at 9 this morning." Mail from Laramie "snowed in at Mud Springs and must return." It would "probably" be several weeks before mail could get through.[2]

In spite of the weather, prisoners escaped from Fort Laramie's guardhouse. On January 16 a deserter who "had been in irons for three months" awaiting sentence—possibly

[2]Unrau, *Tending the Talking Wire*, 79; *O.R.*, I, 34, pt. 2, pp. 15, 25, 28–29.

"death"—from the War Department fled. He decamped at night, taking along two horses "and another man" from Company E who "had served a short time." Before the escape, thirty dollars and a Colt revolver had been stolen from the post barber, and the gunsmith lost "some six shooters and a small breechloading rifle." Presumably, the escapees took the items as they planned their departure.[3]

A scouting party brought the fugitives back five days later. They were put in irons, along with a third man who was suspected of taking the horses. About a week later, yet another man from Company E tried to desert. He stole a pony belonging to "the son of one of the officers," rode along the telegraph line, without arms or provisions, and had to stop at a telegraph station about sixty miles south. The telegraph operator kept him there until a couple of troopers arrived to take him into custody. He joined the others in leg irons. Even so, one of those confined managed to escape again, irons and all. About thirty troopers hunted for him, with "orders not to take him alive." He was never found.[4]

Johnson noted that, along with his regiment, he was issued a Spencer repeating rifle. He explained, "metallic cartridges are used for loading it, seven cartridges are fired from it one after another with great rapidity, and it is loaded with seven more much quicker than the old pieces are with one."[5] The Spencer increased the fire power of a unit immeasurably, and proved its worth on the frontier many times over. Relatively few Civil War Union troops were as fortunate.

Meanwhile, the military administration of the department changed once again. On January 1, Major General Samuel R. Curtis took command of the Department of Kansas, including the state of Kansas and Nebraska, Colorado, and Indian

[3]Unrau, *Tending the Talking Wire*, 81.

[4]Ibid., 82–83, 87, 89, 91.

[5]Ibid., 92. The carbines the regiment purchased last May finally arrived.

Territories, with headquarters at Fort Leavenworth. Colonel Chivington commanded the District of Colorado. Companies C and F, under Major Mackey, were stationed at Fort Halleck, while Collins had the rest of the regiment at Fort Laramie and along the line north and west to South Pass. The 1st Colorado staffed all of the other posts in Colorado Territory. The 7th Iowa policed the road in Nebraska. Just 63 officers and 1,235 men covered the vast District of Colorado that January, including for a time forts Halleck and Laramie.[6]

Collins wondered why the Oregon and Overland roads guarded by the 11th had been transferred to Chivington's command. On February 17 Collins put that question to his new department commander. It took Curtis a little over two weeks to reply. "I do not know why you were shifted from the [District of] Nebraska," said Curtis. Collins was to report to Denver (Chivington) as assigned, but "you may always write directly to these headquarters on any and all matters of interest to your regiment and the posts you command." Curtis observed that supplies for the 11th "most economically" had to come from Iowa, not Denver, since those came from Iowa as well.

Curtis continued, "no inclination exists on my part to change [the disposition of] your troops, but I wish heartily your regiment was full. I anticipate a great rush of armed gold hunters to your neighborhood, and we may have to escort

---

[6]*O.R.*, I, 22, pt. 2, p. 768; 34, pt. 2, pp. 205–7. Chivington soon loomed like a black and ominious storm cloud over the overland roads. Born in northeastern Ohio, he began preaching at age twenty-three. He arrived in Denver in 1860 and spread the gospel in many area mining camps, but when the Civil War broke out he accepted a major's commission. After the Union victory at Glorietta Pass in New Mexico, in which he played a leading role, he received a hero's welcome in Denver and a promotion. By 1864 he commanded the military District of Colorado. Despite Union demands for Colorado troops, he refused to send his 1st Colorado Cavalry east, but kept them in his district. Close friends with Colorado governor Evans, he appeared to share Evans's plans and ambitions.

them." Curtis was pessimistic about finding additional troops. "I fear if we would try to raise them we would be filled up with gold hunters that desert to the mines the moment they come near them. Many think you will suffer greatly by desertions." But, he added, "I shall continue to feel great anxiety about your command, and therefore [will] support you by every means in my power." Curtis asked for "all the intelligence you can give of routes" to, and information about the mines (in Montana and Idaho), and "also the friendly or hostile conduct of the Indians north of you." Curtis also proposed to visit Fort Laramie if he could "when the snow is gone."[7]

Collins apparently stimulated Curtis to redraw district boundaries, as less than three weeks later the Oregon and Overland roads, and the 11th Ohio, returned to an enlarged District of Nebraska, removing them from Chivington's grasp. Collins now reported to Brigadier General Robert B. Mitchell, newly appointed to the command. When he reported at Fort Leavenworth, Mitchell brought with him a letter to Curtis from Secretary of the Interior John P. Usher. Usher complained that the military had promised to protect Indians "in their peaceable agricultural pursuits" but had not kept its word. Usher thought Mitchell would not disappoint him that way. Curtis believed the secretary's criticism was aimed at Major General James G. Blunt, who commanded that part of the District of the Frontier (southern Kansas, especially along the Arkansas River) contained within Curtis's Department of Kansas. Curtis betrayed his own views by telling Blunt "you will . . . see that no officers promise peace and security in time of war to anybody." Yet it was incumbent upon the military to "do what we can to prevent assaults of any kind upon loyal Indians and white men. . . .

[7] *O.R.*, I, 34, pt. 2, pp. 510–11.

This [is] all we can do, and I have so written to the honorable Secretary."[8]

Early in March Collins sent a detachment of about forty men after a wagon train that had just left Fort Laramie moving north. Collins had learned the train was carrying arms for Indians, and so it seemed. The detachment returned with "about thirty kegs of powder, several hundred pounds of ball, shot and lead, and about a bushel of percussion caps." Collins stored the materials at Laramie. Although the merchant had a license to trade with tribesmen, and the munitions might have been part of an annuity payment, Collins feared the consignment could have been used against his troops or emigrants, and not just for hunting game.[9]

Ever since he arrived at Fort Laramie, Collins had listened to complaints by the Sioux of mistreatment by Indian agent John Loree, in charge of the Upper Platte Agency. In March 1864, matters came to a head. Loree alienated his Sioux charges by cheating them and stealing from their annuities for his own profit. Outraged, Collins feared Loree would drive the Sioux into open hostility. He managed to arrange an interview between Mitchell and John Hunter, who was married to a Sioux. Mitchell found Hunter "honest and intelligent" and accepted Hunter's indictment of Loree. Mitchell gathered other evidence as well, which boded ill for Loree. After all, Mitchell had befriended Loree's superior,

---

[8]Ibid., I, 34, pt. 2, pp. 533, 684–85. Mitchell had a stellar Civil War record. While a colonel of the 2nd Kansas, he was badly wounded while riding with Brigadier General Nathaniel Lyon, who was killed at Wilson's Creek. Mitchell served with Curtis at Pea Ridge, and won promotion to brigadier general. At Perryville he commanded a division, earning a reputation as an energetic leader. In the Stone's River affair, he commanded at Nashville, after which he headed the 1st Cavalry Division of the Army of Cumberland. Mitchell fought in the Middle Tennessee campaign and at Chickamauga. His old wounds bothered him, however, and he asked for a less demanding command. Assistant Secretary of War Charles A. Dana called him "a shrewd, energetic man." After temporary duty in Washington, D.C., he was sent west to join Curtis. *O.R.*, I, 31, pt. 2, pp. 62–63; 34, pt. 2, pp. 348, 464.

[9]Unrau, *Tending the Talking Wire*, 96.

DEER CREEK STATION
Drawing by Private Charles F. Moellman.

the secretary of the interior, Usher. In addition to Collins, Loree had upset Seth Ward, sutler at Fort Laramie, as well as other traders, all of whom also energetically worked for his expulsion. The pressure on Loree became so intense that subsequently, in fear for his life, he resigned on September 30, 1864.[10]

In late March, several detachments of the 11th left Fort Laramie to relieve their fellows who had spent the winter at the small posts on the Oregon road from Laramie to the South Pass. According to Johnson, Company E caused considerable trouble at Deer Creek station, about ninety miles northwest of Laramie. He claimed nearly all in Company E were drunk, and one could not even sit his horse. Another, a "Sullivan," hit the officer of the day and was promptly fired upon and wounded. Company E finally settled down.

[10]*O.R.*, I, 34, pt. 2, p. 720; Remi Nadeau, *Fort Laramie and the Sioux* (Englewood Cliff, NJ: Prentice-Hall, Inc., 1967), 161–67; Becher, *Massacre Along the Medicine Road*, 24–25.

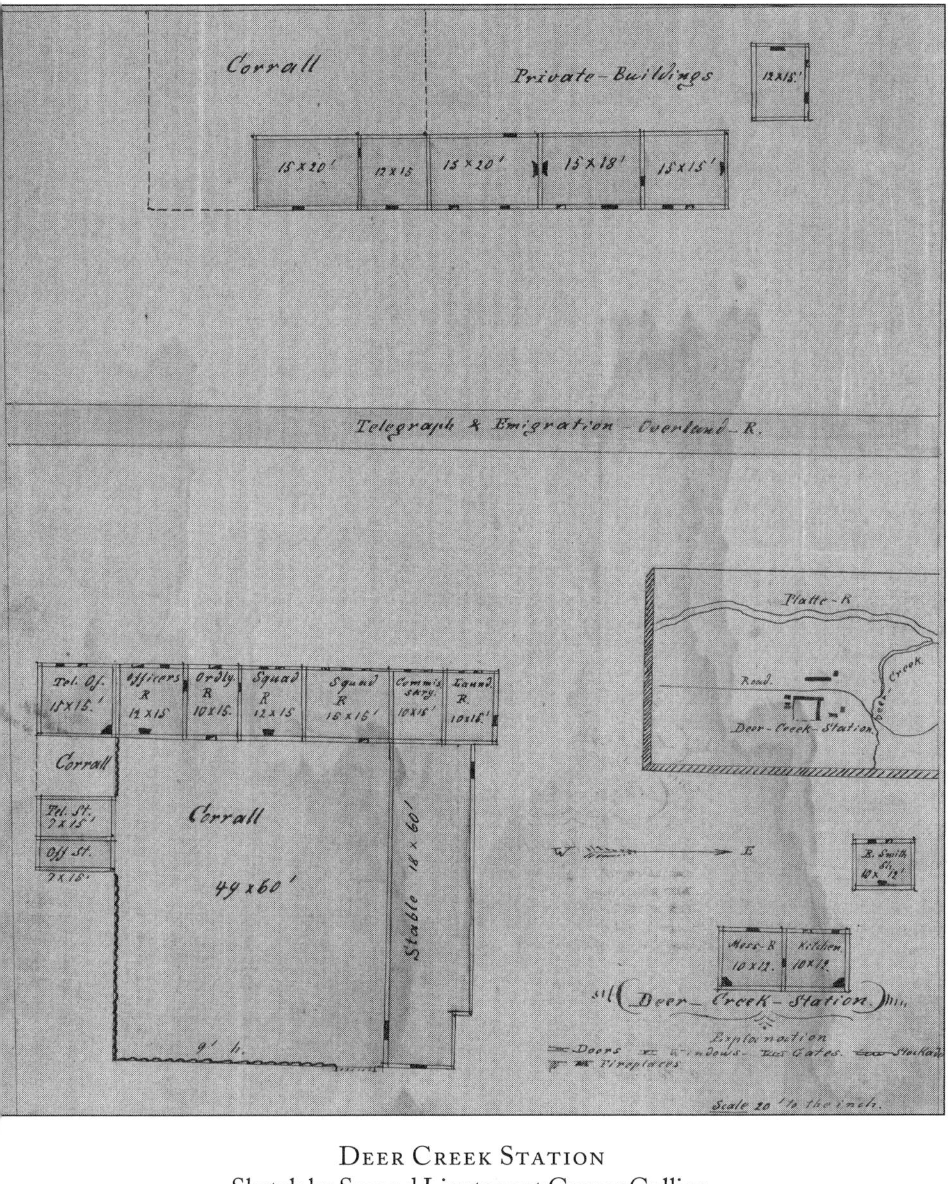

Deer Creek Station
Sketch by Second Lieutenant Caspar Collins.

Though Johnson remained at Deer Creek, "a very pleasant place," some of his company, G, went on to Platte Bridge, and part of E even farther west. Company E replaced H, ordered back to Laramie because, Johnson reported, there were "so many desertions from it." Arnold, on duty all winter near Platte Bridge, now joined Company E "further west along the telegraph line."[11]

Major General John Pope, commanding the Department of the Northwest (Minnesota and the Dakotas), planned an expedition into the Dakotas for spring or early summer. In mid-March he asked Curtis to send him a battalion of cavalry, but Curtis replied, "I could not spare a man," short-handed as he was. In addition, he pointed out that "an immense emigration is concentrating in the Platte Valley en route for the Bannock mines, and they are liable to create trouble with the tribes northwest of Laramie whose territory they will undoubtedly invade." Curtis's predictions proved to be quite accurate.[12]

Curtis faced yet another problem. He foresaw a serious Confederate threat to southern Kansas, and searched for reinforcements. If Chivington and Mitchell continued to keep their parts of the frontier quiet, he might be able to use some of their troops. On March 26 he told Colorado Governor Evans he was "obliged to draw every man who can be spared from the Indian frontier to operate against rebels" who threatened Kansas. At that point, Curtis siphoned no troops from Colorado, but Evans and Chivington certainly feared he would. They needed to make their troops indispensible to Colorado.[13]

On April 7, 1864, Mitchell, apparently not yet acquainted

---

[11]Unrau, *Tending the Talking Wire*, 103–7; Crawford, ed., *Rekindling Camp Fires*, 65; Merrill, *Bound for Idaho*, 171.

[12]*O.R.*, I, 34, pt. 2, pp. 652–53.

[13]Ibid., p. 743; Becher, *Massacre Along the Medicine Road*, 85.

with all his officers or the geography of his command, asked the "Commanding Officer, Fort Laramie" if he knew anything about 175 head of stock "the Indians have stolen . . . from near Denver, in your district." If so, he ordered Collins to "take the necessary measures to recapture the stock, and, if possible, the Indians." Collins would then report the result to Chivington. Curtis knew that this was Chivington's business even if Mitchell did not, and on April 8 Curtis told Chivington he should not "let district lines prevent pursuing and punishing" tribesmen, and to cooperate with Collins. Then on April 9 Chivington let Curtis know that four days previously "a party of Cheyenne Indians stole 175 head of cattle from the Government contractors, Irwin, Jackman & Co., from the headwaters of the Big Sandy, on the Smoky Hill route of the overland stage line. . . . I have sent out a section of artillery and a company of cavalry in pursuit" to recover the stock and "chastise" the Indians if they refuse to return it. On April 10 Collins asked Chivington for information on the alleged depredation and told him if he needed help, he could call on Major Mackey's 11th Ohio at Fort Halleck.[14]

Irwin, Jackman and Company had contracted for much of the government's freight business. During the winter they pastured many draft animals on Bijou Creek by the South Platte. On April 5 company herders reported many animals were gone, probably stolen by Cheyennes. Herders often blamed their losses on Indians, when the stock simply strayed. It gave Chivington an opportunity to use his cavalry against Cheyennes.[15]

George Bent saw this incident from the Cheyenne's viewpoint. He claimed a party of young Cheyennes went out in early April to fight the Crows who had killed a Northern Cheyenne the previous summer. They found four stray mules

[14]*O.R.*, I, 34, pt. 3, pp. 85, 98, 113, 123–24.

[15]Becher, *Massacre Along the Medicine Road*, 85–86.

as they approached the South Platte, but a "white man" claimed them, and told Colorado soldiers Cheyennes stole them. On April 12 a detachment of the 1st Colorado Cavalry charged a party of Dog Soldiers, a Cheyenne warrior society. Bent called this the Fremont's Orchard fight. A Cheyenne killed an "officer" with an arrow, and the troops fled. "We did not wish to kill them as we were not at war with the whites," Bent wrote. Two Cheyennes were wounded, and the Dog Soldiers returned to their village, forgetting about the Crows. The village then moved to a new camp on the Smoky Hill River, "to keep out of the way of the whites." The Cheyennes strenuously objected to the soldiers attacking them without even trying to talk to them first.

Almost simultaneously, a few Cheyennes ran across some oxen straying in the sand hills, and took them into camp without knowing to whom they belonged. But herders from Irwin, Jackman and Company told Colorado soldiers that the Cheyennes had driven off their entire herd of 175 animals. "I never believed this story," said Bent, for "the Indians had no use for the oxen" since there was plenty of buffalo, which they preferred.[16]

On April 13 Chivington told Collins that Lieutenant Clark Dunn and a detachment of the 1st Colorado Cavalry "had a fight with a band of Cheyennes near Fremont's Orchard" on the 12th, with "4 men wounded, 2 fatally; several Indians killed. They have gone with stolen stock in your direction. Look out for them and kill them. They are stealing in every direction, and refusing to give up stock when caught." Other cavalry patrols went out to hunt Indians, with no result. Collins sent detachments of the 11th Ohio out as well, but failed to find any Cheyennes. Collins himself led a patrol along the Oregon road as far east as Camp Cottonwood, where he met a company of the 7th Iowa Cavalry.

[16]Hyde, *George Bent*, 122–24.

Young Lieutenant Eugene F. Ware, 7th Iowa, thought Collins "a very fine old gentleman, rather old for military service, but finely preserved, energetic, and soldierly."[17]

April brought a burst of activity for Collins and his 11th Ohio. At Deer Creek, troopers of the 11th captured five deserters from Company H, put them in irons, and brought them to Laramie. Although early in the year, emigrant travel on the Oregon road began to pick up dramatically. Collins telegraphed Mitchell: "Immigration is coming rapidly; trouble with Indians may be expected." Collins wanted to know if he was obligated to provide escorts "through Idaho." A large party, Collins claimed, planned to use the Bozeman Trail. "The new route will be at least 200 miles shorter, through a country that ought to be opened, but a strong military party will be necessary." This worried Collins, especially since "deserters and secessionists are thronging into the territory and even good men make trouble through ignorance." Curtis replied through Mitchell that Collins could send "one proper escort" over the new trail, but he thought the "immigration [was] large enough to defend itself. We cannot control it." Complicating matters further, Captain Alfred de Wattewyl, Swiss army, arrived at the end of the month, accompanied by the acting consul general of Switzerland, Dr. John Hitz, Jr., with a Smithsonian expedition. From Fort Kearny to Fort Laramie they traveled with some two hundred recruits bound for the 11th. They came to Laramie to collect natural history specimens, something Collins had already begun to do.[18]

---

[17] *O.R.*, I, 34, pt. 3, pp. 150, 151, 167, 188, 219; Ware, *Indian War*, 120, 443. The post was designated Fort Cottonwood in May 1864; it was built two miles west of Cottonwood Springs at the intersection of the Oregon road and a heavily used north-south Indian trail. See Lass, *From the Missouri to the Great Salt Lake*, 151.

[18] *Collins Family Papers*, items 74, 76, 77; Ware, *Indian War*, 452–53; Unrau, *Tending the Talking Wire*, 114–15; *O.R.*, I, 34, pt. 3, pp. 304–5, 330; Lewis B. Hull, "Soldiering on the High Plains: The Diary of Lewis Byram Hull, 1864–1866," ed. by Myra E. Hull, *Kansas Historical Quarterly* 7, no. 1 (February 1938): 9.

Private Johnson reported from Deer Creek on April 22 that about a dozen wagons with fifty men passed that station headed for the Bannock mines. Another seventy-five wagons went by earlier. Johnson thought the emigrants were from Missouri, though they denied it. "They are nearly all copperheads," he wrote. He also believed he might be part of an escort over the Bozeman Trail, but he would not want to go "under Col. Collins. . . . I would prefer being under an Officer of the regular army one who has been out there and who understands indian *tactics*." Two weeks later Johnson noted "Emigration continues to pour along in a continual stream. copperheads are plenty." He predicted there would be "trouble" with the "south platte Cheyennes." He heard they were "being pursued by colorado soldiers and are trying to get on the north side of the north Platte." Johnson knew they would go after stock and horses. "We are not afraid of them attacking us, but if they attempt doing any mischief in our neighborhood, somebody will be apt to get hurt." Spencer repeating rifles doubtless boosted his confidence. By mid-May, Johnson wrote, "Emigration continues to pour along, sometimes as high as one hundred and twenty wagons pass in one day."[19]

Overland travel reached "unprecedented proportions" in 1864 and 1865. Part of the reason for increased freight activity was provisioning the road ranches that supplied the influx of emigrants, as well as the increase in military activity along the Platte Valley routes. After the gold strikes in Montana and Idaho in 1862 and 1863, John W. Bozeman with John M. Jacobs and James Stuart blazed a shorter route to the claims in the spring of 1863. Their route led through the heart of Sioux country, a direct violation of the Fort Laramie Treaty of 1851. Yet many argonauts and freighters opted to try the new trail in 1864, another reason for increased travel. In fact,

[19]Unrau, *Tending the Talking Wire*, 119, 124–25, 127.

Bozeman led a body of miners over his trail, and in April Jim Bridger piloted a wagon train of emigrants to the gold fields along a route west of Bozeman's, up through the Big Horn Basin, which later became known as the Bridger Trail. The Bridger expedition included about 62 wagons with 300 persons, and two more emigrant trains followed close behind. Yet another, with 150 wagons, 461 people, 636 oxen, 194 cattle, and 79 horses came later. But it was Bozeman's trail that disturbed the Sioux, Cheyennes, and Arapahos who hunted in that area, and whose villages dotted the river valleys.[20]

Not until early May did Collins hear from headquarters about his seizure of ammunition back in March. Orders came to retain the material until "further orders. . . . In any case it should not be permitted to be sold so as to fall into the hands of hostile Indians." Mitchell ordered that "trade with warlike Indians be stopped," but it was up to Collins to decide if he needed to restrict trade "with the other tribes to prevent the hostile Indians from profiting thereby."[21]

In Colorado, Chivington received reports of depredations by tribesmen and consequent fear among settlers, especially along the South Platte. Lieutenant George W. Hawkins reconnoitered the country east and south of Camp Collins, Colorado, on April 25 but found no hostiles, just "very friendly" Sioux. Even so, Chivington kept "three separate commands out after Indians, who are stealing in every direction." He asked Mitchell to return "the companies of my regiment" in his district.[22]

---

[20]Lass, *From Missouri to the Great Salt Lake*, 144; Hebard and Brininstool, *The Bozeman Trail*, vol. 1, 123, 219–20; Alter, *Jim Bridger*, 304–7; Dorothy M. Johnson, *The Bloody Bozeman: The Perilous Trail to Montana's Gold* (Missoula, Mont.: Mountain Press Publishing Company, 1983), 27, 50, 110, 129; James A. Lowe, *The Bridger Trail* (Spokane, Wash.: The Arthur H. Clark Company, 1999), 85–118. Bridger's route, though more difficult than Bozeman's, was safer. It went west of the Big Horn Mountains, away from hostile Indian country. Bridger's route was used only in 1864.

[21]*O.R.*, I, 34, pt. 3, pp. 503–4.

[22]Ibid., pp. 291, 292, 303–4.

Chivington heard from Major Jacob Downing on April 27 that "a party of Cheyennes . . . had stolen about $800 worth of horses." Downing followed them, found their village, and destroyed their lodges and contents, but the Indians eluded him, fleeing east toward the Republican River. Downing complained he had neither the men nor the horses to "successfully pursue them." George Bent said that "those in camp at Smoky Hill first heard of [the action at] Fremont's Orchard," then of other skirmishes with soldiers from other chiefs. He could not understand the need for these attacks unless they were politically motivated, to avoid sending Colorado troops east and to build political support for Governor Evans and Chivington by killing Indians. Bent thought Evans and Chivington only wanted to make the Indians hostile.[23]

Along the Oregon road west of Platte Bridge, Arnold's detachment of Company E, 11th Ohio, went west to staff the Three Crossings station on the Sweetwater River. Arnold remembered that the duty was good, the "location all that could be desired." When a supply wagon failed to arrive, a courier found the empty wagon standing alone without its six-mule team. Along with two others, Arnold tracked the culprits who had stolen the provisions and the mules. They followed the track north for twenty-five miles before they lost the trail and returned empty-handed. Next, Arnold participated in a small detachment that escorted a Mormon party headed east to "Sweetwater Bridge," where other troopers waited to take the Mormons to Platte Bridge. At Sweetwater station he learned from a friend that "Crawford," a member of his detachment, suspected that it was he who had implicated the mutineers last year. Crawford had been one of them, and the word followed that he would seek revenge. Even if Crawford did not, "there are enough

[23]Ibid., p. 314; Hyde, *George Bent*, 124–27.

Knights of the Golden Circle left that we know of to make trouble" for Arnold.[24]

This news disturbed Arnold. "[I]n reporting the mutineers . . . I had done what I thought was my duty. Now it looked like I was to pay for it. . . . I felt that either Crawford would kill me or I would be compelled to kill him. . . . I decided that whatever happened I must avoid bloodshed." Arnold noted that in the "wilderness" there was no other post he could easily transfer to, and besides, he would be "ashamed" to tell the company commander of his fears. "I was no coward," he wrote, but desired to avoid trouble. It was "for this reason that I resolved to . . . desert." Arnold failed to see that desertion was much of a crime; after all, he had done it before and many others had deserted as well.[25]

Arnold figured he would need a gun and a saddle that belonged to the "government," but he had his own pony, purchased from some emigrants. He also calculated he had more in wages due than the value of government property, "so I could take them without any qualms." He had ten dollars in cash. "So one day I started out hunting, as I had often done before, . . . but this time never to return." Thus Arnold disappeared. Never apprehended, he headed for the gold fields as others had, then moved on to other places in the West, where he remained for the rest of his life. He "never had the courage to face the people back in Ohio . . . and who . . . might brand me for my desertion from the army." He became another deserter from among those Collins had recruited in 1863.[26]

---

[24]Crawford, ed., *Rekindling Camp Fires*, 67, 74. The Knights of the Golden Circle were a pro-Confederate secret society found in southern parts of Union states and border states.

[25]Ibid., 75–76.

[26]Ibid., 76–77, 303. Arnold married in South Dakota in 1878 and had several children. He died in 1922. He had two brothers in the Union army, one of whom was killed at Atlanta [ibid., 138, 306–7]. See also a capsule biography of Arnold in Nellie Snyder Yost, ed., *Boss Cowman: The Recollections of Ed Lemmon, 1857–1946* (Lincoln: University of Nebraska Press, 1969), 143–46. Lemmon gives a quite different and fanciful account than Arnold does.

In May and June 1864 most violence took place on portions of the overland roads away from the reach of the 11th Ohio. But these activities would affect it before many weeks passed. The 7th Iowa, stationed along the Oregon road east of Julesburg, heard on May 3 that Mitchell had ordered them "to exert a controlling influence over the Indians," keep the tribesmen from disturbing each other, and "prevent soldiers or other parties from committing outrages upon the Indians." Given the army's reputation in the West, Mitchell insisted "the shooting of Indians for trivial or supposed offenses by soldiers must not be allowed under any circumstances, and every effort [must be] used to allay any ill-feeling that may exist." Unfortunately, that order was directed at Iowa, not Colorado or even California troops. Then, a week later Company F, 11th Ohio, moved into Colorado to garrison Camp Collins, relieving the 1st Colorado and at the same time solidifying the 11th's control of the Overland mail route. It also was a part of Chivington's plan to concentrate his troops on the Arkansas River.[27]

Farther east along the Oregon road, the telegraph operator at Plum Creek, just west of Fort Kearny, reported on May 21 that Cheyennes had killed ten soldiers at Box Elder Creek, 175 miles southwest, and claimed that they would kill all white men and soldiers on the Oregon road. He estimated the Cheyennes had over 1,600 warriors and they would be at Plum Creek within a day. When Major George M. O'Brien received this report at Fort Kearny, he understood this was far away. He calmly noted that "Indian troubles are much magnified." There was "nothing to cause serious alarm here,"

[27] *O.R.*, I, 34, pt. 3, pp. 354, 425–26, 541. On June 9 Company F, 11th Ohio, was flooded out of the camp by the rushing Cache la Poudre River. They relocated the post on higher ground nearby (see Lass, *From Missouri to the Great Salt Lake*, 152) and called it Fort Collins. Today it is the site of the city of Fort Collins, Colorado. Also see Hafen and Young, *Fort Laramie*, 151–52. Camp Collins previously was La Porte stage station.

along the Platte, he reported.[28] The "alarm" would sound sooner than O'Brien thought.

Accounts of fighting elsewhere continued to mount. On May 16—the report not reaching either Chivington or O'Brien until May 25—a detachment of Colorado troops under Lieutenant George S. Eayre was attacked by perhaps as many as four hundred Cheyenne warriors near the Smoky Hill River. According to the information, the detachment arrived back at Fort Larned (on the Santa Fé road) May 19, with a loss of four troopers killed and three more wounded. Eayre claimed the Cheyennes lost twenty-eight killed. But apparently it was Eayre who had attacked, killing a chief called Lean Bear. Lean Bear had come forward to show his peace medal, given to him in Washington in 1862, to claim his group was peaceful. Then the Cheyenne fought back until another chief, Black Kettle, managed to call them off, as he believed the Cheyennes should not fight against the whites. George Bent told the Cheyenne story. The Cheyennes, Bent said, captured fifteen cavalry horses, completely equipped, noted that three tribesmen had been killed and many wounded, and "if Black Kettle had not stopped the fight, not one of Eayre's men would have escaped." But some young Cheyennes retaliated for Lean Bear's death by raiding the stage line along the Santa Fé road between forts Riley (northeast of Fort Larned on the Kansas River) and Larned.[29]

Bent observed that in spite of the attacks on them, most of the Cheyennes were opposed to war. An exception was the fraternity of Dog Soldiers. The remainder of the Cheyennes removed south of the Arkansas River and camped with the Kiowas, Comanches, Prairie Apaches, and Arapahos. William Bent, George's father, went among them counseling

[28] *O.R.*, I, 34, pt. 3, p. 711.

[29] Ibid., pt. 4, pp. 38–39; Grinnell, *The Fighting Cheyennes*, 144–46; Hyde, *George Bent*, 130.

peace, and even took some chiefs with him to Fort Larned, but was rebuffed by the commandant. That angered the chiefs. The troops there had been ordered to keep the tribesmen at a safe distance, and when a sentry drew on a Kiowa chief who had come with friendly intentions, the Kiowas sent two arrows through him. The post went quickly on alert, but the Kiowas ran off with the post herd, including 240 horses and mules. When some friendly Arapahos came by Larned with an offer to return the herd, they were fired upon. They left and ran off another herd near Fort Lyon. After a short time, the southern tribesmen cooled down, still expecting to keep the peace.[30]

Chivington's 1st Colorado appeared to be deliberately provoking the Cheyennes. George Bent and his father thought so, as did brevet Brigadier General Christopher "Kit" Carson, a legend on the southwestern frontier, and Jesse Leavenworth, Indian agent for the Kiowas, Comanches, and Apaches. Carson said he had "heard it publicly stated that the authorities in Colorado . . . determined to get up an Indian war. . . . I know of no acts of hostility on the part of the Cheyennes and Arapahos committed previous to the attacks made on them." Leavenworth testified that if Colonel Chivington "was not stopped in his course of sending" the 1st Colorado "after the Indians we should get into a general Indian war on the frontier." Also, George Bent wrote that he "could never understand why the soldiers made these attacks on the Cheyennes. . . . There was no reason for it. . . . The attacks were evidently planned at headquarters, for the troops went after our people at about the same time at widely separated points." Chivington needed "to attack the Indians and stir them up. The troops would then be needed in Colorado."

---

[30]Hyde, *George Bent*, 133–35. Fort Lyon, formerly Fort Wise, was Bent's old trading post on the Santa Fé road, west of Fort Larned.

Bent added, "on the frontier, this was the shortest road to the [white] people's hearts."[31]

Before the Cheyennes "cooled down," as Bent put it, they, along with others, probably Kiowas and Arapahos, raided all along the Santa Fé road and left it nearly deserted. Thomas O. Osburn, United States marshal for Kansas, reported these attacks. Osburn said one white man, left alive because he had married a Cheyenne woman, told him the tribesmen "intended to kill all the whites they could find." He found ranches "deserted and sacked" and two wagon trains "robbed." Osburn noted that "the stage stock is all off the road for 100 miles and every station keeper has left."[32]

Chivington and Evans kept General Curtis in the dark concerning their decision to force an Indian war and failed to keep him up to date on events in Colorado. About ten days later they presented him with the results of their activity, when it was too late for him or anyone else to do anything about it. Meanwhile, George Bent remained with his father on the Purgatorie River, south of the Arkansas, not far from Fort Lyon. Bent recalled that some Cheyennes, especially the Dog Soldiers, along with some Sioux, sent small raiding parties out to hit the Oregon road along the Platte. But other Sioux, especially Brulé and Oglala, did not want "to get mixed up in the war," so they gathered near Fort Cottonwood.[33]

On May 28 Governor Evans paraded his problems before General Curtis. He knew Curtis wanted Colorado troops for use elsewhere, but Evans continued to claim he could not spare them since "now we have but half the troops . . . and are at war with a powerful combination of Indian tribes who are

[31]Becher, *Massacre Along the Medicine Road*, 88–89; Hyde, *George Bent*, 127. Becher quotes Carson and Leavenworth's testimony concerning the above attacks from the later Congressional investigation into the Sand Creek Massacre.

[32]*O.R.*, I, 34, pt. 4, pp. 149–50.

[33]Hyde, *George Bent*, 137.

pledged to . . . drive the white people from this country." Evans noted that he had been in Washington to visit the Indian Bureau and the War Department to prepare for the anticipated conflict. He asked for carbines and he got them, but that was all that could be done to strengthen "the posts on the plains in Kansas and Nebraska . . . by springtime." His informants told him, he said, that the Sioux and Arapahos in his country would keep the peace, but "all of the Cheyennes . . . with the Kiowas and Comanches, are allied and now [are] carrying out their hellish purposes" and "are in strong force on the plains" and had skirmished with Colorado troops. In his opinion the hostiles had to be chastized "severly and at once" or a delay would bring a long and bloody war, costly in lives and property. Then on May 31, Chivington told his 1st Colorado Cavalry "the Cheyennes will have to be soundly whipped before they will be quiet. If any of them are caught in your vicinity kill them, as that is the only way. Take their stock and turn it in to the quartermaster." Evans told Curtis conflict was at hand and he needed to be ready for it; Chivington declared war against the Cheyennes.[34]

Officers of the 7th Iowa at Fort Cottonwood knew that General Mitchell intended to come out from his Omaha headquarters that spring to council with the Sioux in hopes of getting their pledge of peace. He also hoped to convince them to leave the Platte Valley. In fact, they learned from an officer of the 1st Colorado how important it would be to keep the Sioux away from the Cheyennes since Colorado troops planned to campaign against them. Otherwise it seemed likely the war would spill over into the Platte Valley with the Sioux and Cheyennes allied. It was important that Mitchell succeed in neutralizing the Sioux. What none of the military realized was how close the Sioux and Cheyenne were. They, along with other plains tribes, had been historically allied for

[34] *O.R.*, I, 34, pt. 4, pp. 97–99, 151.

many years. If nothing else, the Cheyenne Dog Soldiers and Sioux had intermarried often.[35]

Mitchell met with some of the Brulé and Oglala at Fort Cottonwood in May and listened to their complaints about the whites who brought them alcohol and caused drunkeness and discord, and about surveyors who it seemed were mapping out a new road along the Niobrara River, north of the Platte. Mitchell seemed to throw his good will away when he mentioned he wanted them to leave the Platte Valley. Though angered, the Sioux agreed to meet with him again.[36]

Mitchell doubtless had qualms about the success of any meeting since just before his arrival at Fort Cottonwood a young Sioux war party killed two travelers just across the Platte River in full view of the fort. They also taunted the troopers, waving bloody scalps at them. The soldiers could do nothing, as the Platte was too high with snowmelt to ford; there could be no pursuit.[37]

Mitchell also wanted intelligence concerning the Sioux-Cheyenne connection. Obligingly, Major O'Brien sent out two white men who had married Indian women, Alfred Gay and John W. Smith, to seek information "in regard to impending hostilities between the whites and Cheyennes and other Indians" and to convince the Brulé and Oglala Sioux to meet again. Gay and Smith soon ran across a band of both Cheyennes and Sioux. When they returned with a report, they noted the Cheyennes wanted to kill them on the spot, but the Sioux intervened. They had learned that the Cheyennes—probably Dog Soldiers—had scouts in the Sioux camps. "They have their spies out in every direction; they are met on the Platte traveling as Sioux. . . . They are in

---

[35]Ibid., pt. 3, p. 711; Becher, *Massacre Along the Medicine Road*, 87.

[36]Becher, *Massacre Along the Medicine Road*, 87, claimed this meeting took place in April, citing Ware, *Indian War*, 105. Becher overlooked Clyde C. Walton's note on 456 that Mitchell couldn't have been at Cottonwood then.

[37]Ware, *Indian War*, 142.

the Sioux camp." Notwithstanding advice they received from the Cheyennes, the Brulé and Oglala were willing to talk again.[38]

On June 8 Mitchell next met with the Brulé and Oglala Sioux near Fort Cottonwood. Major O'Brien, 7th Iowa, asked the Sioux if they intended to remain at peace, and received an affirmative reply. Next he asked, "if you had to fight, which side would you take, Cheyenne or white?" The Sioux replied they had no desire to fight either one, only to be allowed to live and hunt in peace, under the protection of their "white brothers." Then Mitchell told the Sioux that if they wanted peace, they would have to "keep your people off the Platte Valley road" and not "interfere" or trade with the emigrants, and leave the Pawnees alone as well. If the Sioux agreed to this they would be treated as friends; otherwise, enemies. According to Mitchell, the Sioux agreed to everything, but wanted assurances that if the soldiers went after the Cheyennes, they would not be molested. The Sioux also said they wanted to hunt south of the Platte and would like a white man with them who could protect them from the soldiers. They also wanted their annuity goods distributed to them at a place ten miles north of Cottonwood, since it was difficult to go to Fort Laramie to receive them. Mitchell replied that he could not promise the annuities would be delivered as the Sioux requested, but he would recommend it. Mitchell also reported that the Sioux thought the Cheyennes were "fools" for making war on the whites, but they knew the Cheyennes boasted "they will kill all the whites on both the Platte Valley and Santa Fé roads." According to Mitchell it was a friendly conference; his report was optimistic.[39]

George Bent again held a different opinion. He thought Mitchell had been arrogant when he "ordered" the Sioux to

[38]Ibid., 143; *O.R.*, I, 34, pt. 4, p. 461–62.

[39]*O.R.*, I, 34, pt. 4, pp. 458–60.

stay out of the Platte Valley. In reference to the May meeting between Mitchell and the Sioux, Bent noted that Sioux chief Spotted Tail had claimed "the valley belonged to his people and that they would come there to trade and cross north and south of the river whenever they liked." Bent added that both the chief and Mitchell lost their tempers, "but after a while the General cooled down and told the Sioux to come back for another talk," which they did on June 8.[40] Even at the June 8 meeting, Mitchell had not been able to address all the Sioux questions, and yet a third council was scheduled. Mitchell doubtless discovered that commanding on the plains proved quite different from other military commands he had held. He sincerely tried to keep the peace with the Sioux, and though they wanted it, the Brulé and Oglala were only two of many Sioux tribes.

Mitchell's third meeting with the Sioux took place July 19. Although the Brulé and Oglala who met with him were anxious to avoid war, this meeting failed. A company of Pawnee scouts, recently recruited and equipped as cavalry, were present, exacerbating tensions. Mitchell demonstrated little knowledge of Native American affairs, or he would have known the Sioux and Pawnee had been bitter enemies for over a hundred years. Both tribes were upset and violence clearly threatened, but Mitchell and a detachment of the 7th Iowa, with a brass cannon, came between the groups. Bent reported that Mitchell had "to send the Sioux away in a hurry." Even though the Brulé and Oglala had wanted to hunt south of the Platte, they went north instead, hoping to avoid getting caught up in any disturbance. This peace effort came to nothing, dashing Mitchell's hopes of establishing peace with the Sioux. A few days later a small war party of young Sioux ranged east of Fort Kearny to kill Pawnees. In the dark they mistook a party of whites for their enemy,

[40]Hyde, *George Bent*, 137. Bent also thought the first council had been in May.

killing several. Mitchell sent troops out to hunt down the Sioux war party, an act of open hostility on his part.[41]

More trouble came to Colorado. About sixty-five miles from Denver an emigrant family camped along Bijou Creek by the South Platte River. They reported that six mounted Indians stampeded their stock, six horses and four mules, stranding them. There were no casualties, but worse was to come. Ward Hungate, a ranch manager, rode out to look for stray stock on June 12, and before long saw smoke rising from the ranch. By the time he returned, he found the ranch engulfed in fire and his wife and daughters dead. The raiders, still on hand, then killed Hungate. A search party found the Hungates that afternoon. Hungate had been mutilated and scalped; his wife stabbed and scalped; his daughters' throats slashed. Thirty head of horses and mules were missing. As the ranch was but twenty miles from Denver, the gruesome bodies were carried to Denver and put on exhibition in an effort to compel "the military in force [to] proceed against the Indians at once."[42]

Quickly, on June 14, Governor Evans went over Curtis's head to Secretary of War Stanton. "Indian hostilities on our settlements commenced," Evans wrote, as he had predicted "last fall." This war is at hand, "murdered and scalped bodies brought in today." Would Stanton authorize "a regiment of 100-days' men" or would he federalize the militia?[43]

On June 15, 1864, Major Thomas I. McKenny, Curtis's inspector-general for the Department of Kansas, reported from Fort Larned that he was convinced

> if great caution is not exercised on our part there will be a bloody war [with the Indians]. It should be our policy to try and conciliate

[41]Grinnell, *The Fighting Cheyennes*, 151; Hyde, *George Bent*, 138; *O.R.*, I, 34, pt. 4, p. 585; Ware, *Indian War*, 157–65, presents a detailed account of the July 19 fiasco.

[42]*O.R.*, I, 34, pt. 4, pp. 353, 354–55, 405; Becher, *Massacre Along the Medicine Road*, 101–2.

[43]*O.R.*, I, 34, pt. 4, p. 381.

> them, guard our mails and trains well to prevent theft, and stop these scouting parties that are roaming over the country who do not know one tribe from another, and who will kill anything in the shape of an Indian.

McKenny continued, "It will require but few murders on the part of our troops to unite all these warlike tribes of the plains, who have been at peace for years and intermarried amongst one another. I do wish," he told Curtis through his adjutant, "that some prudent, good man could be placed in command of the troops along the roads."[44]

Major Henry D. Wallen, 7th United States Infantry, just back in Kansas City after a journey on the plains, echoed McKenny. His information, he said, indicated that "an expensive Indian war is about to take place between the whites and the Cheyennes, Kiowas, and a band of Arapahos. It can be prevented by prompt management."[45] Unfortunately, McKenny's and Wallen's common sense attracted too little attention.

Even if McKenny's assessment had been heeded, it was already too late. The "few murders" had already happened, and thoroughly aroused Native American war parties struck back. Not only the Cheyennes, but also Kiowas, Comanches, Arapahos, and Sioux, especially their young men, participated in raid after raid. The chiefs, who knew the ultimate consequences of war, could not restrain them. War parties struck the roads along the Platte, Arkansas, and Smoky Hill; they attacked stagecoaches and emigrant and freight wagon trains, destroyed ranches and stage stations, ran off hundreds of head of livestock, and in the process killed dozens of people. Writing of these raids, George Bent admitted "they were terrible affairs, but after all, the Indians were wild people in those days; they had been attacked again and again by the

[44]Ibid., p. 404.

[45]Ibid., p. 476.

troops without any cause, and they were retaliating in the only way they knew how."[46]

Governor Evans finally had his war, and he knew it. On June 16, he begged Curtis to let Chivington operate against "these infernal Indians" and bring "into service" Mitchell's troops from "Laramie, Cottonwood, and Kearny" as well. He sent along communications from two of his civilian correspondents who testified to the need for action against the Indians. When Evans had received no reply from Curtis by June 22, he became surly. "I had supposed that the information I have given you was sufficient to satisfy you that this Indian war is no myth but a terrible reality," he wrote Curtis that day. If Curtis thought otherwise, he should tell Evans, but he was "at a loss to perceive" how that could be so.[47]

With other pressing matters at hand elsewhere in his department, Curtis ignored Evans and instead sent instructions directly to Chivington. Curtis told Chivington that he had a message from Major McKenny that criticized the report of the 1st Colorado's attack May 16 that resulted in the death of Lean Bear. That was "not so well reported," said Curtis. He told Chivington that if he were attacked, of course he could fight, but "it is bad economy to divert needless numbers in pursuit of Indians." Curtis frowned on search-and-destroy tactics. He also cautioned Chivington against allowing troops to "chase after buffalo, an amusement which breaks down stock and delays marches." When Chivington reached Fort Larned, he was to see that James W. Parmetar, 12th Kansas, "the drunken captain" who had rebuffed the Cheyennes, Arapahos, and Kiowas, "is immediately relieved, superseded, or arrested." Besides, "letters from Larned give many reports of Indian barbarities, which are not authenticated." He wanted "careful reports" from Chivington.[48]

---

[46]Hyde, *George Bent*, 139.

[47]*O.R.*, I, 34, pt. 4, pp. 422–23, 512–13.

[48]Ibid., p. 595.

Curtis finally got back to Evans on July 5. "I may not have all you have seen and heard, but I am sure I have a great deal on the subject which you have not seen nor heard." They should be prepared for trouble, Curtis wrote, but should "not exhaust our efforts in pursuit of rumors." Curtis only wanted to hear "information of outrages" that were "fully ascertained." Curtis noted how short of horses the entire department was, and how necessary it was "to avoid waste in this branch of service." Though they might fear "a general Indian war," they should not decide one is "in actual existence before doing all in our power to prevent such a disaster." Nothing Curtis heard convinced him such a war was at hand.[49] So far as Curtis was concerned, that was the end of the matter.

But it was not the end. Before Evans received Curtis's July 5 missive, Evans had published a proclamation on June 27, a proposal of his to provide sanctuary for "friendly Indians." According to this document, Evans directed "all friendly Indians to keep away from those who are at war, and go to places of safety." Such among the Cheyennes and Arapahos were to "go to Major [Samuel G.] Colley, . . . Indian Agent at Fort Lyon, who will give them provisions and show them a place of safety."[50] Kiowas and Comanches would be received near Fort Larned.

Evans should have known his scheme would not work. Not only were hostiles and friendlies "hopelessly intermixed," but also he heard that Congress would not "appropriate funds" for such a purpose. "It is not contemplated that the Indians should be collected and fed on the reservations, but they should be concentrated, if anywhere, about the buffalo range" where they can take care of themselves. Evans' proclamation was nothing more than smoke and mirrors.[51]

---

[49]Ibid., 41, pt. 2, p. 53.

[50]David A. White, compiler, *News of the Plains and Rockies, 1803–1865* (Spokane, Wash.: The Arthur H. Clark Company, 1998), vol. 4, 293.

[51]Ibid., 293–94.

Chivington finally arrived at Fort Larned, but not before Kiowa braves made off with many army horses. Although Arapaho Chief Left Hand had warned Captain Parmetar that such would happen, he had been rebuffed. The captain ordered his men to shoot any Indian who came near Larned, and even friendly Arapahos were fired upon. Chivington obeyed Curtis's order and replaced Parmetar with Captain William Backus, 1st Colorado. But it came too late to keep angry young Arapahos from leaving to join with the warlike Dog Soldiers.[52] Misguided and misinformed whites managed to provoke a major war on the Great Plains.

---

[52]Becher, *Massacre Along the Medicine Road*, 106–7.

CHAPTER SIX

Roads, Recruits, and Danger: Summer 1864

In May and June 1864 the 11th Ohio faced only minor disturbances along the Oregon and Overland roads. Northern Cheyennes and Sioux conducted hit-and-run raids on emigrant parties, inflicting some casualties but mostly running off livestock. Collins could do little to protect the many emigrant trains, for the marauders evaporated before pursuit could be organized. On May 24, a civilian died and another was wounded in such a raid near Fort Laramie, and though a detail from Company H searched for those responsible, they found no one.[1]

Also that May, Lieutenant John K. Wright, Company B, 16th Kansas, detached from duty at Fort Leavenworth, brought about two hundred recruits for the 11th Ohio to Fort Laramie. They had left Leavenworth on March 12 and, since they were without horses, walked the seven hundred miles to Laramie (except when a few sometimes rode in supply wagons or on mules). Fortunately, their two-month-long trek was mostly uneventful; the few Native Americans they met were not hostile. At Mud Springs in May they met an escort from Laramie, and on May 8 they camped four miles from the post, in quarantine. Those at the fort were "afraid of smallpox," as

[1]Robrock, "The Eleventh Ohio," 31.

something similar had been reported among the recruits back at Fort Kearny. Colonel Collins met them at their camp May 10, bringing along the "band . . . from the fort" to serenade them. The recruits gave "three cheers" for the colonel and another round for Lieutenant Wright. On May 25, the newcomers moved into the fort. Private Lewis B. Hull and eighty-four others became the nucleus of Captain Jacob L. Humfreville's Company K; many joined Captain Jacob F. Apt's Company I, and still others were dispersed ultimately to Companies E, F, G, and H.[2]

North of Fort Laramie at Deer Creek, Private Johnson of Company G reported on June 16 that the "Indians are getting very mischievous" and killed a few emigrants and stole "a great deal of emigrant stock." Emigration was brisk; he claimed to have seen a wagon train "near a mile long." They were headed for the gold fields in Montana "without escort." Colonel Collins, he wrote, claimed there were no men to spare for escort duty, but Johnson thought Collins "was afraid of the natives. . . . The Col might make a good farmer but he aint fit to command a regiment. . . . The boys have to laugh at him." Johnson continued, "at 'dress parade' he draws his saber so gracefully . . . gives commands with such accuracy, then returns his sword to the scabbard, the wrong side foremost and works half an hour to get it out and put it in right." Johnson continued to poke fun at the officers, for whom he had very little regard.[3]

---

[2]Hull, "Soldiering on the High Plains," 6, 8–13; *Official Roster of the Soldiers of the State of Ohio*, pp. 560–73. Hull came from Highland County, Ohio, as did Hervey Johnson of Company G and Colonel Collins. Hull was a veteran of the 60th Ohio Infantry until captured at Harper's Ferry on September 15, 1862. Paroled and then discharged November 19, 1862, he enlisted in the 11th Ohio on February 3, 1864. He was promoted to sergeant on June 30, 1864. Apt, a lieutenant in Company D, was promoted to captain and took over Company I in May 1864; Humfreville, a lieutenant in Company A, won promotion to captain and took over Company K that same May, though their commissions officially arrived October 31.

[3]Unrau, *Tending the Talking Wire*, 139–40.

On June 23 Johnson drew a detail to inspect the horses and mules of the emigrants to see if any had "US" brands. Of the several hundred he checked, he found only two. "We take them right out of the team where we find them. . . . the Capt [Levi M. Rinehart] goes for everything they have that is contraband. he took a cavalry saddle from a man this morning." Civilians had to have papers to prove ownership of government-issue items, even blankets and clothing. This was not an unusual procedure. Julius Merrill, traveling along the Oregon road in 1864, mentioned a similar inspection at the hands of the 7th Iowa at Fort Cottonwood in July.[4]

Johnson also told how the emigrants left mail with the soldiers. Troopers charged ten cents for each letter they posted. "One of the boys took down about four hundred [letters] the other day [to post]. quite a business place our town is when forty or fifty wagons stop here, the boys trade horses and ponies with them, steal their dogs and anything else they can lay hands on." They also bought "worn out" cattle from emigrants "for little or nothing an let them run on the prairie two or three weeks" by which time they are healthy enough to be traded for other worn out cattle. Another money maker for soldiers involved learning how to operate the telegraph. "[N]early all the [telegraph] offices . . . are run by soldiers they get 65 dollars per month besides their soldiers wages." Johnson thought that was pretty good business, too.[5]

Except for petty theft, the emigrants doubtless saw these things a little differently. Posting their mail provided a service for them, even at soldier rates: there was no other way to manage that. The replacement of worn oxen and other animals also proved useful and often necessary, for the road ranches that performed that same service were far behind them, and emigrants knew of no others ahead. The soldiers

[4]Ibid., 139; Merrill, *Bound for Idaho*, 46.
[5]Unrau, *Tending the Talking Wire*, 139–40.

were not required to provide such services at all, and while emigrants might grumble about the cost, they had no other choice.

From Fort Laramie, Hull reported "emigrants plenty in camp" on June 15 and, five days later, "emigrants lining the road." Not only did travelers abound, perhaps nervous about the road ahead, but also ninety more 11th Ohio recruits arrived on June 23, to be spread among Companies E through K. Yet another company, L, was sworn in June 30. This one, captained by Ewell P. Drake, was made up of eighty-two men transferred from Companies A, B, C, and D whose enlistments would not expire until 1866, three more from Company F, including Drake (promoted from lieutenant), one from Company E, and three recruits—the whole, officers and men, totaling ninety.

The garrison planned a big Independence Day celebration for all, not just the newcomers, constructing an evergreen arbor and making table decorations for the dinner. At noon on July 4, a salute of fifty guns boomed out, followed by the "splendid dinner" of beef, veal, "mutton tongue, pies, cake, etc." That evening "good" entertainment took place, "consisting of pantomime, burlesque, songs," and the like. At eleven that night came another salute of fifteen guns, "a fine sight." A few days later Hull became "acting secretary for the minstrels." On July 7 he sold $107 worth of tickets for the performance. Tickets went for 15 to 50 cents, depending on seat location. Colonel Collins mentioned he was "pleased with the results."[6]

From Deer Creek on July 5, Johnson, newly promoted to corporal, wrote that Indians took forty-two horses from emigrants "about eighteen miles below" Deer Creek. A detachment of the 11th chased the Indians, recovered twenty-seven

---

[6]Hull, "Soldiering on the High Plains," 14–16; *Official Roster of the Soldiers of the State of Ohio*, pp. 577–80.

horses, killed four tribesmen, and wounded others. He had been out with a scouting party five days and admitted that the vastness of the plains still amazed him. On the 18th he reported, "have been out scouting after the indians . . . sometimes twice and three times a day." Johnson noted the emigrants "are collecting in large trains" for better protection. "A great many have been killed, their wagons plundered and property burned, dead and wounded men are picked up every day and buried by soldiers and emigrants."[7]

Also on July 18 Johnson reported "two hundred men and two pieces of artillery" arrived "yesterday" from Fort Laramie. Rumor had it that a plan existed to "hunt up and attack the indian village," but he had no hard information about that. He knew, though, that three soldiers rode south "last week" for about eighteen miles when Indians drove them back to Deer Creek. They claimed the road was "strewn for miles with arrows clothing beds flour bacon salt" and other plunder, six dead men "all of them . . . killed by arrows. . . . Three men, two badly wounded . . . are the only survivors." Two women and two children were captured. On the 17th a scouting party found the body of a little girl and buried it. Johnson said he "got over the notion" that he would never try to kill anyone. He now "could shoot an indian with as much coolness as I would a dog, and I will do it if [I] can."[8]

Johnson referred to the July 12 attack on the Kelly-Larimer train at Little Box Elder Creek, about ten miles south of Deer Creek. A Sioux war party attacked the two wagons with eleven people, killed four of the men, and took Mrs. Fanny Kelly and her young niece captive, along with Mrs. Sarah Larimer and her eight-year-old son. The next wagon train along buried the dead and told the story to Captain Rinehart, Johnson's commanding officer. Rinehart sent for reinforce-

[7]Unrau, *Tending the Talking Wire*, 141, 147.

[8]Ibid., 147, 150.

ments, to which Collins responded by sending Company E and some troopers from Companies I and K, along with two pieces of artillery (the "two hundred" men Johnson mentioned above), with orders for them to pursue the Indians and rescue the captives. Captain Levi G. Marshall spoke with Mrs. Larimer on July 17, after she and her son escaped from their captors and walked about forty miles to Deer Creek. On July 18 Marshall and 160 men rode out to find Mrs. Kelly. They scouted for eleven days, but failed to find the woman. They met with Indians several times and claimed to have inflicted about forty casualties among them. An arrow found Second Lieutenant John Brown of Company E, the first officer of the 11th to die in action.

Shortly after Marshall's scout for Fanny Kelley, Collins sent patrols out to search the country for hostiles within a twenty-five–mile radius of Fort Laramie. Returning troopers reported they found none. No sooner had they unsaddled their horses on the parade ground in the center of the fort, than thirty tribesmen appeared from nowhere, galloped across the parade ground "yelling, shooting, and waving buffalo robes. They stampeded every animal . . . and made away with them in a cloud of dust." About a hundred soldiers of the 11th Ohio and 7th Iowa quickly saddled up other horses and began a pursuit that lasted several days and covered a hundred miles, with Charles Elston as "guide and scout." All they found was "only a dozen worn-out horses the Indians had abandoned." About the same time, another contingent of the 11th raced from Deer Creek to rescue Platte Bridge, threatened by perhaps a hundred Indians, and chased them for miles, killing about twenty and taking another twenty prisoner.[9]

[9]Robrock, "The Eleventh Ohio," 32–33, 34; Hafen and Young, *Fort Laramie*, 320; Ware, *Indian War*, 207–10; Merrill, *Bound for Idaho*, 167; McDermott. *Frontier Crossroads*, 36. Elston, married to a Sioux, lived near and traded at Fort Laramie.

Meanwhile, raiders hit the South Platte again. On July 17, two emigrants died at Bijou Ranch, eighty-five miles from Denver. Marauders took seventeen horses there, going down the line, running off stock belonging to the stage company and taking sixty horses from a nearby station. Colorado soldiers recovered the stock and reported that they killed five Indians tending the herd. Another raid followed the next day, and shortly thereafter a passing stagecoach reported they found two more whites killed and scalped. General Mitchell, on July 22, stopped all emigrant and freight wagons at Julesburg on hearing this news, and ordered travelers to move in groups large enough to defend themselves.[10]

General Mitchell told Curtis on July 19 that "Indians [are] cleaning out the valley above Julesburg" and were headed toward it "in force." Mitchell took two companies of cavalry and a section of artillery "to meet them." Lieutenant John A. Wilcox, acting assistant adjutant general, reflecting Mitchell's report wrote: "The Indians appear to be in great force on the North Platte, committing depredations" both "above and below Laramie."[11] Mitchell intended not only to find the raiders, but also to strengthen the Julesburg-Laramie-South Pass line.

Curtis, meanwhile, somewhat exasperated with both Chivington and the Cheyennes, decided to have a look for himself. On July 21, Curtis noted that while things were under control in Kansas, he was "going to look after the western portion" of his command. Two days later he reached Fort Riley, intending "to rally a force on the border fifty miles west of Salina for the purpose of suppressing the mischief." He asked for seven hundred militia, and hoped to have a thousand men at hand. He ordered "one piece" of artillery from the 9th Wisconsin Battery and a crew to handle it. All the "well men" of Captain

[10]Hafen, *Overland Mail*, 256–57.

[11]*O.R.*, I, 41, pt. 2, pp. 276–77.

Henry Booth's Company L, 11th Kansas Cavalry, would meet him at Salina, Kansas, "tomorrow night."[12]

Curtis thought the militia "gather slowly," but Lieutenant James H. Dodge, 9th Wisconsin, reported on July 24 that Company L, 11th Kansas, and one section of the 9th Wisconsin Battery were on the way to join Curtis. Ultimately, by July 27, a regiment of Kansas volunteer militia under Colonel John T. Price, another Kansas militia regiment under Colonel D. W. Scott, and a "battalion" of "U.S. Volunteers" commanded by Captain Henry Booth joined Curtis. The Kansas militia totaled about three hundred men; in all, Curtis had less than four hundred. By July 28, reaching the north bend of the Arkansas River, he reported that "the Indians have scattered before our arrival," but he would try to impose on them "the severe chastisement due for their offenses."[13]

Although there had been many reports of Indian raids, they failed to materialize for Curtis. By July 30, he arrived at Fort Larned. Just as he did so, four companies of the 1st Colorado arrived. He scolded Colonel Chivington for not having sent them "six weeks" earlier, as he had ordered. If Chivington had done so, "a great portion of the murders and loss of stock that have occurred in this region" could have been prevented. Curtis had intended to march on to Denver, but other matters required his "immediate and further attention." He said he feared Chivington's "attention is too much attracted" by political affairs in Colorado and too little to his orders. He also had not heard from him for ten days.[14] If Curtis believed this rebuke to Chivington would straighten him out, Curtis was mistaken.

By August 8 Curtis had returned to Fort Leavenworth. He reported to Halleck that on leaving Fort Larned he divided his forces "in all directions," while he scouted "southward toward Red River." He thought he "scared them [the Indi-

[12]Ibid., pp. 314, 368, 369.

[13]Ibid., pp. 378, 379, 428, 445–46.

[14]Ibid., pp. 483–84.

ans] away from the Santa Fé route, where stages and trains again move regularly." He noted that he created the District of Upper Arkansas, which included forts Lyon and Larned, removing them from Chivington's control, and put them in the hands of Major General James G. Blunt. He also had set up a new post, Fort Zarah, at Walnut Creek, the north bend of the Arkansas River. He believed he "increased and improved the organization of troops" as well.[15] He had traveled about five hundred miles in two and a half weeks, quite a feat for the commander. But if he thought he was due any rest, he was mistaken again.

Meanwhile, Mitchell was on his way west from Fort Kearny. Since Mitchell took two companies of the 7th Iowa, D and F, with him, it became necessary to reinforce Kearny and Cottonwood. Company A, 7th Iowa, left Dakota City for Fort Kearny, and Colonel Robert R. Livingston volunteered the services of his veteran 1st Nebraska Cavalry, then on furlough. Curtis told Mitchell to have Collins send some of the 11th Ohio to Fremont's Orchard and Camp Collins to "make the overland stage route as secure as possible." That would also relieve the 1st Colorado of those duties and make them more available around Denver and the South Platte. Along the way to Fort Laramie, Mitchell heard that there were a thousand lodges of "Missourias and Sioux, all hostile," within seventy miles of Laramie. He told Curtis he had all his cavalry "in the field."[16]

Mitchell arrived at Fort Laramie on July 27. By telegraph he told Curtis, "just arrived here. Find Collins' troops almost all

[15]Ibid., pp. 491, 610. Blunt, age thirty-seven, was born in Maine, served in the merchant marine, then took a medical degree in Columbus, Ohio. He moved to Kansas and became active in antislavery politics. He became a lieutenant colonel in the 3rd Kansas, but soon commanded a cavalry brigade. In April 1862 he was promoted to brigadier general and commanded the Department of Kansas. He took the field and won several important victories, was promoted again, and beat Confederates in Arkansas in several engagements. He was a uniformly successful commander, if a difficult person to get along with.

[16]*O.R.*, I, 41, pt. 2, pp. 276, 277, 302, 370, 399, 428, 447, 448, 449.

on different lines of communication. His battalion extends on this line over 500 miles of country. He also has three companies on the Denver line from Julesburg to Fremont's Orchard." Mitchell concluded, "the only safety to emigrants, stages, or telegraph lines will be to patrol the whole country from Kearny to South Pass, and to do this I must have more soldiers. The Governor of Nebraska has kindly offered to call out two companies of militia." They might be of some help, but "depredations are committed daily on the lines of communication. From present appearances you may expect a general Indian outbreak in all this western country." Mitchell laid it out very clearly: he needed more help; his line was very thin.[17]

The two companies of the 7th Iowa camped just north of Fort Laramie on the 27th. The next day, Mitchell relieved Collins as commander of Fort Laramie, and instead gave him charge of "all posts and detachments west of Julesburg, including both lines of communication westward," the Oregon road and its telegraph, and the overland stage road. "Lieutenant-Colonel Collins will make such changes as he deems necessary for the better protection" of the communication lines. Mitchell placed Major John S. Wood, 7th Iowa, in command of Fort Laramie, with his companies D and F as the garrison. The chief responsibility remained the protection of the overland roads, and to that end the 7th Iowa garrison would be "subject to orders from Lieutenant-Colonel Collins." Collins remained the overall commander, freed from responsibility for the fort itself. By putting all of the 11th Ohio on the roads, with two companies of the 7th Iowa in reserve, Mitchell strengthened his westernmost command as much as he could.[18]

---

[17]Ibid., pp. 302, 429.

[18]Ibid., pp. 448–49. As of June 30, portions or all of companies B, D, G, and H of the 11th Ohio garrisoned Fort Laramie. The new companies, I, K, and L, were organizing there, but by the end of July some of them had been sent to Deer Creek for the expedition referred to above, returning to Laramie July 29.

Lieutenant Eugene F. Ware, 7th Iowa, became post adjutant at Fort Laramie. He had light duty, he said, which gave him time to look around. He found what he called the "Squaw Camp" about a mile above Laramie, where friendly Indians came to camp and trade. Indian wives of some trappers lived there, as did "a lot of half white Indian papooses." He struck up an acquaintance with Jim Bridger, then living at Laramie, and was fascinated with him, as were many others. Ware also met Elston, Indian trader Julius Ecoffey, and Pallady, the frontiersman who was a friend of Colonel Collins. Like Bridger, they too had many stories to tell and advice for the young officer.[19]

On July 29 Mitchell again pleaded his case for more troops to Curtis. "With two or three more companies I can secure this line against Indians. My forces at different points have had several skirmishes and been successful. . . . The Indians are strung out in small parties all along the line. I have my troops," Mitchell claimed, "patrolling the entire line for 500 miles." Collins had charge of the roads and watched "the movements of Indians from Julesburg west." Mitchell put Colonel Samuel W. Summers, 7th Iowa, on the same duty from Julesburg east. In addition he had two companies of "Nebraska militia" and he intended to make a permanent post at Julesburg. With his new troop disposition, Mitchell tried to be as ready as he could for the war that he expected would follow along the roads.[20]

His anticipated war came sooner than he wished. On July 22, Mitchell ordered Summers to send "an officer and twenty men to Plum Creek at once." At Fort Kearny, Summers worried if he would have a garrison large enough to defend the post, especially if the Cheyennes to the south hit the Platte: Mitchell had already taken two companies of the 7th Iowa, Company A was a week away to the east, but en route. Sum-

[19]Ware, *Indian War*, 197–202, 462–63.

[20]*O.R.*, I, 41, pt. 2, pp. 462–63.

mers advised the emigrants and freighters to move only in large groups, as he had no way of escorting them. Summers sent Captain Wilcox and Company B to check out the Cheyenne camp reputed to be south on the Republican River, to determine their strength and attitude. The Cheyenne were there all right, but the troopers failed to find them. For a brief time it appeared quiet along the Platte. The constant movement of troops, reinforcement of forts Kearny and Laramie, and military scouting activities in late July seemed to make the Indians cautious. The military, as well as freighters and emigrants, relaxed.[21]

War erupted along the Platte the second week of August. On the 8th, Cheyenne tribesmen attacked wagon trains at Plum Creek, about thirty-three miles west of Fort Kearny. Fourteen men were reported killed, with three trains burned and robbed. Three more people died near Gilman's Ranch, sixty-three miles west of Fort Kearny, and Indians ran off stock from Cottonwood eighty-five miles west of the fort. Then on August 7 raids commenced in the Little Blue River Valley, southeast of Kearny. Several more whites were killed; Mrs. Lucinda Eubanks, her two children, and Miss Laura Roper were taken captive. The driver of an eastbound mail coach reported that he passed several burned trains and counted eleven dead bodies. The previous day six others had died at Thirty-Two Mile Creek. Dwellings and outbuildings burned. White ranchers and farmers fled the valley for the safety of larger settlements closer to the Missouri River, leaving the countryside east of Kearny depopulated.[22]

Around the first of August, Curtis ordered Captain Henry E. Palmer, Company A, 11th Kansas, to take sixty recruits

[21]Becher, *Massacre Along the Medicine Road*, 118–19.

[22]Ibid., 132–249, passim; Hafen, *Overland Mail*, 258; John G. Ellenbecker, *Tragedy at the Little Blue: The Oak Grove Massacre and the Captivity of Lucinda Eubank and Laura Roper* (revised 2nd edition, Niwot, Colo.: Prairie Lark Publications, 1993), 21–22: the date given here for the capture is August 7.

assigned to the 11th Ohio from Fort Leavenworth to Fort Kearny and turn them over to Captain Jacob L. Humfreville, Company K, 11th Ohio, who would be there to receive them. These men were now "galvanized yankees," former Kentucky cavalrymen of Morgan, captured with him in Ohio. On August 8 they met fugitives from the raids along the Little Blue, and the next day they saw for themselves the results of the attacks, including ruins of the Eubanks ranch and the bodies of the three small children. As troops were arriving to defend the valley, Palmer moved the 11th Ohio recruits on to Fort Kearny.[23]

At Julesburg on August 8, Mitchell informed Curtis of the Plum Creek massacre, though not all the details. He "just learned a train was burned at Plum Creek this morning between Cottonwood and Kearny." He desperately needed "at least 800 horses" and the 1st Nebraska cavalry that was then on furlough. He mentioned at least two other attacks on the road, one east of Kearny. He told Curtis half of his troops were "in this district on foot," thus the need for mounts. At the same time Governor Evans told Curtis that doubtless the news of Plum Creek had reached him, and declared Denver to be in "a desperate condition on account of our communications being cut off by Indians." None of these communications reached Fort Leavenworth until the 10th.[24]

That day Nebraska's Governor Alvin Saunders also reported to Curtis that "several trains have been attacked and destroyed in the Platte Valley" just west of Kearny "and all the men along with them killed." He advocated "active measures" or "complete abandonment" of the Platte Valley. Also, there were no horses available for the 1st Nebraska. Then an agent of the Overland Stage Line delivered another blow to

[23]Henry E. Palmer, "History of the Powder River Expedition of 1865," *Transactions and Reports of the Nebraska State Historical Society*, vol. II, 197–98; Dee Brown, *The Galvanized Yankees* (Lincoln: University of Nebraska Press, 1986), 183–84.

[24]*O.R.*, I, 41, pt. 2, pp. 612–13.

Curtis with the message, "Indians have murdered all families on the Little Blue. . . . Fifteen are known to be killed. All families are moving in for safety." The entire road from near the Missouri River to Denver was under attack.[25]

Just returning from his expedition to the south, and faced with many other problems in his Department of Kansas, Curtis nonetheless reacted as well as he could. He asked Kansas for militia; requested Colonel Summers at Fort Kearny to get after the Little Blue raiders if possible; and told Mitchell to send Kearny's troops as well. He even telegraphed Halleck in Washington, D.C., with news of the raids, and asked if "some of" Brigadier General Alfred Sully's men, in Dakota, could not "move down to Nebraska." This last was a vain hope because even if any of Sully's troops could be spared—and they could not—they could not have arrived in time. But by now Curtis was desperate.[26]

All this violence gave Colorado's Governor Evans an opportunity to gloat. He told Secretary of War Stanton that as he predicted "last winter" the Indians were allied and on the warpath and it would take "a large force, say 10,000" troops, "to defend the lines and put down hostilities." Evans told much the same thing to the commissioner of Indian Affairs: the immense Indian war was under way "as apprehended last winter. . . . extending from Texas to the British" border (Canada).[27]

Response to the Indian threat along the Oregon road came quickly. The governor of Nebraska called up twelve militia companies, and Governor Evans in Colorado received permission to recruit a regiment of hundred-day volunteers. On August 11, Curtis sent a company of the 16th Kansas Cavalry and a howitzer from Fort Leavenworth to the Little Blue Valley, and wired Mitchell to "buy horses," since no others were available.[28]

---

[25]Ibid., pp. 642–43. [26]Ibid., pp. 641, 643. [27]Ibid., p. 644.
[28]Ibid., pp. 659, 695; Becher, *Massacre Along the Medicine Road*, 188–89.

On August 13 Colonel Summers sent Captain Edward Murphy and Company A, 7th Iowa, along with sundry others and ten days' rations, to check out the Little Blue Valley. Only 50 of Murphy's 125 men were mounted. Fortunately, along the way Murphy found some additional mounts that belonged to the stage company and pressed them into service. Colonel Summers disapproved of the requisitioning of private property, but Murphy desperately needed horses. Curtis, meanwhile, was on his way to Omaha, planning to go into the field again himself. Unfortunately he chose to go by river, but the Missouri was very low and he was delayed.[29]

The army hunted simultaneously for horses and the equipment for them. The latter proved to be a serious problem too, for none could be found at hand. The 1st Nebraska needed both before it could be a factor. The Nebraska militia also required arms, ammunition, transportation, and rations. The adjutant at Omaha, who could not find Curtis, even asked Mitchell at Fort Cottonwood to help him.[30]

Murphy's column met the Kansas militia in the Little Blue Valley on August 14. The Kansans had buried a number of bodies, and all were eager to find the Indians and recover as much stock as they could. Also, by the same date the 16th Kansas and more Kansas militia had arrived at Marysville, on the Oregon road just before it entered the valley of the Little Blue. They planned to strike out after the Indians, believed to be on the Republican River to the west. That information was also reported to Curtis, with the Indians gathered there supposed to be about "2,000 strong"; at least he knew where his foe was encamped.[31]

On the 16th Murphy's men and some militia stumbled into a skirmish with Sioux and Cheyennes near Elk Creek along

[29]Becher, *Massacre Along the Medicine Road*, 192–93.

[30]*O.R.*, I, 41, pt. 2, p. 672.

[31]Ibid., pp. 708, 721; Becher, *Massacre Along the Medicine Road*, 196–98.

the Little Blue, ending with the loss of two men and a hasty retreat to the safety of Little Blue station where other militia were camped. Murphy did not have a strong enough force to deal with the large numbers the Indians could throw at him, so on the 17th he returned to Fort Kearny.[32]

Curtis finally arrived in Omaha on the 16th. There he found a dispatch Mitchell sent from Fort Kearny the day before. "I find Indians at war with us through the entire District of Nebraska from South Pass to the Blue, a distance of 800 miles and more, and have laid waste the country, driven off the stock, and murdered men, women, and children in large numbers." He advocated mounting a strong expedition to "exterminate the leading tribes engaged in this terrible slaughter." He also believed "every party of Indians on this line has been led by white men."[33]

Mitchell reported to Curtis again the next day. "The amount of damage done west of here [Fort Kearny] is hard to estimate. There have been 20 persons killed between here and Cottonwood and one train burnt. The ranchmen have all run." The agent for the Overland Mail refused to move stages between Julesburg and Cottonwood. Mitchell ordered companies of the 11th Ohio from Fremont's Orchard and Camp Collins to extend "two posts towards Julesburg" and placed a company of the 7th Iowa at the latter. Detachments of Captain Jacob S. Shuman's Company H, 11th Ohio, garrisoned the Ficklin and Mud Springs stations, while the remainder of the company built Camp Shuman, later Fort Mitchell, about three miles west of Scotts Bluff. Also, Captain Levi G. Marshall's Company E, 11th Ohio, built Camp

[32]Becher, *Massacre Along the Medicine Road*, 203–7.

[33]*O.R.*, I, 41, pt. 2, p. 722. There were numbers of half-bloods among the Native Americans, and the military thought they saw white men. They believed these reported whites were at least Southern sympathizers, but there was little evidence to support this frequent claim. Along with Mitchell on his return from Laramie was Colonel Collins's wife, on her return to Ohio, among others.

CAMP MARSHALL
Drawing by Private Charles F. Moellman.

Marshall about fifty-seven miles west of Fort Laramie. "We occupy the road west from [Camp] Collins to the South Pass. My troops are just scattered enough to be cut up by detail." Captain Edward B. Murphy, 7th Iowa, "has been on the Blue since last Thursday" [August 11], but Mitchell had not heard from him since he left Pawnee Ranch. Major George M. O'Brien at Fort Cottonwood reported "today" that his troops clashed with Cheyennes at noon "six miles east of Cottonwood."[34]

Curtis faced a very serious situation. The Indians threatened to overwhelm the entire Oregon-Denver road, and he had too few troops to deal with the situation. The news seemed all bad. At Fort Kearny on August 18, Mitchell told Curtis he had finally heard from Murphy about his patrol along the Little Blue and the fight with "500 well-armed

[34]Ibid., p. 734; Ware, *Indian War*, 216, 219. Camp Shuman was built of sod and adobe. Ware noted Ficklin was nine miles east of Scotts Bluff (p. 227), and Mud Springs forty-six miles east of Scotts Bluff. Shuman kept pickets on Scotts Bluff (p. 226).

Indians." Mitchell was disheartened. "Things look blue all around this morning," he told Curtis. Bad news or not, Curtis was already in the field, marching to Kearny. Somehow the army found sixty horses and mounted some of the 1st Nebraska, who accompanied Curtis. Also, equipment for five hundred horses had arrived at Leavenworth.[35]

Curtis headed west from Omaha with Company G, 11th Kansas Cavalry; three companies, A, C, and K, of the 1st Nebraska Cavalry; and Company B of the 1st Battalion, Nebraska Cavalry (formerly the 2nd Nebraska), all veterans of other Civil War campaigns. Captain Thomas McFadden and the Pawnee scouts, over seventy strong and arch enemies of the Sioux and Cheyenne, also joined Curtis. Kansas militia remained along the Little Blue section of the road, and Curtis found Grand Island defended with two small forts the settlers had built. His troops reached Fort Kearny on August 23.[36]

The department's field commanders, Curtis and Mitchell, planned the Plum Creek Expedition to hunt down and chastize what proved to be very elusive hostiles. Colonel Samuel W. Summers and his companies of the 7th Iowa joined the column. Summers, who had been stung by criticism of his slow response to the Plum Creek massacre earlier on August 8, looked for a chance to refurbish his reputation. He gave up command of Fort Kearny to go into the field with his men, Companies A and B of the 7th Iowa. Also included in the expedition were Captain Humfreville and a detachment of 11th Ohio Cavalry recruits (those "galvanized yankees" on their way to Laramie), Lieutenant Thomas Flannigan and a battery of artillery from Fort Leavenworth, Captain Thomas B. Stevenson and four companies of the Nebraska militia, and McFadden with his Pawnee scouts. The force numbered about 620 officers and men.

---

[35] *O.R.*, I, 41, pt. 2, p. 765.

[36] Ibid., p. 981; Becher, *Massacre Along the Medicine Road*, 212, 305–6.

They moved out to Plum Creek on September 1, and headed into the field southwestward toward the Republican River on September 3. By September 7 they reached Solomon's Fork of the Kansas River, and having found no Indians, divided the expedition. Curtis headed east with the 1st Nebraska, a company of the Nebraska militia, Humfreville's 11th Ohio detachment, and a company of the 11th Kansas. Mitchell took the others and went west. They found no Indians the entire time they were in the field, from September 1 to the 26th. George Bent noted that Mitchell had a "strong force" of cavalry, "but he could not reach the Indians who were raiding in small parties and were careful to keep out of the reach of the troops."[37]

Up north at Fort Laramie during the first week in August, Catherine Collins left to go home. She had been planning to return to Ohio since May, and she could no longer put off her departure. Her husband was on the line with his troops, so General Mitchell kindly allowed her, along with eleven-year-old Florence Schnyder, to travel with him as far as Fort Kearny. Dr. Hitz, returning east, was also in the party. Mrs. Collins provided Mitchell company in his "four mule ambulance" and escort of twenty cavalrymen. They spent evenings in tents pitched in "broiling sun" where grass was "alive with grasshoppers." Mitchell dismissed the escort at Pole Creek, a day's travel west of Julesburg, where Mitchell expected to find two more companies of cavalry. They had not arrived, however, and worse, Mitchell heard about the massacre ahead at Plum Creek. Even so, Mitchell and Mrs. Collins continued east by themselves. Mrs. Collins traveled for a day "amidst loaded revolvers" and wished she knew how to use them. Late on the second day, east of Julesburg, the new escort met them. Mitchell detached twenty to serve as far as

[37] *O.R.*, I, 41, pt. 1, pp. 244–47; pt. 2, p. 965; Becher, *Massacre Along the Medicine Road*, 306–7; Hyde, *George Bent*, 142. Technically, Humfreville was still a lieutenant then.

Fort Kearny, where they arrived on August 14. Mitchell could go no farther east, as he had a great deal to do. But Mrs. Collins and Florence with luck found a stage bound for Omaha; though it was crowded with eleven other travelers, she made it safely there in three days. She doubtless passed Curtis's column as he headed for Kearny.[38]

As Catherine Collins left Fort Laramie that August, perhaps a dozen women remained there. Besides officer's wives, there was the sutler's wife, as well as seamstresses and washerwomen. Most lived in terrible boredom. The women were not allowed off the post, as it was considered far too dangerous. Some officers took Native American women as wives, including two from the 11th Ohio, one of whom was Captain Rinehart of Company G. Some enlisted men married as well; other troopers visited the "Squaw Camp" occasionally. These "marriages" seldom were permanent, but they often produced fair-complexioned children.[39]

The major army post west of Fort Leavenworth, Fort Laramie seemed like a city, compared with the solitary minor posts and stations scattered along the overland roads, to troopers who spent so much time away from any civilization. It was a gathering place for freighters, emigrants, even friendly Indians, and the garrison lived fairly well. Jim Bridger remained at Fort Laramie much of the time, with entertaining stories for those who would listen. Soldiers bored and lonely after duty in tiny frontier stations found recreation and relaxation when

[38]*Collins Family Papers*, items 27, 28; Spring, ed., "An Army Wife Comes West," 267–69, and note 34; Hull, "Soldiering on the High Plains," 18. Hull noted that Mrs. Collins took "Flora Schneider [*sic*] with her to give her an education; a prairie flower for sure." Florence, or "Flora," was the postmaster's daughter at Fort Laramie. He gave Mrs. Collins three hundred dollars for the girl's "benefit." From Omaha, Mrs. Collins took a steamboat to St. Joseph, staying over a few days to see relatives in the vicinity. She continued home by train.

[39]Nadeau, *Fort Laramie*, 151–53; Robrock, "The Eleventh Ohio," 36–37; Ware, *Indian War*, 213. Ware claimed the officers of the 11th Ohio had "bought" their wives and kept them at the Squaw Camp, though Rinehart kept his at Deer Creek.

rotated to Laramie. Even the drill, inspections, target practice, and battle maneuvers for infantry, cavalry, and artillery gave them something to do. Because liquor was available at Laramie, considerable imbibing took place, sometimes leading to rowdiness. Besides the holiday parties, many evening "performances" and dances, such as those Sergeant Hull described, took place, as well as games of baseball and horseshoes. Soldiers could also get passes to fish and hunt, and in winter some even skated on the frozen Laramie River. Three drummers and three fifers made up the post band, but sometimes entertainments included "violin, guitar, melodeon, and brass band," with itinerant musicians such as "Mr. Raymond from Salt Lake" on the melodeon. Many troopers kept pets: dogs, cats, even a tame antelope. Dog owners had to watch over their favorites closely or the Indians would use them for stew. Laramie seemed like a fairly safe place for most of 1864, even during the August raids elsewhere along the Platte.[40]

The adjutant at Fort Laramie, Lieutenant Ware, 7th Iowa, observed that emigration by the post had almost stopped entirely and that no stages had come past "for months." Actually, the stages were on the Overland stage and mail route to the south, when they could run, bypassing Laramie. Farther north, at Deer Creek, Private Johnson mentioned that "about 20,000 persons passed Deer Creek headed west" so far this year, but on August 11 he echoed Lieutenant Ware: "emigration has pretty much ceased. scarcely a train a week passes." Even so, "we have been bothered to vexation almost by importunate questions of emigrants. A hundred men will pass in a day and all ask the same questions such as how far is it to grass? any wood there? is the road sandy?" How far to this place, or that, what is the route like? "We generally tell them anything we think of at the time."[41]

---

[40]Nadeau, *Fort Laramie*, 150, 154–56; Hull, "Soldiering on the High Plains," 15, 16, 21, 26. A melodeon was a small pump organ.

[41]Ware, *Indian War*, 210; Unrau, *Tending the Talking Wire*, 159–62.

But by August 19 Johnson learned about the trouble down south along the Platte, as did everyone else up north. "Everything indicates indian war," he wrote. Yet he remained untroubled by the news. He loved to include gossip in his letters. He thought Captain Rinehart would resign. Johnson claimed Rinehart neglected his duties by "trading a good deal, buying and selling stock, he laid out seven or eight hundred dollars a few days ago for cattle, has been buying merchandise" from emigrants. It appeared that Rinehart planned to set up his own trading post. "It would be the most profitable busines that a man could engage in." He also wanted to impress his readers back home with tales of bed bugs, flies, and grasshoppers that harassed him.[42]

Mixed-blood George Bent left his father's stockade that summer, and at Solomon's Fork, south of Fort Kearny and west of the Little Blue River, he found Cheyennes, including the Dog Soldiers, along with Sioux and Arapahoes "all camped close together. It was one of the largest villages I ever saw and the camps were full of plunder." War parties went out every day, while others returned "loaded with plunder and driving captured herds of horses and mules." He saw "fine silks heaped on the ground in the lodges, and cloaks, groceries of all kinds, ladies fine bonnets, canned goods, bolts of fine cloth, sides of bacon, bags of coffee and sugar, boxes of crackers, boots and shoes—everything you could think of." Many "young warriors were wearing fine silk shirts of bright colors and stripes which the women had made out of captured bolts of silk." George had "a half-dozen of these silk shirts made for me and wore them for some time." He also noted the Platte road was completely blocked and remained so for six weeks.[43]

The incursions along the Platte that provided such rich

---

[42]Unrau, *Tending the Talking Wire*, 168–72.
[43]Hyde, *George Bent*, 140–41.

plunder for George and his Cheyenne brothers virtually cut Denver off from the east. Yet, on August 25 a mail coach managed to get through. It brought news of further Indian attacks in Kansas and Nebraska at least equal to those in Colorado. Though mail service from the east was disrupted, that from Denver west remained in operation. A great deal of mail, over two tons of it, accumulated at Latham (between Fremont's Orchard and Fort Collins) on the South Platte. Other mail piled up at Atchison (on the Missouri River), and was returned by rail to New York, then sent to California by water, then to Salt Lake and Denver by eastbound coach, which took "several weeks." An eastbound coach left Denver on the 23rd over the Platte road and managed to make it through safely.[44] The depredations brought cries for vengence from the white community. Colonel Chivington stood ready to exact it.

---

[44]Hafen, *Overland Mail*, 260–61.

Horse Shoe [*sic*] Station
Drawing by Private Charles F. Moellman.

CHAPTER SEVEN

Bad News from Sand Creek, Fall 1864

Diligently guarding their assigned sections of the Oregon and Overland roads, the 11th Ohio remained remote from the bloody onslaughts south and east along the Platte. Any large-scale action of the Plains tribes would necessarily involve them sooner or later, but for now the route along the Platte River in Kansas, Nebraska, and Colorado became the focus of combat along the overland roads. The Native Americans who attacked along three hundred miles of the Platte road the second week of August 1864 inflicted an estimated fifty white casualties, burnt ranches and wagon trains, swept up about three thousand animals, and halted the mail, freight traffic, and emigrants. Damages to white property totaled perhaps a million dollars. The superintendent of the Overland Mail lamented that the Indians maintained that the land belonged to them alone, and they intended to regain and keep it, "if they have to destroy every white man, woman, and child" to attain their goal. Colorado's Governor Evans believed him.[1]

Few tribesmen had followed Evans's earlier dictum that peaceful Indians congregate at specified sanctuaries, so on August 11, he issued another proclamation. This time he

---

[1]*News of the Plains and Rockies*, vol. 4, 294.

authorized "all citizens of Colorado" to arm themselves and "go in pursuit of all hostile Indians." Evans instructed citizens to leave those Indians who gathered peacefully at his specified "rendezvous" points alone, but urged them to "kill and destroy, as enemies of the country, wherever they may be found, all such hostile Indians." Citizens could take and keep "all the property of said hostile Indians that they may capture." He believed this way he could augment his Colorado cavalry. But by declaring open season on all "hostile Indians"—turning civilians into vigilantes, and not specifically exempting Indian women and children—the proclamation appeared "to sanction extermination" of the Plains tribes.[2]

About the same time, appalled by the bloodshed, William Bent implored the Cheyenne chiefs to make peace. Shortly thereafter, George Bent, along with his brother-in-law, Edmund Guerrier, wrote letters dictated by the chiefs asking for peace, provided all other tribes could be included with the Cheyennes. They offered, in return, to give up white prisoners taken in the raids. Dated August 29, one letter went to Major Edward W. Wynkoop, who commanded at Fort Lyon, and another to Samuel G. Colley, agent for the Cheyennes and Arapahos. Chief Black Kettle also asked Colley how they might move across the plains without facing attacks by troopers or white vigilantes. The letter to Wynkoop was necessary since Black Kettle did not, with good reason, trust Agent Colley. Two Cheyenne couriers took the letters to Fort Lyon, only to have Wynkoop promptly arrest them and throw them in the guardhouse.[3]

Wynkoop knew he had to rescue the captives if he could.

---

[2]Ibid.

[3]Dee Brown, *Bury my Heart at Wounded Knee: An Indian History of the American West* (New York: Holt, Rinehart & Winston, 1970), 75; Grinnell, *Fighting Cheyennes*, 158–59; Hyde, *George Bent*, 142. Colley said on August 26, "The orders are to kill every Indian found in the country, and I am inclined to assist in carrying the orders into effect." *News of the Plains And Rockies*, vol. 4, 294–95.

About September 15, accompanied by 125 men of the 1st Colorado Cavalry, he went to the Cheyenne camp. Chief Black Kettle prevented any altercation that might have developed when the troops appeared. Wynkoop told the chiefs he lacked authority to make peace, but if they would surrender the captives he would take some chiefs to Governor Evans and see what could be done. The Cheyennes turned over three small children and young Laura Roper. Two of the children and Laura Roper had been taken along the Little Blue, the other at Plum Creek.[4]

As he promised, Wynkoop escorted the chiefs to Camp Weld, outside Denver, where they met with Governor Evans, Colonel Chivington, and others. Evans told the chiefs he could not make peace with them; they would have to deal with the military. Speaking for Colorado's soldiers, Chivington ended the meeting by warning the chiefs that when he fought "white men or Indians," he did so "until they lay down their arms and submit to military authority. They [he indicated the chiefs] are nearer to Major Wynkoop than anyone else, and they can go to him when they are ready to do that." Bewildered, not knowing if peace was possible, the chiefs returned to Fort Lyon and sought out Wynkoop as Chivington had suggested. When they reached the post, Wynkoop "told them to bring their people in near the fort and they would be treated as prisoners." Even so, Wynkoop appeared friendly. Meanwhile, General Curtis warned Chivington "the chiefs . . . are not reliable and desire to save their friends"; they "are all implicated in the attacks," and "therefore they desire peace, which they cannot have at present."[5] So much for dealing with the military.

---

[4]*O.R.*, I, 41, pt. 3, p. 243; Grinnell, *Fighting Cheyennes*, 159; Hyde, *George Bent*, 142–43; Utley, *Frontiersmen in Blue*, 290; Ellenbecker, *Tragedy at the Little Blue*, 24–27. The three children were Ambrose Asher, Isabel Eubank (both from the Little Blue), and Danny Marble (from Plum Creek). Roper was little more than a child herself at age sixteen. See also Brown, *Bury My Heart at Wounded Knee*, 78.

[5]*O.R.*, I, 41, pt. 3, pp. 495, 525; Brown, *Bury My Heart at Wounded Knee*, 83; Hyde, *George Bent*, 143; Grinnell, *Fighting Cheyennes*, 160.

As the chiefs were on their way to Camp Weld, hoping to make peace, a group of Cheyennes and Arapahos headed for a winter camp near Fort Larned. On September 23 they camped at Ash Creek, and six of their young men went out to attack Pawnees who hunted along the Republican River. On the 25th they ran into an advance guard of General James G. Blunt's expedition, commanded by Major Scott J. Anthony. Blunt was in the field with "about 400 men," having planned to go south of the Arkansas River. But he learned that "a large party of Indians" were on the Smoky Hill, and turned north to investigate. When Anthony's troopers chased the few Indians, noise of the shooting alerted the tribesmen in camp, who mounted up and encircled Anthony's small command. While they defended themselves on a hill, Blunt's main column came up and the Indians broke off hostilities. In the fray, one soldier was killed, another was missing, and seven were wounded. Blunt claimed they counted nine dead Indians, but Bent, who was present, said only one died. With exhausted mounts, Blunt's troopers set out on an unproductive pursuit. Blunt reported "Indian warriors ride fleeter horses than ours, and . . . their war parties cannot be pursued with success." The Cheyennes and Arapahos—George Bent among them—went north to the Republican River, still looking for Pawnees. They camped near Smoky Hill, where their chiefs, returning from their visit with Evans and Chivington, found them. Blunt, on the other hand, had to return east to face a Confederate threat.[6]

Events south of the Platte moved toward a fateful climax. Having in mind the proclamation of Governor Evans from the previous June—which provided sanctuaries for friendly Indians—and desiring to be thought of as such, caused Black Kettle and others to talk with authorities in September and

[6]*O.R.*, I, 41, pt. 1, p. 818, pt. 3, p. 696; Hyde, *George Bent*, 143–46; Grinnell, *Fighting Cheyennes*, 160–61.

to release prisoners. The Cheyenne also needed to prepare for winter by hunting buffalo, and did not want to be hounded by troops and vigilantes. Then encouraged—wrongly, it turned out—by their meeting with Colorado authorities, Black Kettle, George Bent and other Cheyennes, along with a number of Arapahos, went into camp at Sand Creek, near Fort Lyon, expecting a peaceful winter.[7]

Meanwhile, far to the north at Deer Creek more mundane affairs prevailed. Private Johnson of Company G, 11th Ohio, picked up rumors in early October that the old first battalion of the 11th was about to be discharged, since its term of service was drawing to a close. He wrote that it had been "ordered in from the outposts to the fort." His first sergeant, Samuel B. White, was to go with them since he was originally from Company A; but since White had reenlisted as a veteran, he would only go on furlough. More immediately, Johnson learned that all military stations were to be stockaded. "This will give us plenty of work to do all winter. we have about 4 acres to enclose" at Deer Creek. He also heard that Captain Rinehart went to Fort Laramie under arrest. Johnson figured that was for neglect of duty, perhaps for his business affairs, but Johnson would also add "paying attention" to "*squaws*." He thought if a trial followed he would have to testify.[8]

By the end of October, Johnson noted they had not yet begun work on the stockades. They had neither teams to haul material nor enough men for the task even if they had teams. "Our company is scattered along at six different posts and it is probable that we will have to take charge of two more. The length of road we are on is two hundred miles, and if we take two other posts it will be about forty miles longer." It also appeared that the old battalion would not leave for Ohio until spring. By November 6, Johnson and four others had

[7]Hyde, *George Bent*, 146; Utley, *Frontiersmen in Blue*, 290.
[8]Unrau, *Tending the Talking Wire*, 176–78, 182.

been sent from Deer Creek to strengthen Sweetwater Station.[9]

Captain Jacob L. Humfreville and the recruits he brought from Fort Kearny reached Fort Laramie the second week of October. These men had all been in the fruitless reconnaissance that Mitchell and Curtis had made to the Republican River and Solomon's Fork of the Kansas in September. Since the recruits were former Kentucky cavalrymen under Morgan, the campaign had been no special hardship for them, but it had postponed their arrival. Sixteen of the sixty men were attached to Company K, others to Company I. A few days later Companies I and K held elections that ratified the promotions of Apt and Humfreville, followed by a celebration that left "half the company drunk," according to a "perfectly disgusted" Sergeant Hull.[10]

Johnson's speculation concerning discharge of the first battalion reflected some discontent in the ranks of the 11th Ohio. Many had enlisted in 1861 for three years. Also, as the new companies held elections for officers in October, some sergeants of the old companies—A, B, C, and D—believed they, because of their experience, should be commissioned as officers in the new companies. When this failed to materialize for many of them, they petitioned to be sent home. Given the work expected of the 11th Ohio, and the great need for men in the district, Collins could not oblige them. This left some Ohio soldiers unhappy.[11]

On October 5 Mitchell reported to Curtis that he had "troops stationed every fifteen miles from Plum Creek to Julesburg." Mail coaches could now run "with a little care," and those that requested it had escorts "as far as Julesburg." He spoke of an attack September 29, somewhere along the line "evidently made by white men" on a train from Bannock

[9] Ibid., 182–83, 189.

[10] Hull, "Soldiering on the High Plains," 24–25.

[11] Robrock, "The Eleventh Ohio," 37; Hull, "Soldiering on the High Plains," 27.

that carried a large amount of gold. Also on September 29, he placed Colonel Robert R. Livingston, 1st Nebraska Veteran Volunteers, in charge of the "Eastern Sub-District" of his command from Omaha to Julesburg, with Lieutenant Colonel Collins to head the "Western Sub-District" west of, but not including, Julesburg, along "both lines of communication." Collins's duties hardly changed.[12]

Mitchell reported the disposition of troops in his District of Nebraska on October 31. The 11th Ohio still garrisoned the Oregon and Overland roads west of Julesburg by themselves for the most part. They were at Camp Collins (Companies B and F), Fremont's Orchard (Company C), Scotts Bluff (Company H), Horseshoe Station (Company E), Deer Creek (Company G), Sweetwater Bridge (Company A), and Fort Halleck (Company D). These were "company head-quarter" posts with smaller detachments stationed at tiny stations in the vicinity, all for protection of the roads. The exception was Fort Laramie, garrisoned by the 7th Iowa (Company D), still subject to Collins's orders.

Livingston's Eastern Sub-District had twenty companies from Nebraska and the 7th Iowa strung along the line from Omaha to Julesburg, with four companies (A, C, F, and K) of the 1st Nebraska at Fort Kearny and three more companies (E, G, and H) at Plum Creek. Chivington's District of Colorado had sixteen companies of the 1st and 3rd Colorado Cavalry (the 3rd were hundred-days' men) scattered across Colorado, except for six companies of the 3rd at Camp Elbert, near Denver.

Along the Santa Fé road, the District of the Upper Arkansas, eleven companies stood guard. At Ellsworth, Company H, 7th Iowa; at Fort Larned, Company H, 12th Kansas, and two companies (B and L) of the 1st Colorado; at Fort Lyon, Company K, 1st New Mexico, along with three

[12] *O.R.*, I, 41, pt. 3, p. 652.

companies (D, G, and K) of the 1st Colorado; at Fort Riley, Company A of the 17th Kansas, L of the 11th Kansas, and a section of the 9th Battery, Wisconsin Light Artillery; and at Salina, one company (G) of the 7th Iowa. On all the roads, there were 3,269 officers and men actually present for duty. Most of them, 1,570, garrisoned the Eastern and Western Sub-Districts in Mitchell's District of Nebraska, and half of those were troopers of the 11th Ohio.[13]

By September the roads opened to travel again. Many small Indian raids continued into the fall, but there was not much actual bloodshed. In late October Lieutenant Ware, 7th Iowa, at Fort Laramie commandeered, with the approval of Collins and Mitchell, an empty Mormon wagon train headed east for supplies. He had it loaded with pine timber cut near Courthouse Rock to be delivered at Julesburg for the use of the soldiers who were building Camp Rankin nearby. Ware also noted that in spite of sporadic Indian raids, traffic had picked up on the Oregon road. He suspected that wagoneers trusted to their luck and ability. "But more than this," he said, "the great majority of the pilgrims and whackers rather enjoyed the prospect of having a little skirmish with the Indians . . . so as to have something to enliven the trip and something to tell when they got back to the 'States'." Even so, he added, this was "hard work for the soldiers along the line" charged with protecting the travelers.[14]

In Denver relations with the Cheyennes and Arapahos approached a crisis that fall. Whites in Colorado had been terrorized during the spring and summer. Inhabitants of Denver suffered considerably when the raids stopped shipments of mail, food, and merchandise. Evans and Chiving-

---

[13]Ibid., pt. 4, pp. 374–77, 379.

[14]Ware, *Indian War*, 255, 272–73. Camp Rankin, later Fort Sedgwick, was about a mile west of Julesburg by the mouth of Lodgepole Creek, on the South Platte. See Ware, above, 235–38, and Brown, *Galvanized Yankees*, 18.

ton raised a hundred-day regiment of volunteers, the 3rd Colorado Cavalry, men who were hungry to fight Indians. Then the large group of Cheyennes and Arapahos came in to camp at Sand Creek, near Fort Lyon, professing peace. If Colorado authorities actually made peace, they would antagonize local citizens who howled for revenge; the 3rd Colorado Cavalry's enlistment would expire without its ever having been used; federal authorities would question the governor's dire predictions of an awful Indian war; and who could say the whole problem with the Cheyennes and their fellows would not be repeated the next year?[15]

When Black Kettle and the others arrived at Sand Creek, they discovered Major Wynkoop had been replaced at Fort Lyon. Curtis had told Chivington on September 28 that he wanted "no peace till the Indians suffer more. . . . No peace must be made without my directions." Yet Wynkoop had rescued the white captives, brought the chiefs in to talk with Evans and Chivington, and the tribesmen came into Sand Creek mistakenly thinking peace was at hand. While Black Kettle and the others believed Wynkoop would protect them, it seemed a direct contradiction of Curtis's order. Major Scott J. Anthony, who replaced Wynkoop, disarmed the Arapahos and confiscated some of their stock before the Cheyennes arrived. He forbid the Arapahos any further entrance to Fort Lyon at all. Suspicious, some of the Arapahos then moved south of the Arkansas River, though a few stayed at Sand Creek. They warned the Cheyennes to be very careful. Even so, Black Kettle and other chiefs went to Fort Lyon to parley with Major Anthony, who told them they could remain at Sand Creek until "he heard from his superiors."[16]

Colonel Chivington saw the situation quite differently.

[15]Utley, *Frontiersmen in Blue*, 290–91.

[16]Ibid., 292–93; *O.R.*, I, 41, pt. 3, p. 462; Hafen and Young, *Fort Laramie*, 325; Grinnell, *Fighting Cheyennes*, 165; Hyde, *George Bent*, 146–47.

General Patrick E. Connor, who commanded the District of Utah, arrived in Denver in mid-November. As early as August, Evans had sought Connor's assistance against hostile tribesmen in Colorado. In Washington, Halleck had heard from both Evans and Ben Holladay, the stage line owner, with similar requests for Connor's help. In October Halleck told Connor he should do what he could for the overland road between Kearny and Salt Lake. Welcomed by Denver citizens as a "fighter," but receiving no cooperation from his counterpart, Colonel Chivington, Connor returned to Salt Lake on November 30. Still Chivington feared Connor might replace him. He considered the Sand Creek Indians hostile, and hastened preparations to attack them. That would solve many of the dilemmas both he and Evans faced. Though some protested his plan, Chivington claimed "it to be right and honorable . . . to kill Indians that would kill women and children" and "damn any man that was in sympathy with Indians." Under strict secrecy, his column arrived at Fort Lyon at noon, November 28.[17]

Chivington had about seven hundred men in his expedition: the new 3rd Colorado regiment, over half the 1st Colorado, and four mountain howitzers. The hundred-days' men of the 3rd Colorado had been "hastily recruited from among the worst class of frontier whites. They had little discipline, were not uniformed, were eager to kill Indians." Major Anthony objected to the proposed action, but Chivington ignored him. Anthony warned Chivington that if he attacked at Sand Creek, "there was not a large enough force of troops in Colorado to deal with a new outbreak." Soon enough, Anthony would be proved right. On the evening of the 28th, Chivington's force departed for Sand Creek, with

[17]Utley, *Frontiersmen in Blue*, 293–94; Brigham D. Madsen, *Glory Hunter: A Biography of Patrick Edward Connor* (Salt Lake City: University of Utah Press, 1990), 119–20; *O.R.*, I, 41, pt. 4, pp. 24, 63.

George Bent's brother Robert as an unwilling guide: he had to show the troops the way or be shot.[18]

Chivington attacked at dawn the next day. About a hundred lodges of Cheyennes and ten of Arapahos were at Sand Creek when the troops attacked. Chivington would later claim his troops killed between 500 and 600 Indians, with a loss of 10 soldiers killed and 38 wounded. George Bent later calculated 137 Indians died, while his brother-in-law, Edmund Guerrier, counted 148. Nine of the chiefs were slain, but Black Kettle escaped. Women and children made up as much as two-thirds of the Indians slaughtered. Soldiers took over a hundred Native American scalps with them back to Denver, where the troops received an enthusiastic welcome. They also seized over four hundred Indian ponies and mules, all of which the victors neglected to turn over to the government as the army required. Chivington ordered the Indian lodges burned, but the soldiers plundered them first.[19]

George Bent received a hip wound, but with the help of others made good his escape. Bent and other survivors managed to reach a Cheyenne camp some fifty miles away at the headwaters of the Smoky Hill. There they mourned the dead and cried for revenge. Word of the brutal Sand Creek massacre crossed the plains like wildfire, inflaming winter camps of all central plains Indians. By the time George Bent next reached the large village on the Cherry Creek fork of the Republican River, the war pipe had been smoked by Sioux, Cheyennes, and Arapahos. Around 1,500 warriors and their families gathered at Cherry Creek, ready for raids that would engulf all the overland roads.[20]

Flushed with his cruel victory, Chivington thirsted for

---

[18]Hyde, *George Bent*, 148–49; Utley, *Frontiersmen in Blue*, 294; *O.R.*, I, 41, pt. 1, pp. 948–49.

[19]*O.R.*, I, 41, pt. 1, p. 949; Hyde, *George Bent*, 159, 162; Grinnell, *Fighting Cheyennes*, 173–75; Utley, *Frontiersmen in Blue*, 296.

[20]Hyde, *George Bent*, 165, 168; Utley, *Frontiersmen in Blue*, 300–301.

more blood. He proposed to General Curtis on December 16 "if all companies of the First Cavalry of Colorado and the Eleventh Ohio Volunteer Cavalry . . . were ordered to report to me, I could organize a campaign which . . . would effectually rid the country between the Platte and Arkansas Rivers of these red rebels." As revulsion over Chivington's attack at Sand Creek grew, nothing came of his new plan. Within three weeks Chivington resigned, and an official inquiry into the massacre began. Chivington escaped a court-martial only because he retired from service before the procedings could take place. Governor Evans, whose actions touched off the Sand Creek massacre and the violent Indian war that followed, survived only another six months, his reputation withering under the spotlight of the investigation.[21]

Up north, the implications of the Sand Creek massacre had not yet become apparent. On the Sweetwater River, 167 miles northwest of Fort Laramie, young Lieutenant Caspar Collins wrote to his uncle in Ohio on December 13. He had charge of four "block stations," he noted: Sweetwater Bridge, Three Crossings, Rocky Ridge, and South Pass. But at this time he was temporarily at Laramie, detailed to a court-martial. It took him five days to get there, in "awful" weather, with the temperature at minus ten. His normal duty included visiting the block stations every two weeks. Sweetwater Bridge and Three Crossings had been palisaded by then, but not the others. The Indians never visited Rocky Ridge, he said. Even in winter game abounded, he added. Sweetwater's garrison also included Private Johnson. He thought Lieutenant Collins "a smart scholar, but a perfect boy, and incapable of holding the position of Lieutenant. The Sergeant here has to see to everything."[22] They and others in the regiment would soon be tested by events far to the south.

[21] *O.R.*, I, 41, pt. 1, p. 950; 48, pt. 1, p. 416; Grinnell, *Fighting Cheyennes*, 175–76; Bain, *Empire Express*, 191.

[22] *Collins Family Papers*, item 13; Unrau, *Tending the Talking Wire*, 211.

By December 31 the disposition of troops along the roads changed. The 11th Ohio still garrisoned the Oregon and Overland roads, as they had in October, with some small alterations. Collins still commanded the Western Sub-District, with his Ohioans at Camp Collins (Companies B and F, as before); Fremont's Orchard (Company C, as before); Fort Halleck (Company K replaced D); Camp Marshall (Horseshoe Station, still Company E); Camp Mitchell (Scotts Bluff and vicinity, still Company H); Platte Bridge (Company G moved up from Deer Creek); and at Fort Laramie, with Collins in command there again, Companies A, D, I, and L, plus 7th Iowa, Company D.

Livingston's Eastern Sub-District now included nineteen companies from Nebraska and the 7th Iowa on the line from Omaha to Julesburg. Colonel Summers commanded Fort Cottonwood with two companies of the 7th Iowa (one of recruits) and one of the 1st Battalion Nebraska Cavalry. Three companies of the 1st Nebraska Cavalry garrisoned Plum Creek, and four companies of the 1st Nebraska Cavalry with one of the 1st Nebraska Militia at Fort Kearny. Kearny, Cottonwood, and Plum Creek had the largest concentrations of troops.

Colonel James H. Ford of the 2nd Colorado Cavalry assumed command along the Santa Fé road, replacing Blunt as head of the District of Upper Arkansas. Curtis needed Blunt to take over the District of South Kansas and pursue Confederates operating near there. Ford kept twenty-two companies heavily concentrated at Fort Lyon (where Major Anthony still commanded), including nine from the 1st Colorado and one from the 1st New Mexico; and at Fort Riley Ford located eight companies of the 2nd Colorado Cavalry with one from the 9th Wisconsin Artillery. The others were strung out along the line or were noted in reports as en route.

Chivington still commanded in Colorado when the year-end report was made. Only six companies were listed, three each from the 1st and 3rd Colorado. The rest of the 1st Colorado were under Colonel Ford's control at Fort Lyon, but the remainder of the 3rd Colorado had disappeared from the report, since, as hundred-days' men, they had been discharged. As in October, Mitchell's District of Nebraska had the largest number of troops present for duty—1,612—and Colorado had the fewest with 362. On all the roads, there were 3,119 officers and men present for duty that December: much the same as in October.[23] With the Cheyenne and Arapaho still smarting from Sand Creek, planning revenge, and smoking war pipes with the Sioux, the guardians of the roads, including the 11th Ohio in the north, would need all the troops and then some on duty in the days to come.

Some Colorado citizens disapproved of Chivington's bloodletting at Sand Creek and feared even greater danger from reprisals. With the 3rd Colorado mustered out and the 1st Colorado close to the end of its enlistment, if the Sand Creek massacre drove the tribes to seek revenge, alarmed settlers wondered who would protect them. Not only Coloradoans but also others who lived on the frontier in Kansas worried about the reaction that Sand Creek could cause among all of the plains Indians. Colonel Ford heard from settlers who voiced precisely that uneasiness. He mentioned this to Curtis first on January 3, 1865; then on January 8, he told Curtis how "enraged" citizens of Kansas were at Chivington, and how now Sand Creek had "precluded all possibilities of peace, and it is now war to the knife." Ford's scouts reported large numbers of Indians congregating on the Smoky Hill, triggering proposals for new posts he saw as necessary; he also asked for reinforcements, if only to keep the roads open. Ford toured part of his district and concluded "all the tribes will have to be conquered," but it could not be

[23]*O.R.*, I, 41, pt. 4, pp. 989–93.

done in one campaign. "We will have a lively time this summer."[24]

Reflecting on the political ambitions of those in charge in Colorado, as well as Kansas, Curtis proposed to Halleck on December 31 that if he could get troops "disconnected" from local affairs he might get "an honest, impartial determination of facts" in those areas. He would "shift" the troops "so as to put officers and men out of their home localities" which, he thought, "would greatly improve" his command. Curtis may also have believed his allegation of "so much political and personal strife" that colored the information he received would temper his share of responsibility for the debacle at Sand Creek.[25]

Already, Curtis began to put this exchange of command and troops into being. Ten days before he explained his plan to Halleck, he directed Colonel Thomas Moonlight of the 11th Kansas Cavalry to take over the District of Colorado from Chivington in Denver, and ordered the 11th Kansas Calvary to follow. It took Colonel Moonlight until January 4 to reach Denver, and his regiment arrived much later.[26] The strategy envisioned by Curtis would be sorely tested in the new year.

---

[24]Ibid., I, 48, pt. 1, pp. 407–8, 461–62.
[25]Ibid., I, 41, pt. 4, pp. 970–71.
[26]Ibid., I, 41, pt. 4, p. 909; 48, pt. 1, p. 416.

Camp Mitchell
Drawing by Private Charles F. Moellman.

CHAPTER EIGHT

Indians Strike Back

The winter of 1865 not only brought the usual piercing cold with arctic snow, but also a revival of widespread hostilities. Angry over the deplorable news from Sand Creek, about a thousand Cheyennes, Arapahos, and Sioux moved north from their village on Cherry Creek bent on revenge. Very determined, their soldier societies acted like military police to keep the warriors from straggling and to prevent eager young men from raiding prematurely. They targeted Julesburg, an important junction point for the Oregon, Denver, and Overland roads. A home station on the stage line manned by about forty people, it boasted a large cedar-log station house, an express office, a telegraph station, blacksmith and repair shop, a large store, a warehouse brimming with supplies, and stables and corrals. About a mile west of Julesburg, Company F, 7th Iowa Cavalry, commanded by Captain Nicholas J. O'Brien, garrisoned Camp Rankin, a small adobe post built only the previous summer.[1]

About dawn on January 7 tribesmen began their assault. First, just a few, perhaps ten, appeared before Camp Rankin

[1]Grinnell, *Fighting Cheyennes*, 182; Hyde, *George Bent*, 169. A thick sod wall about five feet high surrounded the few structures of the "fort." On September 27, 1865, with some improvements, Camp Rankin was renamed Fort Sedgwick; see the brochure from the Fort Sedgwick Historical Society, "Fort Sedgwick, Colorado Territory," FSHSociety Documentation Project, 1996. It was named after Major General John Sedgwick, who was killed at Spotsylvania, May 9, 1864.

and attacked its pickets. O'Brien responded, sending out about sixty troopers to drive the attackers away. The Cheyenne plan to decoy soldiers from the little fort, then destroy them, nearly worked. Once the 7th Iowa cavalrymen rode out, a thousand warriors flowed over the sand hills and charged them. Leaving fourteen of their number dead on the field, they promptly fled back into the fort. Thus they avoided the catastrophe planned for them. At nearly the same time that the soldiers had ridden out, a westbound stage came into Julesburg, and its passengers and crew, along with station hands, a storekeeper, and a telegraph operator, all from Julesburg, raced into the fort followed by the hastily returning cavalrymen. Thwarted by the failure of their plan, but not wishing to storm the fort, the tribesmen turned to plunder Julesburg. George Bent and his brother Charles, in full war regalia, were among them. Bent wrote, "at the station breakfast had just been put on the table and was still hot. I sat down with several Indians and ate a good meal."[2]

Indian women arrived with ponies, loaded them with plunder, and took the loot to their camp, often making several trips back and forth. An army paymaster had been on the stage with "a big tin box" full of green paper that the Indians broke open, sending pieces of paper sailing across the plains. Bent noted that he "came up and secured a good deal of the money." He also found an express package addressed to an army officer in Colorado that contained a new uniform. "I took this," he said, "and later wore it during the fighting on the Powder River." The Indians remained at Julesburg most of the day, so thoroughly looting the place that it took them three days to cart the plunder to the village at Cherry Creek.[3]

[2]Grinnell, *Fighting Cheyennes*, 184–86; Hyde, *George Bent*, 170–72; Ware, *Indian War*, 324–26.

[3]Grinnell, *Fighting Cheyennes*, 187–88; Hyde, *George Bent*, 172–73. It would appear that by taking an active part in this attack, George Bent broke his parole, given upon his release after his capture at Corinth in 1862. George, however, doubtless considered this a different war, since he was not fighting as a Confederate even though he fought the army that paroled him—if he thought about it at all.

Army reports listed from thirty-five to fifty-six Indians killed, but Bent claimed they lost none. Once the Cheyennes, Arapahos, and Sioux returned to Cherry Creek, their camps full of loot, they participated in scalp dances as a certain festiveness replaced their mourning for the dead of Sand Creek. The chiefs then decided to move north to the Black Hills and Powder River country to ask their northern brothers to join the war, but first they would ravage the South Platte Valley. Black Kettle, in spite of Sand Creek, still opposed the war, and led eighty families south of the Arkansas River to join some of the still-peaceful southern Arapaho tribesmen.[4]

Immediately upon receiving the news about Julesburg, Mitchell amassed six hundred cavalry, four mountain howitzers, and a hundred wagons at Fort Cottonwood. On January 15 he headed for the Republican River in a bitter winter march of about three hundred miles, but found no hostiles. He returned to the Platte eleven days later. Mitchell failed to look in the right place. On January 27 the Cheyennes, Arapahos, and Sioux launched vigorous attacks along the South Platte. They laid waste to seventy-five miles of the Denver road, burning stations and ranches, driving off herds of cattle, destroying wagon trains, and tearing up the telegraph line. A party of Cheyennes stumbled upon some men recently mustered out of the 3rd Colorado who were headed east. They discovered these men carried momentos of Sand Creek, including two Cheyenne scalps. In a rage, the Cheyennes killed and mutilated them. Again, the Indian camps filled with plunder. The tribesmen had never before banqueted so well in mid-winter. They moved their camp again, north of the South Platte about twenty-five miles west of Julesburg.[5]

---

[4]Hyde, *George Bent*, 174–75; Grinnell, *Fighting Cheyennes*, 188; Utley, *Frontiersmen in Blue*, 302.

[5]Hafen and Young, *Fort Laramie*, 328; Grinnell, *Fighting Cheyennes*, 189, 191; Hyde, *George Bent*, 180–82; Utley, *Frontiersmen in Blue*, 302; Ware, *Indian War*, 335–55; *O.R.*, I, 48, pt. 1, p. 463.

On February 2 Indians ransacked Julesburg again, burning the buildings this time, but they failed to lure any soldiers out of the fort. Helpless in the face of a thousand warriors, the few men of the 7th Iowa could only watch as Julesburg went up in smoke. The Indians liberated the only booty left, a large store of shelled corn. They divided into three groups after that, raiding along the river again, and in the process captured a wagon train that contained bottled liquor destined for Denver. The main Indian village moved north on February 3, into nearly empty country between the forks of the Platte. They continued to destroy the telegraph, chopping down poles or burning them and carrying away wire or tangling it up and leaving it.[6]

Even as Julesburg burned, Colonel Moonlight reported Indian raids along the South Platte had Denver "hemmed in," though large, well-guarded trains could still get through. His outnumbered command was "fighting every day," and "quite a number" of his soldiers had been wounded. General Mitchell announced that in the face of "such large numbers of Indians" he could not protect the roads, and requested "2,000 additional men and supplies." With such a force, he could end "all these Indian outrages in this district." But those "Indian outrages," especially the raids on the South Platte and the interruption of the telegraph brought panic to Denver once again.[7]

The Cheyennes, Sioux, and Arapahos continued to move north. They burned the telegraph station at Lodgepole Creek on February 3, fortunately while the operator was absent. On the morning of February 4 their advance came

---

[6]*O.R.*, I, 48, pt. 1, pp. 88–90; Hyde, *George Bent*, 182–83, 186; Grinnell, *Fighting Cheyennes*, 192–93; Ware, *Indian War*, 359–75.

[7]*O.R.*, I, 48, pt. 1, pp. 726, 735; Hafen and Young, *Fort Laramie*, 329. On January 25, raiders struck the American Ranche on the Platte and took Sarah Morris and her two children captive after killing her husband and others. She was rescued June 21, 1865, near Fort Rice, on the Missouri River; see Brown, *Galvanized Yankees*, 97–99.

upon the telegraph station at Mud Springs. Nine soldiers and five civilians, including the telegraph operator and herders, also employees of the telegraph company, were there. The herders had charge of a small collection of cattle, horses, and mules that they wintered nearby. The Indians quickly ran off the cattle and about twenty horses, but ignored the white men in the station. Frightened in the face of overwhelming numbers of warriors, the telegraph operator wired Camp Mitchell and Fort Laramie for help before the lines were destroyed.[8]

As soon as he received the telegram from Mud Springs at Fort Laramie, Colonel Collins ordered Lieutenant William Ellsworth, commanding Company H, 11th Ohio, at Camp Mitchell, to rush all the men he could spare to the relief of the station. Ellsworth and thirty-six troopers rode all night and reached Mud Springs about daybreak on the 5th, making about fifty-five miles in twelve hours through bitter cold. At the same time Collins turned out 120 men from Fort Laramie, detachments of various companies of the 11th Ohio and part of Company D, 7th Iowa. They reached Camp Mitchell, but because of below-zero weather, several men could go no further. Collins and twenty-five men hurried on, however, arriving at Mud Springs not long after Ellsworth. The Indians returned later in the morning, appeared surprised at the increase in manpower facing them, fired some shots, then retired to the hills. They remained in sight all day.[9]

Bent later wrote that "the soldiers were all inside the buildings (which were very strong)" and shot through "loopholes. It was a hard place to attack successfully." The tribesmen thought "it was not very interesting," and by noon the war-

[8] *O.R.*, I, 48, pt. 1, p. 92; Grinnell, *Fighting Cheyennes*, 195; Hyde, *George Bent*, 187–88; McDermott, *Frontier Crossroads*, 40.

[9] *O.R.*, I, 48, pt. 1, p. 92.

riors were "tired of wasting their ammunition and arrows in that sort of fight." Some returned to their camp about ten miles east of Mud Springs. But at daylight on February 6, Indians came over the bluffs from all directions trying to cut off the main detachment of soldiers led by Captain William D. Fouts, 7th Iowa, as they arrived about 8:00 A.M. The men, Collins wrote, were fatigued, chilled, and frost-bitten. Collins thought the station "utterly indefensible," but the troops held on though arrows and rifle fire showered upon them. Seven soldiers and many horses and mules were wounded. Collins telegraphed Fort Laramie to send him a howitzer. About 2:00 P.M. the warriors withdrew, but watched from the hills until dark. The telegraph line was cut then, and Collins sent a party to repair it; it was cut still again, and again repaired. Bent claimed no tribesmen died, though Collins thought his men killed perhaps thirty. Collins admitted it was impossible to know for certain, as the Indians carried off their dead and wounded. Collins estimated the attackers numbered close to a thousand, were well-armed with revolvers and rifles, as well as bows and arrows, and had plenty of ammunition.[10]

While Collins prepared for renewed attacks, the tribesmen crossed to the north side of the Platte River. They sanded the ice so the animals could cross easily and camped about five miles into the bluffs. They were prepared to stay about four days, resting their ponies for the hard trek through the desolate country they knew was ahead. Bent remembered that scalp dances went on long into the night. In the morning Collins found no warriors around Mud Springs, but reconnaisance found many Indian trails. Scouts concluded that an Indian village was perhaps ten miles away at Rush Creek. The howitzer arrived before daybreak February 8, with fifty more troopers after a thirty-four-hour journey from Fort

[10]Ibid., Collins's report, pp. 92–98; Hyde, *George Bent*, 189–90.

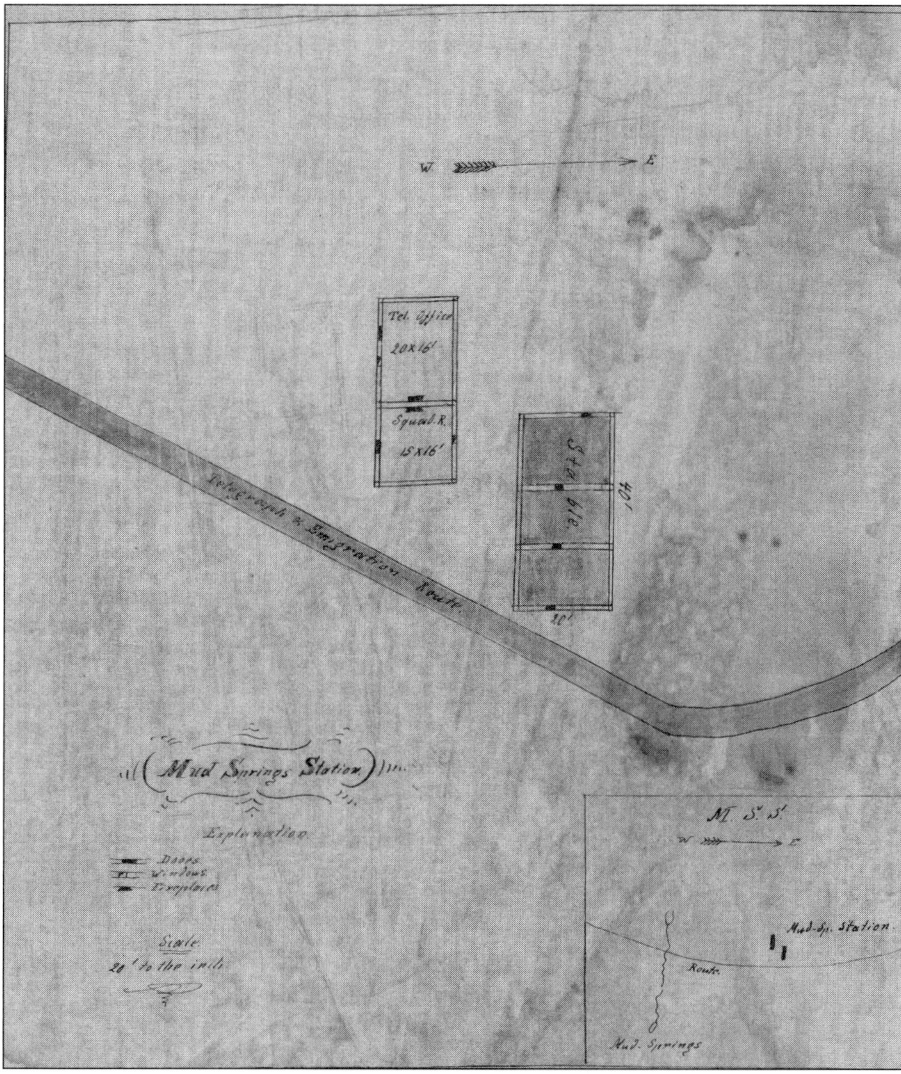

Mud Springs Station
Sketch by Second Lieutenant Caspar Collins.

Laramie. Collins then moved out to Rush Creek, but the tribal village was gone. His troopers found evidence of slaughtered cattle; empty oyster, meat, and fruit cans; flour sacks; codfish; and other spoils from ranches and trains. They then followed the Indian trail to the mouth of Rush Creek at the Platte River and saw warriors on the other side grazing their horses. Through field glasses, Collins saw no women and children and surmised they had gone on ahead, as indeed they had. But Collins raised his estimate of warrior numbers to two thousand.[11]

As Collins looked for a way to cross the frozen river, the warriors began to cross over toward him. "We barely had time to corral the wagons," Collins reported. The Cheyennes "attacked boldly" at first, but then resorted to "their old game of skulking and sharpshooting." At one point, Collins ordered a cavalry charge against a position that overlooked his, scattering the tribesmen at a cost of two troopers, one from the 7th Iowa and one from the 11th Ohio. The body of the man from the 7th Iowa was recovered intact, but the dead soldier from the 11th Ohio, not recovered until the next morning, was "horribly mutilated with ninety-seven arrows sticking in it." At dusk, the warriors broke off and recrossed the frozen Platte River.[12]

Through his field glasses, George Bent watched the affair at Rush Creek from across the river. He observed that soldiers had dug rifle pits all around the wagon corral for defense. Once the warriors determined "there was no chance of getting at the horses and mules inside the corral," they dismounted and crept as close as they could. Some found a good position in Collins's rear, Bent wrote, but a cavalry charge cleared them out. They mounted their ponies and fled, with one wounded. Other warriors already on horseback chased

---

[11] *O.R.*, I, 48, pt. 1, p. 94; Hyde, *George Bent*, 190; McDermott, *Frontier Crossroads*, 40–41.

[12] *O.R.*, I, 48, pt. 1, pp. 94–95.

the cavalry into their corral of wagons "at a hard gallop." Bent thought only about half of the troopers made it back. One cavalryman on a very fast horse dashed through the Indians and got away west along the "Laramie road," but eventually the warriors caught and killed him. "They found on him a paper and after the fight brought it to me" to read. The note, an order to another commander (Bent could not remember who), said Collins "was fighting three thousand Indians and needed aid at once." Later, Bent discovered Collins had sent two men out with identical orders, but the other went undetected. Bent claimed the Indians lost none killed and only two wounded.[13]

About sunrise on February 9, some warriors returned—Collins guessed around four hundred—while many others remained alert on the north bank of the river. They skirmished with the troops for a time, then returned to the other side, and with many of their fellows rode rapidly northward into the bluffs. By noon most had gone. Collins believed they left to join their families. Bent reported that the tribesmen gave up their plan to stay four days in camp north of the bluffs, and instead moved on, traveling forty miles that day. Collins noted that his casualties at Mud Springs and Rush Creek totaled "28 disabled and killed," which included 2 dead, 16 wounded, and 10 seriously frostbitten in night marches, out of 175 men. He estimated Indian dead at between 100 and 150.[14]

Collins wisely decided that pursuit was useless. The vast number of warriors would only compel them to corral again and fight on the defensive. Also, a pursuit in the sand hills would provide no subsistence for their stock. Collins broke camp about 2:00 P.M. and moved up the Platte nearly fifteen miles, where he divided the command. Lieutenant William

[13]Hyde, *George Bent*, 191–93.

[14]Ibid., 194; *O.R.*, I, 48, pt. 1, pp. 96–97; Nadeau, *Fort Laramie*, 172–75.

H. Brown, Company A, took most of the men back to Camp Mitchell and Fort Laramie, while the remainder, about seventy-five, followed Collins back to Mud Springs. The next morning he went on to Pole Creek station to open communications with Julesburg. At Pole Creek, he encountered Captain John Wilcox with some of his 7th Iowa, working to repair the telegraph. The station had been burned, and between it and Mud Springs even the telegraph poles were gone for over ten miles. Wilcox told him that east of Pole Creek the poles were missing for an even longer distance. Collins replied that the Indians obviously had "got over their superstitious idea that it is bad medicine to touch the telegraph." On February 11, Collins left to return to Fort Laramie, arriving three days later.[15]

In very cold wintry weather Collins's force had marched over four hundred miles in ten days, often spending nights without tents or shelter, sleeping on the frozen ground without a fire, living on short rations and forage, and courageously meeting "a brave and cunning foe" while outnumbered ten to one. Collins praised the officers and men who shared this experience. The troopers obeyed orders, fought systematically, and demonstrated both prudence and adroitness in imitating Indian cunning, Collins reported. He noted the howitzer proved useless as the ammunition was old and unreliable, reflecting its storage at Fort Laramie for eight or ten years. Collins correctly observed that fighting in Indian country was little understood by the military and could only be learned by actual combat. Collins learned fast, since this was his first and only experience leading troops in the field against Indians.

Collins's report continued with an observation that the attacking party was rarely equalled in size during winter

[15] *O.R.*, I, 48, pt. 1, pp. 96–97. Detachments of the 1st Nebraska, 7th Iowa, and 11th Ohio repaired the Denver telegraph line by February 12, the Laramie line by the 17th, and west to California by the 18th; ibid., pp. 90–91.

months because it was difficult for large numbers of warriors to remain together for lack of subsistence that time of year. On this foray, though, they had enough stolen stock and plundered stores to provide them with adequate supplies. He thought the party of warriors included mostly Cheyennes and Oglala and Brulé Sioux, with some Kiowas, Arapahos, and others, about eight hundred to a thousand lodges in all. He correctly assumed they were moving north to the Powder River country to join their compatriots there. They could be expected to continue their depredations on the North Platte. Collins advised that they were well armed, had many rifled muskets with plenty of ammunition, and were bent on revenge for the loss of their people at Sand Creek. He knew his posts at Deer Creek and Platte Bridge, within reach of the Powder River, were vulnerable, and that more troops were sorely needed in his sub-district. He suggested that large expeditions should be carried out in the spring to penetrate the center of the northern Indian country. His report in some respects resembled a lawyer's brief—lengthy, detailed, and soundly reasoned.[16]

Meanwhile, things were not going well for Curtis at department headquarters at Fort Leavenworth. He was supposed to investigate Sand Creek and perhaps bring Chivington up on charges, but he believed that nearly impossible since Chivington was "probably out of service"; and anyway, officers who could staff a court-martial were "widely scattered" and otherwise occupied. Then, too, Chivington was only partly to blame as "the popular cry of settlers and soldiers on the frontier favors an indiscriminate slaughter" of Indians, "which is very difficult to restrain." Chivington "may have transgressed" Curtis's "orders concerning Indian warfare and otherwise acted very much against" Curtis's

[16]Ibid., pp. 96–98; the report is also found in *Collins Family Papers*, items 52 and 53.

"views of propriety in his assault at Sand Creek, . . . it is not true . . . that such extra severity is increasing Indian war." But obviously it did just that, though Curtis either could not see it or refused to admit it. He knew the tribes were "more united" now, but only because "they are in a destitute condition." Curtis also blamed Wynkoop, who erroneously allowed Indians to camp at Sand Creek and let them believe it was a refuge. Chivington should be "severely rebuked," even so, for violating "known arrangements of that sort," Curtis wrote to Halleck on January 12.[17]

A West Point graduate and able administrator, and now chief-of-staff of the army, Halleck knew very well that things were not as they should be in the Department of Kansas. He had heard excuses from many officers as they tried to cover up poor performance, and clearly Curtis tried to dodge responsibility for the trouble in his department. No one in the Department of Kansas had been able to keep the overland lines of communication open and bring an end to Indian raids. Politics continued to cloud departmental affairs even in areas that had nothing to do with Indians. But Sand Creek seemed to be the last straw, and Halleck determined to clean house throughly.

The changes came on January 30. "By direction of the President," the order from the War Department began, the Department of Kansas was merged with the Department of the Missouri, headquarters at Fort Leavenworth. Curtis was sent to command the Department of the Northwest, headquartered in Milwaukee, Wisconsin. Major General Grenville M. Dodge, who headed the Department of Missouri, assumed command of the combined departments. A new command level established the military Division of the Missouri, which included the Departments of Missouri and the

[17] *O.R.*, I, 48, pt.1, pp. 502–3.

Northwest, headquarters at St. Louis, under the oversight of Major General John Pope (who formerly commanded the Department of the Northwest).[18] It took some time before the new commanders arrived, but that made little immediate difference to those involved at Julesburg and Mud Springs.

Halleck informed Grant about the new appointments the next day, and at the same time told Pope clearly "it is highly important that the roads to New Mexico, Colorado, Utah, and Idaho should be properly protected from Indian hostilities, so that there may be no interruption in the transmission of supplies and the mails." Halleck admitted that he had no idea if Indian raids were "greatly exaggerated" or not, or if they were excuses by the mail company to "cover their frequent failure to transport the mails" on schedule. Both Pope and Dodge especially would soon learn that hostilities were not exaggerated at all.[19]

The rampaging tribesmen had left the Platte roads and settlements "an appalling shambles." For better than a month not a mail coach, supply train, or telegraphic dispatch reached Denver. The telegraph lines to Salt Lake and Denver had been destroyed over long distances. For eighty miles from Julesburg toward Denver all of the ranches and stage stations were destroyed. The warriors had killed as many as fifty people, stolen at least 1,500 head of cattle, burned a hundred tons of government hay, and "carried off stores beyond calculation of food, forage, and other merchandise." One

[18]Ibid., pp. 686, 780. Major General John Pope, age forty-two, a West Pointer and career officer, had led the Army of Mississippi to victory at Island No. 10, and then the Army of Virginia to defeat at second Bull Run. Since 1862 he capably ran the Department of the Northwest, overseeing several successful campaigns against the Sioux. Grant trusted him. Major General Grenville M. Dodge, an engineer who built railroads, had been a corps commander in the Army of Tennessee in Sherman's Atlanta campaign. Wounded in August, 1864, he was on leave until he took over the Department of the Missouri in December 1864.

[19]Ibid., pp. 694, 714.

historian claimed "these raids . . . were the most savage and persistent in the history of the Overland Trail." Without the plunder, the Indians could never have reached the Powder River on a winter march. On February 6 Colonel Moonlight put Denver under martial law and ordered businesses closed until 365 men could be raised to open the road to Julesburg. General Pope received authorization that same day to recruit two regiments of enlisted "rebel deserters" from prisoner of war quarters at Rock Island, Illinois, to reinforce western roads, though it would take time to outfit and transport them.[20]

Even while Collins fought at Mud Springs and Rush Creek, reports of Indian destruction in the area reached General Pope from Dodge. On February 9 when he reported the demolition of the telegraph from Julesburg west and to Denver, he advised "new poles are on the way from Cottonwood. . . . We are compelled to haul poles from 130 to 145 miles." No communication existed with either Denver or Fort Laramie. The Overland stage "cannot run through" and "everything is destroyed." Pope relied, "send as many troops as are necessary and as soon as you can" to get the roads open. Dodge ordered the 11th Kansas Cavalry from Fort Riley to Fort Kearny to be "prepared to make a campaign . . . immediately." On February 10 Dodge claimed he would have the telegraph open to Denver and Salt Lake by "Sunday," February 12.[21]

Dodge promptly threw himself into action to open the overland roads along with the mail route and telegraph lines. He received lengthy reports on February 9 from Mitchell and Livingston enumerating the broad scope of the Indian attacks, destruction of property, the precious little protection

[20]Utley, *Frontiersmen in Blue*, 303; Nadeau, *Fort Laramie*, 172, 176; *O.R.*, I, 48, pt. 1, pp. 760–61, 763–64.

[21]*O.R.*, I, 48, pt. 1, pp. 793–95, 806. See also footnote 15, above.

they could afford with the few resources at hand, the terrible seriousness of this full-scale war, and the urgent pleas for more troops from field commanders. So informed, Dodge received permission to raise two companies of Indian scouts on February 10. The same day he ordered all westbound wagon trains organized and armed, with no less than a hundred armed men. Civilian trains could join government trains, but the military escort would be in command. The Overland Mail would be well-protected by cavalry who would also report and repair "immediately" any breaks in the telegraph.[22]

Finally, on February 11, news of Collins's fights at Mud Springs and Rush Creek reached Dodge with the plea, via Captain Wilcox, for more troops to protect the posts north to Laramie and beyond. That day Dodge ordered the 16th Kansas Cavalry, with howitzers (manned by a detachment of the 15th Kansas) to Julesburg, for Mitchell to use. That regiment was supposed to "press forward as fast as possible." Then Dodge asked Livingston, who commanded the eastern sub-district, "where is Mud Springs? Where are Colonel Collins' troops stationed? Say to Colonel Collins our posts must be held. As fast as troops can march they will go to your aid." Dodge, just arrived on the scene and unfamiliar with his command, had no idea who Collins was, or even the command structure west of Julesburg. Dodge learned quickly, however, as evidenced by his reply when the equally new Pope asked him a few days later, "what is General Mitchell doing in Omaha while the Indians are overrunning his district? . . . order him to his proper station." Dodge told Pope, "Mitchell's district headquarters are at Omaha. He has been on the plains all winter" tending to business as he should have been.[23]

---

[22]Ibid., pp. 793–94, 807–8.
[23]Ibid., pp. 815–17, 821, 849.

While frantic communications flew in and out of Dodge's headquarters at Fort Leavenworth, up north near Deer Creek on February 13, Captain Rinehart, Company G, 11th Ohio, died. Rinehart had been under arrest and awaiting court-martial, but was relieved and returned to his company. Rinehart learned that Indians had plundered a camp of mountaineers and stolen horses some twenty miles from Deer Creek. With ten troopers he rode quickly to the source of trouble, then immediately charged the Indians, who promptly killed him. Private Johnson, at Sweetwater station, told his sister a slightly different story. According to his version, Rinehart "and a drunken crew of perhaps 12 soldiers and two Swiss civilians went out to rescue horses stolen by Indians, and Capt. Rinehart was shot by one of his soldiers by mistake. Rinehart was drunk too."[24]

As part of the rotation of units in the field, Sergeant Hull and Company K had left Fort Laramie for Fort Halleck in late November. They relieved Company D, which returned to Laramie. Fort Halleck looked good to Hull, who wrote December 1 that he had a "fine time at the dance. Six ladies present." A midnight supper followed, which proved "splendid!" But it was winter, and a lot of snow and bitter cold followed. In mid-February two of his men froze to death minding cattle. The winter snows remained troublesome until May.[25]

Meanwhile, in Omaha Mitchell reported that he had sent scouts out to track the Indians Collins fought, and was "satisfied" they were headed north. Dodge told Mitchell "troops

---

[24]*Collins Family Papers*, item 87; Robrock, "The Eleventh Ohio," 36, 40–41; Unrau, *Tending the Talking Wire*, 223. To give some credence to Johnson, see Brown, *Wondrous Times*, 237, who wrote "officers of the frontier army also had a weakness for firewater," as did enlisted men. There was plenty of evidence of this in Hull's diary as well.

[25]Hull, "Soldiering on the High Plains," 28–35. Hull wrote of "Iowa boys" he found at Halleck when he arrived, but failed to mention D Company. The *Official Records* neglected to mention Iowans.

are on the road," and Mitchell should meet them at Fort Kearny. Dodge continued, "as soon as troops reach Kearny be ready to push right out against the Indians, and follow them until they are entirely broken up and so chastized they will not return." Yet Dodge wanted no "such outrages as were committed by Chivington." Then Dodge suggested to Pope that "troops at Sioux City and Fort Randall [Dakota Territory] should move across the country to Fort Laramie at the same time" he moved north from Julesburg.[26] Dodge's concept, though sound enough militarily, failed to take into account the logistics and distances involved in winter on the plains, never mind that troops and officers new to the area had virtually no knowledge of the vast terrain north of the Platte, much less how they might be supplied.

Dodge had wasted no time discovering what troops he had on hand and where they were in the District of Nebraska. One of his first actions was to send his inspector general to locate them all. That report came back February 15. "Near Cottonwood Springs" were seven companies of the 1st Nebraska Veteran Volunteers, along with five companies of the 7th Iowa. At Fort Kearny was another company of the 1st Nebraska, and yet another was located at Plum Creek; at Columbus, Nebraska Territory, a company of the 7th Iowa; at Dakota City and Omaha two more companies of the 1st Nebraska; at Fort Laramie, Companies A, D, I, and L of the 11th Ohio; at Camp Mitchell, Company H, 11th Ohio; at Fremont's Orchard, Company C, 11th Ohio; and at Camp Collins, Companies B and F, 11th Ohio. It was not a full report, as the inspector omitted the 11th Ohio companies on station north and west of Fort Laramie and at Fort Halleck. But it gave Dodge a general idea of the disposition of his command.[27]

Dodge had difficulty getting reinforcements on the roads.

---

[26] *O.R.*, I, 48, pt. 1, pp. 853, 859.

[27] Ibid., pp. 861–62.

The 11th Kansas, ordered transferred from Fort Riley to Fort Kearny ready to campaign, was ill-prepared. The troopers had few horses. Dodge told Mitchell to "mount" them on "mules, or put them in forts and take mounted men from your posts." He still wanted troops from Sioux City, but they were not in his department and in the end he would not get them. Pope asked Dodge if Kansas had "arms . . . for two regiments from Rock Island?" At least Dodge could assure Pope there were "plenty of arms" at Fort Leavenworth.[28]

On February 20 the first two companies of Rock Island men left Illinois, to be armed later at Fort Leavenworth. Within a week other elements of the 2nd and 3rd United States Volunteers followed. Mitchell reported the Indians who fought against Collins were on the Powder River, north of Fort Laramie. Other scouts in the vicinity of Loup Fork failed to report. Subsistence trains were on the way west as well, in the vicinity of Fort Kearny. Mitchell noted that he planned to head for Kearny in the morning (February 24), and asked Dodge if he could strike "Indians on Powder River at an early day." Dodge again revealed how little he knew of the geography involved. "Where is the Powder River, and how far from Julesburg?" Mitchell's answer probably dismayed him. "Powder River is 150 miles north of Fort Laramie, on direct line 250 or 300 miles." Though Mitchell wanted to mount a winter campaign, Major Thomas L. Mackey of the 11th Ohio cautioned him he was daily "expecting trouble" from Laramie west and his "posts are weak." Mitchell qualified his own desire for an early campaign by telling Dodge that guarding the overland mail stages was "using up an immense amount of horses," and "our supply for the troops . . . is sadly deficient. Roads are very bad."[29]

---

[28]Ibid., pp. 863, 885, 916. The Rock Island regiments were former Confederate war prisoners who chose to enlist in the Union army rather than remain in federal prison at Rock Island, Illinois. These were designated "United States Volunteers."

[29]Ibid., pp. 921, 961, 962, 971; Brown, *Galvanized Yankees*, 15.

On February 25 the concept of a winter campaign received still another blow. Mitchell told Dodge "we are in the midst of a terrible storm today, and very cold." His scouts reported "snow so deep they cannot follow trail." On top of that, streams were "all swollen and bridges reported gone." Obviously, there could not be a campaign under these circumstances, at least not yet. From Julesburg, Collins told Mitchell the need for an attack still existed. Dodge agreed, "we must strike them [the Indians] as soon as possible. If the [reinforcements] do not get up let Collins and Livingston combine" and do the job. Mitchell certainly agreed also; all he needed was troops, supplies, and moderate weather.[30]

Simultaneously, Dodge wired Brigadier General Connor in Salt Lake to leave the District of Utah "in charge of a good officer" and go to Denver where new orders would reach him. "If you have any spare troops take them with you." An impatient Dodge advised he still wanted "to strike the Indians before grass grows." That day, February 27, Mitchell told Dodge "snow too deep for work." His sources told him it would be impossible to reach Indians on the Powder River before spring. To make matters worse, the Kansas troops had not yet reached Kearny, perhaps "delayed by high water." But, reflecting his superior's desire to launch a campaign, if he had "troops and supplies sufficient" he would move against the Powder River Indians "regardless of snow." Realistically, Mitchell knew enough troops and supplies would not be available for a winter strike. This could be no small campaign. Indian scouts placed 1,800 to 2,000 lodges of hostiles around Powder River, which meant the presence of thousands of warriors. Those tribesmen already had warned friendly Sioux at Fort Laramie to leave, as "they intend to clean the country." Fort Laramie needed more troops "at as early a day" as possible. From Laramie, Major Mackey opined "things are looking

[30] *O.R.*, I, 48, pt. 1, pp. 979, 1001.

more serious than I ever saw them before." Dodge, though, seemed unimpressed. "All you can do," he said, "is work the troops up toward Julesburg and Laramie as fast as you can, . . . and then make a quick dash at them. . . . You can strike them with 1,500 or 2,000 well-mounted men. Subsistence and forage enough have been forwarded," or so he thought.[31]

The February 28 report of troops on station in Mitchell's District of Nebraska revealed no increase in strength, the troops deployed very much as they had been on the 15th. Kansas troops remained unreported, as they would not arrive at Kearny until the next week. Essentially the troop buildup Dodge envisioned materialized very slowly. Worse, the first battalion of the 11th Ohio departed for home, subtracting many veterans from the ranks. The first battalion's enlistment had expired in December 1864. As early as August, Collins warned Mitchell his men were due out in December, and that the veterans wanted to know when they could leave. In October, he posed the same question to Mitchell twice, with no response. Clearly they were still badly needed, even if the troopers thought their time was up. They could quite properly be kept in service for their three-year term *or during the war*, as others discovered later to their chagrin. Even so, with many new troops supposedly on the way, the first battalion left for Ohio on March 7, just three months late. Collins called the men of Companies A, B, C, and D, 11th Ohio, from their various duties in the field as February ended and led them east. His son, Lieutenant Caspar Collins, remained behind on station with Company G.[32]

Caspar stayed on duty because his commission dated from June 1863, so his enlistment had not expired. Neither had that

---

[31]Ibid., pp. 1001, 1014, 1015.

[32]Ibid., pp. 1040–41, 1104; *Collins Family Papers*, file folder 17; Fred A. Shannon, *The Organization and Administration of the Union Army, 1861–1865* (Gloucester, Mass.: Peter Smith, 1965), vol. I, 36.

of the 104 replacements in Companies A, B, C, and D, most of whom came on hand in 1863. Some others chose to reenlist and not return home. All told, 123 men of the first battalion remained in the West. So did the 17 who had died from sickness or from wounds or had been killed in action, including the pair who froze to death in bitter winter weather. Twelve others had enlisted in the 4th United States Cavalry in January 1863. Another 35 had been discharged earlier, most on a surgeon's certificate of disability; 6 officers had resigned; and 53 troopers had just disappeared or deserted after arriving at Fort Laramie. That left 204 troopers and 12 field and staff, including Collins, who were mustered out at Fort Leavenworth on April 1, 1865.

Many 11th Ohio Cavalrymen remained on duty, even more than had originally come to Fort Laramie in May 1862. The seven companies that had been recruited in the summer of 1863 and early in 1864 numbered about 661 officers and men. They still had a vital role to play.[33]

The departure of Collins and the first four companies of the 11th Ohio forced reorganization of the remainder of the regiment. Major Thomas L. Mackey assumed command, and subsequently, on May 1, 1865, won promotion to lieutenant colonel. No longer a regiment, they became Battalion, 11th Ohio.[34]

On the day Collins departed the Oregon and Overland roads, Mitchell wrote Dodge "Colonel Collins is now en route to Omaha for the purpose of being mustered out, his term of service having expired." Mitchell praised Collins, who "has been in the mountain service three years. He has traversed the mountains in every direction from Laramie to

[33]The statistics are taken from the *Official Roster of the Soldiers of the State of Ohio in the War of the Rebellion*, vol. XI, 549–82.

[34]*Collins Family Papers*, file folder 17; Reid, *Ohio in the War*, vol. I, 175; Robrock, "The Eleventh Ohio," 39. Mackey, age fifty-two, was from Columbus, Ohio.

South Pass for many miles and is probably as well, if not better, posted than any white man that has not made his home with the Indians."[35] Collins's experience, his level-headed, dedicated approach to his job, and his knowledge of and respect for Native Americans would be missed. Collins personally led only one campaign against hostile Indians, that at Mud Springs and Rush Creek, but there he showed initiative and prudence. Otherwise he had no opportunity to prove himself as an Indian fighter or field commander. He never led his entire regiment into battle, as the regiment was never in one place at one time.

Collins proved to be an active commander. He explored adjacent areas, periodically visited and inspected every post the 11th staffed, tried to make army life as comfortable as possible for the troopers, and sought to be fair and impartial in administering military justice and protocol. He made every effort to understand Native American life and problems, produced excellent maps where none previously existed, and studied the flora and fauna, even hosting representatives of the Smithsonian. He was anything but a desk soldier, and would indeed be missed by the remaining Ohio troopers, as well as by General Dodge.[36]

---

[35] *Collins Family Papers*, item 83.

[36] Ibid., items 55, 58, 59, 72–77, 82, 86, 88, 91. His maps have since been lost.

CHAPTER NINE

Connor Takes Over; Campaign Plans

In February 1865 the War Department moved the Territory of Utah into Dodge's Department of the Missouri and ordered General Patrick E. Connor to Denver in preparation for a change in the command structure. This made no difference to Private Hervey Johnson, up north on the line at Sweetwater station; he probably neither knew nor cared about generals hundreds of miles away in Kansas, Missouri, or even Colorado. In March, he wrote that Indians had run off some horses and mules at Sweetwater, and one of his companions suffered a minor wound in a fight that managed to save most of their stock. The telegraph line went down often and was repaired just as often. Travel between Sweetwater and Platte Bridge had been interrupted, and a wagonload of guns and ammunition was lost and a soldier killed. Another raiding party drove off sixteen horses from Camp Marshall and killed a soldier in the process. Another raid at La Prele station cost fifteen horses and the death of a trooper from Company E, 11th Ohio. Johnson's Company G, whose eighty troopers garrisoned six posts from Deer Creek west to South Pass, bore the brunt of virtually non-stop raids along the Oregon road northwest of Fort Laramie that spring.[1]

---

[1] *O.R.*, I, 48, pt. 1, 886, 1001, 1225; Unrau, *Tending the Talking Wire*, 224–30; Robrock, "The Eleventh Ohio," 40.

On March 6 Mitchell told Dodge that quite a number of friendly Sioux at Fort Laramie "are in a starving condition." Mitchell wondered what to do about them because "they dare not leave their camps to hunt or provide for themselves in consequence of the threats of hostile Indians." Mitchell suggested they be fed "condemned and damaged rations," used "as scouts or any way, against the hostile Indians, but under no promise of pay or anything else."[2] These were friendly Indians that Colonel Collins had allowed to remain near Laramie.

Mitchell had still more information for Dodge. The 11th Kansas was about to leave Kearny for Julesburg, but their horses were in poor condition and many of the men were dismounted, and the 16th Kansas had not yet appeared at Kearny. So far as the Indians were concerned, he learned from "Mrs. [Nancy Jane] Morton, lately brought from the Indians on the Powder River, that the Indians are high up on the north fork of the Powder River, where they intend to leave their families for the summer for the purpose of making war on the Platte." Mitchell continued, "She says Cheyennes, Arapahoes [*sic*], Kiowas, Brulé and Ogalalla [*sic*] Sioux and Minneconjous [*sic*] are banded together and determined to make war to the knife. This woman was captured at Plum Creek August last."[3]

Nancy Morton had been captured August 9, 1864, very near Plum Creek. She was carried off by Indians who were with the same group that Black Kettle led, but a different band. When Black Kettle turned over some white prisoners to Major Wynkoop, Nancy Morton had hoped she would be included, but she was not. The band took her north, and

---

[2] *O.R.*, I, 48, pt. 1, p. 1104.

[3] Ibid., p. 1105. The 11th Kansas had only nine companies: three others had already been discharged. Doubtless this contributed to their dissatisfaction; see George M. Walker, "Eleventh Kansas Cavalry, 1865, and the Battle of Platte Bridge," *Collections of the Kansas State Historical Society, 1915–1918*, vol. 14, 332–33.

when they were close to Fort Laramie, her captor thought he might trade for her. He sent a couple of braves to the fort, and Major John Wood, 7th Iowa, in command at the time, tried unsuccessfully to buy her freedom. Though that effort and another attempt failed, toward the end of December he dispatched yet other emmisaries. He sent along his own horse, plus another, and a pack train with food, tobacco, lead, powder, knives, and other items on a long, cold trek through deep snow to the Sioux village some two hundred miles north of Laramie where Nancy Morton was then held.

This time they were successful. In a terrible winter journey the two rescuers and Nancy Morton reached Platte Bridge the end of January, where she was able to ride in an army ambulance the rest of the way to Fort Laramie. At one of the stations between Platte Bridge and the fort she thought she recognized Big Crow, one of the Cheyenne chiefs who had participated in her capture at Plum Creek. She arrived at Laramie on January 31. Major Wood, whom she wanted to thank, was no longer there, replaced by Major Mackey, 11th Ohio, to whom she reported and told of her sighting of Big Crow. Acting quickly, Mackey had the chief arrested and brought to the fort. Sutler William Bullock and his wife cared for Nancy Morton while the Indians burned Julesburg and Collins fought at Mud Springs. It was not until February 26 that it was safe enough on the Oregon road for her to join a wagon train headed east to Fort Kearny, and then procede on to Sidney, Iowa, and her family.[4]

Big Crow, Nancy Morton's tormentor, was locked in the guardhouse at Fort Laramie when Collins's column returned from their fight at Mud Springs and Rush Creek. Those

[4]Becher, *Massacre Along the Medicine Road*, 355–67; Russ Czaplewski, *Captive of the Cheyenne: The Story of Nancy Jane Morton and the Plum Creek Massacre* (Kearney, Nebraska: The Dawson County Historical Society, 1993), various places in Sections One and Two, passim.

troopers, fresh out of sympathy for any Indians, quickly learned of Big Crow's incarceration, rushed the guardhouse, roped Big Crow, and dragged him out, fully intending to kill him. Colonel Collins quickly intervened, cut the rope with his sword, and promised the troops that justice would be done properly. By the time Big Crow's end came, Collins had already led the first battalion of the 11th Ohio home and was not present when "justice" took place.[5]

The troop buildup that Dodge desired interested him far more than the liberation of Mrs. Morton. "Has the 16th and 11th Kansas arrived? Two hundred horses left Fort Leavenworth last week for the 11th Kansas." Mitchell replied that most of the 11th Kansas was on hand, but he heard nothing about the 16th Kansas, ordered to report to him posthaste on February 11; it was now March 6.[6]

On March 10 Mitchell reported to Dodge that "Indians attacked a party of soldiers near Platte Bridge, 130 miles west of Fort Laramie; killed one soldier and captured 1 government wagon. Indians are said to be concentrating there." Still no news of the 16th Kansas; the 11th was on its way to Julesburg; and a company of "Nebraska troops" left Julesburg for Laramie. Mitchell needed the subsistence and forage that he thought must come from Fort Leavenworth. "Additional supplies should be immediately started" for Fort Laramie. When the rest of the troops arrived, Mitchell claimed he would start "the expedition" Dodge ordered. He also noted "stages are running regularly westward" along the roads.[7]

On March 16 Mitchell wired Dodge, "The most miraculous event of the war is the loss of the 16th Kansas. I cannot hear from them by scout or otherwise." Dodge had no knowledge of them either, only that "they had orders to push

[5]Czaplewski, *Captive of the Cheyenne*, Section 1, p. 42.

[6]*O.R.*, I, 48, pt. 1, pp. 817, 1104–5. The 11th Kansas endured a hard mid-winter march on foot from Fort Riley, Kansas. See McDermott, *Frontier Crossroads*, p.45.

[7]*O.R.*, I, 48, pt. 1, p. 1143.

forward as fast as possible without injury to their horses." Over a month had elapsed since he had issued his order, and Dodge felt discouraged. He told Pope, his superior, he knew "the Indians are making extensive preparations for war," but he saw "no very good prospect of moving north from Laramie unless we have better luck getting troops there than we have had thus far." He blamed it on the weather. Two days later he told Pope of a "terrible storm on the plains and a large fire at Fort Kearny; burnt stables and all the hay. . . . This is a hard blow for our stock. The cavalry is snowed in and water-bound all along the road. The elements are evidently partial to the Indians."[8] Dodge could not overcome, among other things, winter on the plains.

Meanwhile, the command structure affecting the overland roads changed. On March 9 Pope reported to General Grant, who now commanded all the armies of the United States, that he had merged the Territories of Utah, Colorado, and Nebraska into one military district, the District of the Plains. He put Brigadier General Patrick E. Connor in charge—Connor then commanded California troops in Utah. Of Connor, Pope wrote optimistically, "I think [with this appointment] no further difficulties of a serious character are likely again to occur on the Overland routes." Dodge still commanded the Department of the Missouri, in which Connor's District of the Plains was located.[9]

By the end of March, the new command structure took shape. As early as March 3 Dodge informed Pope that

---

[8]Ibid., pp. 1194, 1204, 1242–43.

[9]Ibid., p. 1131. In January, Connor drew up a plan for a winter campaign against the northern tribesmen and sent it to the War Department. It was seconded by the Overland Mail Company, the Western Union Telegraph Company, the secretary of the Interior, and the governor of Utah. Grant then forwarded a proposal to create a Department of the Plains under Connor to Dodge and Pope. Pope recommended it to Halleck, and it was done. Dodge already had told Connor February 27; Connor took over, headquarters in Denver, March 28. See Madsen, *Glory Hunter*, 122–26; Varley, *Brigham and the Brigadier*, 197–201.

Mitchell outranked Connor, a small problem, and Pope told Dodge to do what he thought "best." Back in January, Curtis had wrongly rebuked Mitchell for leaving Julesburg virtually undefended when he took a heavy column out in bitter weather on the unsuccessful search for hostiles following the first attack on the town. Mitchell then reacted in anger and frustration by asking Curtis for a transfer to a southern command or he would resign. Mitchell's request still lay on the desk at Fort Leavenworth, so Dodge used it to move Mitchell not to a southern command, but to the District of North Kansas, solving the problem of rank. Connor arrived at Fort Kearny on March 30 to assume command of the District of the Plains. That district then was divided into a South Sub-District, headquarters at Denver, with Brevet Brigadier General Guy V. Henry at its head; an East Sub-District, comprising Nebraska Territory, headquarters at Fort Kearny, Colonel Robert R. Livingston of the 1st Nebraska Cavalry in charge; a North Sub-District of Dakota Territory, including Julesburg but not Fort Halleck, with Colonel Thomas Moonlight, 11th Kansas Cavalry, headquarters at Fort Laramie, in command; and a West Sub-District, the Territory of Utah, headquarters at Camp Douglas outside Salt Lake City, Lieutenant Colonel Milo George, 1st Battalion Nevada Cavalry, directing. The 11th Ohio companies fell under a divided command, those on the Oregon road and telegraph north and west of Fort Laramie under Colonel Moonlight, and those on the Overland mail road under General Henry.[10]

Still at Laramie, Mitchell reported to Dodge on March 29 that ninety lodges of Arapahos were coming to the fort "to give themselves up and want peace." Mitchell could not afford to feed them and asked what he should do. He also

[10]*O.R.*, I, 48, pt. 1, pp. 1069, 1285, 1300; pt. 2, pp. 54–55; Becher, *Massacre Along the Medicine Road*, 398–99.

noted "a large hostile body 190 miles northwest" headed for the North Platte. From Washington, D.C., on March 31, Halleck told Dodge that the "Secretary of War directs that all captured hostile Indians be held as prisoners and confined at convenient military posts till the Department of Interior may see fit to provide for them. They may be made to labor and put in crops for their support." From his desk in Washington Halleck proved he had no understanding of plains Indians or the problem that Dodge faced.[11]

Even as Mitchell wired Dodge from Laramie, the general already had turned his attention to his new district commander. He summed things up for Connor. Troops on hand or en route in the new district amounted to "2,000 or over" cavalry, which should be "pushed right on after the Indians." They had on hand four hundred pack mules, better than wagons for carrying supplies on the sort of expedition Dodge envisioned. The 3rd United States Volunteers (former Confederate prisoners enlisted in U.S. service) were headed for Kearny to relieve the cavalry, and one or two more of the same units would soon be on the way to Leavenworth. A "large number of Canadian horses" would follow soon. Dodge told Connor the plan included pushing Brigadier General Alfred Sully "with a column" west from Sioux City to the Powder River, which Connor would have to supply from Laramie. Dodge reminded Connor that he had control of the whole Overland route, and his troops were to "punish" the Indians so they would have to "keep the peace." Indians had to be kept away from the lines of travel and kept on the defensive. The overland mail and the telegraph "must be protected at all hazards." Connor was ordered to "give the Indians no rest."

There was more. Dodge proposed to have the United States Volunteers, infantry, garrison the posts so the cavalry

[11] *O.R.*, I, 48, pt. 1, pp. 1293, 1294–95, 1303.

could take the field. "Depots should be designated" and well fortified and designed to hold a year's supply for troops in the district, and Dodge sent an engineer out to "examine" the posts to that end. He saw no need for each post to be "a partial depot." Also "Brevet Brigadier General Ford" would shortly leave Fort Larned "with 1,200 men to operate against the Indians" along the Santa Fé road, with assistance from Fort Lyon. Between Connor, Sully, and Ford, Dodge fully intended to intimidate the Indians and keep the roads clear. He challenged Connor: "You are a stranger to me," Dodge reminded Connor, "but I have placed you in command, believing . . . that you will infuse life, discipline, and effectiveness into the forces under you."[12]

In the East on April 3, Grant finally overcame the Petersburg defenses of Richmond, Virginia, and seized the Confederate capital. The news sparked over the telegraph, and on the same day Dodge ordered "a national salute" fired at every post within the department "in honor of the victories." Perhaps the war in the East was winding down, but not that along the western roads. Having had a chance to size up his situation, Connor lamented the want of forage and supplies and warned Dodge his fear that the "expedition will be detained longer than you anticipated, for want of forage and supplies. Corn thus far at Julesburg and Laramie is consumed as fast as received." Neither the 16th Kansas nor the 3rd United States Volunteers had yet arrived at Fort Kearny. Mitchell could have written that dispatch. For all Dodge's hope to move quickly against the Indians, Connor faced the same problems Mitchell had.[13]

Connor made a quick trip to Fort Kearny. He found, he confided to Dodge, "but very little discipline among the troops and but little regard paid to economy, or care given to

[12]Ibid., pp. 1295–96.

[13]Ibid., pt. 2, pp. 21, 30.

public property." Nor did Connor approve of the fortification plans; they were far too costly. He would "do everything in [his] . . . power to expedite the expedition," but "supplies are coming in very slowly . . . and it will take a longer time than you probably anticipate to get it in motion." He asked that supplies be forwarded "as rapidly as possible." He knew Dodge had forbid him from making contracts on his own as he had done in Utah, but he wanted to do that for "such small articles as may be required for immediate use" now. He had always made "careful disbursements of public funds [his] first duty," he said.[14]

Dodge's only reply came on April 6. Angrily, he announced "the commanding officer of the 16th Kansas Cavalry should be brought to account for his delay. It is near two months since he left Fort Leavenworth, time enough to walk to Kearny and return twice." It may have been fortunate for that commanding officer that three days later Connor announced that the 16th Kansas finally had arrived and were at Cottonwood, and that the 3rd United States Volunteers were now at Kearny. Connor distributed the 3rd at Kearny, Cottonwood, Julesburg, and Laramie, with headquarters at Julesburg, as Dodge directed.[15] Though infantry, they relieved the cavalry units previously stationed at those posts.

Meanwhile, north and west of Fort Laramie at Sweetwater station, Private Johnson noted in April that Company E, 11th Ohio, lost a number of horses. A supply train with rations and corn for the "upper posts" camped about seventy miles west of Laramie had their stock stolen "including 12 head of beef for Co. G," his company, and consequently they could not move until replacements arrived to pull the wagons. He also mentioned that Lieutenant Caspar Collins now com-

---

[14]Ibid., p. 36.

[15]Ibid., pp. 42, 60. Two companies of the 3rd U.S. Volunteers marched on to Junction, Colorado, and another two went on to Fort Laramie; Brown, *Galvanized Yankees*, 18.

manded "here but he is next as good as a wooden man." He additonally reported rumors of a soldier's pay increase of four dollars, which would bring him twenty-two dollars a month. Then on April 13 he heard of Lee's surrender and acclaimed, "Hurrah! for Grant. May glory attend him."[16]

Johnson continued describing the raids on the Oregon road in subsequent missives. Two soldiers had died, he wrote on April 21, twenty miles from Deer Creek: one from Company E, 11th Ohio, and one from Company I, 7th Iowa. He observed that reinforcements from the 11th Kansas were headed his way, and in fact, they repulsed an attack twenty miles from Deer Creek on April 22. They pursued the attackers the next day, but to no avail.[17]

While these desultory raids continued, Connor grumbled to Dodge that he did not "deem it practicable . . . to make a campaign at present" and listed his reasons. He could not obtain enough forage because of lack of transportation. Even had he enough grain to feed the horses, it would mean large "cumbersome" wagon trains would have to accompany an expedition, slowing it down and alerting the Indians. When the grass came up he could make forced marches against the Indians with some mobility. The desired expedition would have to wait still longer. The same day Connor ordered Companies L and M of the 2nd California Cavalry from Fort Bridger to Fort Halleck.[18] Although he may not have liked it, Dodge must have been used to postponements by now.

While conditions frustrated Connor's desire to take the field, at Sweetwater station Caspar Collins penned a letter to his mother in Ohio. He told her that the 11th Kansas was strung out between Sweetwater and Fort Laramie, welcome

[16]Unrau, *Tending the Talking Wire*, 233–37; *O.R.*, I, 48, pt. 2, p. 65. Dodge ordered a 200-gun salute "at every post" in commemoration of Lee's surrender.

[17]Unrau, *Tending the Talking Wire*, 237; *O.R.*, I, 48, pt. 1, pp. 198–99; McDermott, *Frontier Crossroads*, 46.

[18]*O.R.*, I, 48, pt. 2, pp. 100–102.

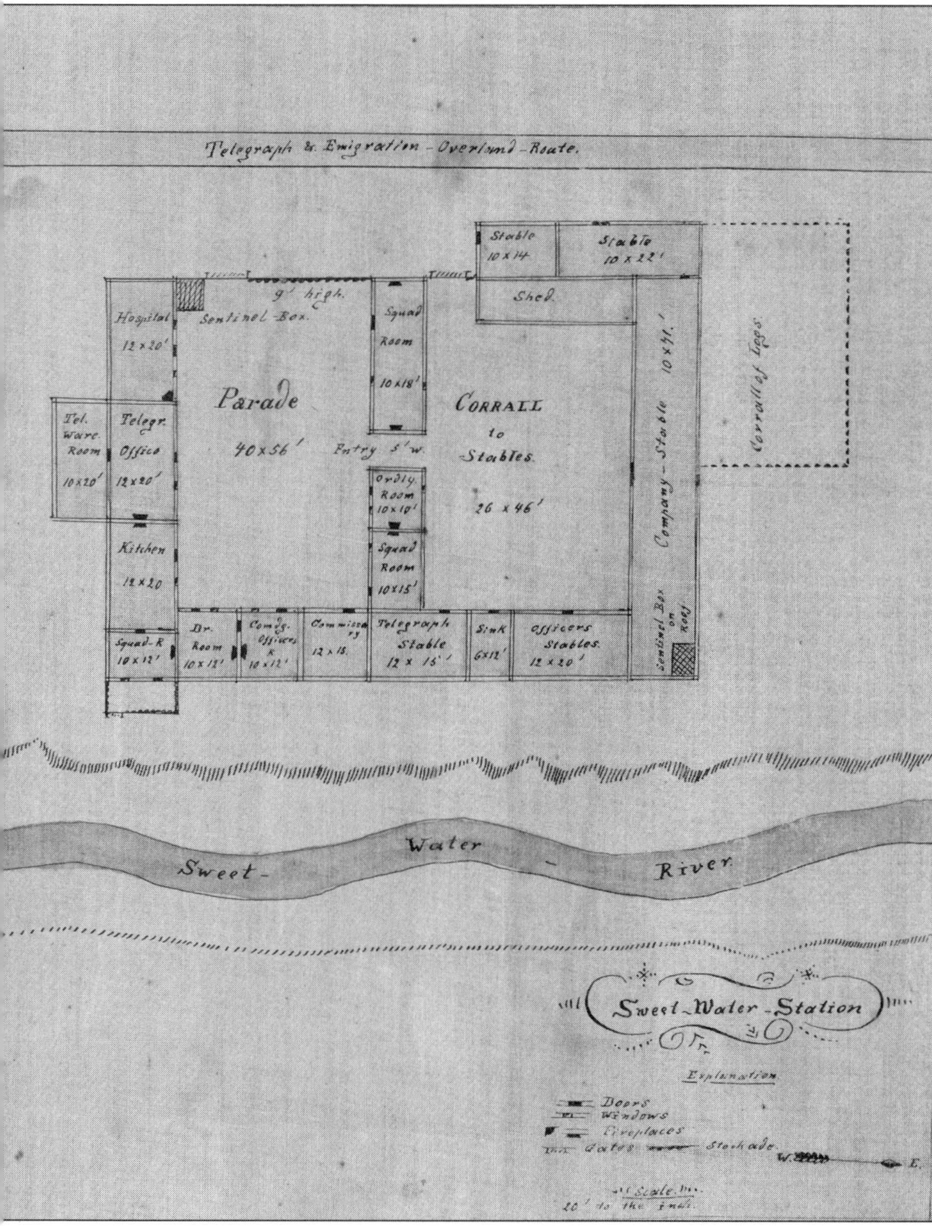

Sweetwater Station
Sketch by Second Lieutenant Caspar Collins.

SWEETWATER STATION
Drawing by Private Charles F. Moellman.

help for the 11th Ohio. Sweetwater, he believed, was well defended now with twenty-six men. Even so, the Arapahos killed one of his troopers, who, along with another, attempted to bring a load of rations in a four-mule rig to the post. The other soldier held the Indians off with his Spencer carbine until dark, then made a thirty-mile dash to safety at the post. "We immediately started in pursuit," Caspar wrote, but the Indians fled "along with the mules which they packed with plunder. The wind obscured their trail, and we couldn't catch them." Also, his troops all rejoiced at the news of Lee's surrender, "but our spirits were thrown into a deep gloom on hearing of the assassination of our beloved president. The country will find it difficult to replace its loss."[19]

Dodge echoed Caspar Collins concerning the assassination in a message to Connor. "A general gloom overspreads the

[19] *Collins Family Papers*, item 14.

community," he remarked. On April 16 the War Department ordered the army to observe a thirty-day mourning period "as far as practicable in a state of war." The colors of all commands and regiments "will be put in mourning for six months." The next day Andrew Johnson was acknowledged as the new president. Among the troops on the roads, news from the East brought elation with news of Lee's surrender, then despair over Lincoln's murder, but no change in their duty. At Fort Halleck, Sergeant Hull allowed that "burning at stake [would be] too mild for [the] assassins' punishment."[20]

Dodge asked Connor on April 24 how the Indian expedition was "progressing." Not well, came Connor's reply. Cavalry horses were on "half rations for want of corn," and transportation remained deficient. Though he would "not be able to accomplish much for some time," he still planned to "take the field as early as possible." Raiding continued "near Fort Laramie." While Connor wrestled with his obstacles, Pope planned a large offensive. About May 15, Sully would take 1,200 men and campaign west from Fort Pierre, Dakota Territory, head north of the Black Hills, and ultimately establish a post on the Powder River in the heart of hostile country. Connor would move north as Sully moved west, wreaking havoc with the Indians in the process.[21]

As April closed, matters of supply continued to concern both Connor and Dodge, with the latter pressuring supply officers at Leavenworth to hurry west with corn. "It is important that Connor gets off before long," he advised them. He also told Connor the same thing if he were to act in concert with Sully. Leavenworth's quartermaster replied to Dodge that twenty-five thousand bushels of corn were "well on the way" and another fifty wagons would "be sent at once."[22] All they had to do was actually reach Connor.

---

[20] *O.R.*, I, 48, pt. 2, p. 104; 46, pt. 3, pp. 788–89; Hull, "Soldiering on the High Plains," 33.
[21] *O.R.*, I, 48, pt. 2, pp. 186, 224, 237.
[22] Ibid., pp. 237–38, 246, 251.

Also on April 30, Pope reported a detailed distribution of troops in the Military Division of the Missouri. Connor's District of the Plains included the overland roads except for the Santa Fé. Livingston's East Sub-District guarded the Oregon road generally east of Julesburg. His strength included elements of the 7th Iowa Cavalry, companies of the 3rd United States Volunteers, the 1st Battalion Nebraska Cavalry, and for the moment the bulk of the 16th Kansas Cavalry. Lieutenant Colonel Milo George oversaw the West Sub-District, with companies of the 2nd California Cavalry, companies of the 1st Battalion Nevada Cavalry, and companies of the 3rd California at various stations.

In Colonel Moonlight's North Sub-District, Connor had begun to gather troops at Fort Laramie for the proposed expedition. Portions of the 7th Iowa remained there, joined by a detachment of the 16th Kansas Cavalry, portions of the 1st Battalion Nebraska Cavalry, and a detachment of the 11th Ohio Cavalry. Elsewhere on the Oregon road Company E, 11th Ohio Cavalry, guarded Camp Marshall; Company H, 11th Ohio Cavalry, held Camp Mitchell; Company G, 11th Ohio Cavalry, lived at Platte Bridge; and the bulk of the 11th Kansas Cavalry camped nearby. At Camp Rankin near Julesburg were two companies of the 3rd United States Volunteers, along with detachments of the 7th Iowa Cavalry and Pawnee Scouts.

Brevet Brigadier General Henry's South Sub-District, in Colorado Territory, included Company F, 11th Ohio Cavalry, at Camp Collins; Company L, 11th Ohio Cavalry, and a company of the 1st Colorado Cavalry at Denver; two 1st Colorado companies at Camp Fillmore; Company K, 11th Ohio Cavalry, at Fort Halleck; and companies of the 1st Colorado at Junction Station and Camp Robbins. A company of the 7th Iowa Cavalry camped at Buffalo Station.

Along the Santa Fé road, the District of the Upper Arkansas, Brevet Brigadier General Ford commanded significant forces in Kansas. At various places he had units of the 2nd United States Volunteers, a company of the 11th Kansas Cavalry, another company of the 7th Iowa Cavalry, the 2nd Colorado Cavalry, unassigned recruits of the 3rd Wisconsin Cavalry, and a company of the 12th Kansas.[23]

These troop dispositions demonstrated quite a gathering of strength along the overland roads. Many units, new to the task at hand, had arrived; most were strung out in company or detachment strength, though the major posts blossomed with the increase of soldiers. The Oregon road as far as Julesburg and Laramie, the overland road to Salt Lake, the road to Denver, and the Santa Fé road now seemed relatively, if temporarily, clear. At the same time, tribesmen gathered in the far north sent small raiding parties against the lightly held portion of the Oregon road between Platte Bridge and the South Pass. There, detachments of the 11th Ohio Cavalry and some 11th Kansas took the sting.

On May 8 Colonel Moonlight reported from Platte Bridge that he had sent sixty men of the 1st Nebraska Cavalry to scour the area around Laramie Peak, west of the fort, but they found no hostile Indians. Yet the many depredations between Platte Bridge and the South Pass convinced him that "a large village of Cheyennes" were "on the Wind River and Big Horn [River]." Determined to move swiftly, Moonlight "concentrated" an "available force with eight days' rations" to "strike that village by rapid night marches." With five hundred cavalry—four hundred from the 11th Kansas Cavalry alone—and detachments of the 11th Ohio and 7th Iowa, and guided by Jim Bridger, he tried to find the foe. The Indians eluded him, moving over to the Big Horn and Pow-

[23]Ibid., pp. 274–77.

der Rivers. Moonlight's fruitless expedition traveled about 450 miles, returning to Fort Laramie May 21.[24]

Also early in May, Captain Jacob L. Humfreville, Company K, 11th Ohio Cavalry, reported from his station at Fort Halleck that "no Indians in this vicinity have come from the direction of the Sweetwater" to the north. In fact, at the moment, all remained quiet at Fort Halleck. Humfreville's scouts knew of only thirty lodges of friendly, trustworthy, and helpful Arapahos, "from Laramie" who camped about nine miles away where they had "plenty" of game and could support themselves. But up north, along the North Platte, raiders continued their work. On May 28 a detachment of the 11th Ohio ambushed Cheyenne raiders for a change when they attacked a wagon train. Troopers hidden in the wagons opened fire and drove off the surprised warriors.[25]

Meanwhile, Connor reported to Dodge that his "troops at Laramie and vicinity" were "nearly out of ammunition." At the same time Dodge continued to do everything he could to forward horses and corn to Connor. But the corn often failed to reach its destination, being requisitioned along the way by officers without authority to do so. Colonel Samuel Walker, of the troublesome 16th Kansas, claimed he had permission for the eighty thousand pounds he took.[26]

On May 10, Pope passed along a blockbuster order from the War Department that threatened the buildup of troops then taking place along the overland roads. He ordered Dodge to "muster out or discharge . . . all officers and soldiers . . . whose term of service will expire prior to May 31, 1865." This was at a time when Dodge and Connor wanted more cavalry for their planned expeditions, not fewer. Dodge immediately protested to Pope, who passed the word along

[24]Ibid., pp. 373, 501; pt. 1, pp. 255–56; Hafen and Young, *Fort Laramie*, 332; McDermott, *Frontier Crossroads*, 46.

[25]*O.R.*, I, 48, pt. 2, p. 344; Robrock, "The Eleventh Ohio," 40.

[26]*O.R.*, I, 48, pt. 2, pp. 285, 288, 455, 500, 524.

to Grant. In the end, Grant told Pope he could "suspend the order for mustering out troops as far as the exingencies of service may require." Grant added more troops would be sent out "soon to enable you to carry out your order." Dodge then told Connor that the "order to muster out of cavalry is suspended in your district. . . . If any such order . . . is out, stop it. . . . no cavalry will leave your district to be mustered out until I replace them, even if it is considered best to muster them out." But troops had indeed heard of the order, and failed to understand the suspension of it, especially the two Kansas regiments, the 11th and 16th. Now Dodge and Connor not only faced the supply problem, but also disgruntled troops who only wanted to go home. Connor had his hands full if he expected to mount his campaign.[27]

Connor kept at it. He sent two companies of the 3rd United States Volunteers to garrison the weak end of his line, Three Crossings, St. Mary's, and Sweetwater, all west of Platte Bridge. Detachments of the same companies also went to Camp Marshall and Deer Creek, between Laramie and Platte Bridge. They were to relieve cavalry, which would then gather at Fort Laramie as Connor readied his expedition. An exception was a squadron of cavalry that remained at Camp Marshall to assist telegraph operators in repairing the line when necessary. And in the distance, more reinforcements, the 6th United States Volunteers, left Fort Leavenworth for Fort Kearny.[28]

None of this made any difference to the Indians who remained determined to drive out the white invaders. Livingston reported from Fort Kearny on May 19 that his forces in the East Sub-District were "too poor" to "run an Indian down" and he needed at the very least "average stock." He had to have capable horses since now "every station" on "the [Little] Blue" east of Kearny between Buffalo and Elm Creek

[27]Ibid., pp. 385, 453, 500–501, 514.

[28]Ibid., pp. 326, 441.

suffered Indian raids. A small detachment, fifteen men of the 3rd United States Volunteers, "sent without arms from Leavenworth were attacked, train captured, seven killed and missing, and rest all dangerously wounded." Cavalry went out to chase after the Indians, Livingston reported, "but have little hope of overtaking them with such unserviceable stock as we have." Actually, it appeared that two died and six were wounded; the lieutenant in charge of the group requested an investigation and punishment of the "unworthy" official who sent them on their way unarmed. Connor so ordered; Livingston carried out what investigation he could.[29]

On the other end of the Oregon road, from Sweetwater, Johnson told of detachments from two 11th Kansas companies (D and I) on their way to Three Crossings, not knowing the place was surrounded by Indians because the telegraph was down. But the wire had been up long enough to alert the garrison at Sweetwater. The Indians pulled back when eighty-five troopers of the 11th Kansas, led by Captain James E. Greer, came on the scene. They had covered the forty miles from Sweetwater as quickly as they could, and on the way found fifty feet of telegraph down near Split Rock. The next morning, May 21, Greer took twenty men and followed the raiders' trail for fifteen miles, but failed to find them. Greer assumed they had gone north to Wind River. Raiders also tried, unsuccessfully, to run off the horses at Sweetwater. Meanwhile, Colonel Preston B. Plumb, 11th Kansas, fought other raiders just seven miles from Deer Creek.[30]

The raids along the Oregon road north and west of Fort Laramie continued almost constantly. On May 22, Connor heard that two hundred Indians attacked Deer Creek and, though repulsed, got away with twenty-two horses. Captain Henry C. Bretney, Company G, 11th Ohio, reported to

[29]Ibid., p. 524; pt. 1, pp. 273–74; Brown, *Galvanized Yankees*, 23–27.

[30]Unrau, *Tending the Talking Wire*, 237–47; *O.R.*, I, 48, pt. 1, pp. 286–87.

Colonel Moonlight, commander of the North Sub-District, that on May 26 Indians had tried unsuccessfully to take the herd from Sweetwater. Two days later raiders returned and took four horses and two mules. The next day about 150 Indians fired the buildings at St. Mary's station, but the tiny garrison of five men of Company G, 11th Ohio, escaped to South Pass. They lost everything but their guns and the clothes on their backs. Of the two horses at St. Mary's, the Indians got one, and the defenders killed the other to keep it from the raiders. Indians also cut four hundred yards of wire and burned the poles. On June 1, they cut the telegraph again and absconded with another hundred yards of wire. From Utah, Dodge reported on May 25 that "Indians attacked stage stations on Green River, west of both Bridger's and the South Pass, and carried off their stock."[31]

Spring finally came to the Overland road, and on May 19th, Sergeant Hull reported from Fort Halleck that emigrants were moving through, and "some camp close." On the 22nd a drove of "4,000 to 5,000 sheep go past, going . . . to California." An ox train passed by on the 25th, and the next afternoon the California troops from Utah, ordered to Fort Laramie by Connor, arrived heading east. But the most excitement came May 17, when an outlaw, one Bob Jennings, killed a frontiersman, Hod Russell, and was subsequently captured by Bill Comstock, a frontier scout and hunter. Taken to Fort Halleck, Jennings was tried, pled guilty, and hanged on May 21. Unrepentant to the end, Jennings's defiant last words were "Hurrah for Jeff Davis and the Southern confederacy."[32]

With renewed raids on much of the Oregon road from eastern Nebraska to the Green River in Utah, Connor closed

---

[31] *O.R.*, I, 48, pt. 1, p. 294; pt. 2, pp. 540, 554, 596.

[32] Hull, "Soldiering on the High Plains," 36–37; Brown, *Galvanized Yankees*, 202–3. Soldiers administered law where there was no civilian court. Presumably Bill Comstock got the $1,000 reward on Jennings head.

it north and west of Julesburg on May 30. He ordered that "no more trains of emigrants, freighters, or others not in government employ" should use the road, but instead would "be required to travel west on the Overland Mail road" past Fort Halleck and west through Bridger's Pass. He continued, "orders have been issued . . . to organize trains . . . not less than 100 wagons each." Even on the overland road, travel could be dangerous and travelers should be well organized. But they could not use the Oregon road.[33]

Also in late May, so august a person as the speaker of the House of Representatives, Schuyler Colfax, with "other gentlemen" of Congress, braved the dangers of the Oregon road on a fact-finding mission. From Atchison, Kansas, as he began his journey on May 22, Colfax reported to the secretary of War. He wrote, "Indian outbreak alarms freighters and emigrants on the plains," and "cavalry re-enforcements seem much needed in this department." Doubtless Connor convinced Colfax of this, for Connor, who had visited Dodge in St. Louis, traveled along with him to Julesburg. Also with the party was newsman Samuel Bowles, who found Connor "most fit and efficient for restraining the Indians." Bowles claimed Connor an "intelligent and accomplished" man. The group also included another prominent New England newsman, Albert D. Richardson. Colonel Livingston provided an escort of "ten mounted men" from the 1st Nebraska and details from the 3rd United States Volunteers. Two days later, from Fort Kearny, Colfax notified Stanton that "indications are that Indians, broken up in small forces, intend attacking [the] whole stage line from . . . Missouri River" west. Dodge and Connor must have been pleased if they knew how Colfax alerted the secretary of War to their predicament. But Colfax's mission would not be so agreeable. This Congressional delegation intended to "inquire

---

[33] *O.R.*, I, 48, pt. 2, p. 690.

into the present condition of the Indian tribes, and especially into the manner in which they are treated by the civil and military authorities of the United States."[34]

Just east of Kearny, Colfax and Connor's party ran into a fierce rain and hail storm that overturned wagons on the road, blew the baggage from atop the stage, and frightened the stage horses. Connor and his passengers quickly left the coach, lest it overturn, and were soaked by the storm. The escort managed to keep the stage upright and quiet its team. The party reboarded the stage, arrived at Kearny, and stayed there long enough to dry out. Both Bowles and Richardson agreed that the plains country was exciting. Bowles thought that it appeared all the men of the East were heading west; there were discharged veterans, politicians, land speculators, Mormons, freighters, railroad surveyors, and others in wagon trains as far as the eye could see. But they also saw the burned ranches, wrecked trains, and fresh graves, evidence of the Indian raids.[35]

Other parties claimed cavalry escorts besides the Colfax group, which Dodge found annoying. He complained to Pope on May 24 that at Leavenworth "five surveying parties under general contract, two Indian agents, one wagon-road company, and others"—all sought protection on the roads.

> It will take at least two regiments, part infantry and part cavalry, to supply the demand. This is getting to be a serious question. . . . If I give escorts I will have to bring troops here to do it. . . . The freight contractors to Utah and New Mexico have to be guarded, and the number of trains leaving on Government account will use up a small army.

Pope could do little except tell Dodge to "give escorts as far as you can without in any manner . . . impeding your military operations. More cavalry will be here soon."[36]

---

[34]Ibid., pt. 1, pp. 281, 1160; pt. 2, pp. 552, 555, 589; Madsen, *Glory Hunter*, 132–33; Varley, *Brigham and the Brigadier*, 213–15; Brown, *Galvanized Yankees*, 28.

[35]Brown, *Galvanized Yankees*, 30–32.

[36]*O.R.*, I, 48, pt. 2, p. 665.

Also, Dodge heard to his dismay that Sully's column—originally ordered to move west from the Missouri River and establish a post on the Powder River in conjunction with Connor's planned move north from Fort Laramie—would not be available. Pope told Dodge on May 29 that Sully instead would have to campaign north to Devil's Lake, Dakota Territory. So, Pope said, "Connor must therefore attend to the Powder River post, and must make an expedition north or northeast from Laramie." Pope added, "Connor must finally deal with these Indians this summer." By way of compensation for the loss of Sully, Pope would forward "all the troops you wish for that service, but it must be done by August."[37]

In the south, the offensive along the Santa Fé road that Brevet Brigadier General Ford had undertaken ran into many obstacles not unlike those faced by Connor. But Ford had the additional complication of Indian agent Jesse H. Leavenworth, who was determined to protect the friendly Comanches and Arapahos in his charge. He had strong political backing in Washington and proved quite influential. By the end of May, a strong movement with the object of making peace with western Indians, rather than fighting them, made itself felt. In Dakota Territory, Governor Newton Edmunds, who also was "*ex officio* superintendent of Indian Affairs," was determined to treaty with the Sioux. James Harlan, President Johnson's secretary of the Interior, demanded that the secretary of War inform him of any military "instructions or orders . . . relating to the Indians" anywhere in the West be sent to him. Armed with reports by Congressional teams then on the roads, the peace advocates generated serious Indian policy debates between the War and Interior Departments. Almost immediately, Ford's expedition was cancelled.[38]

---

[37]Ibid., p. 665.

[38]Ibid., pp. 661–65. See the thorough discussion of Pope's Indian policy in Peter Cozzens, *General John Pope: A Life for the Nation* (Urbana: University of Illinois Press, 2000), 255–59.

Major General Alexander McDowell McCook arrived at Fort Larned on May 30. McCook joined the Congressional committee investigating Indian affairs in "Kansas, New Mexico, &c." He told Pope that the committee was "anxious to carry out your views about Indian affairs," including moving the Indians to reservations "and keeping white men away from them." Agent Leavenworth and the committee believed that peace could be made with the tribes by keeping them south of the Arkansas River. The Santa Fé road would be open except for stray Sioux and Cheyennes "supposed to be on the south waters of the Platte." So, "in your name," McCook wrote, "I have suspended Colonel Ford's expedition." There were also military reasons for doing so, he continued. Ford did not have enough men "to accomplish anything"; the Comanches in the area were not hostile, so war with them was "not desirable"; if the campaign were cancelled the Indians could be put on reservations south of the Arkansas; "an extensive war . . . would require 6,000 men and cost millions" of dollars; and while a war was in progress the road would be "poorly protected." Ford's campaign against the Comanche, Kiowa, Cheyenne and Arapaho tribes was off.[39]

Two parts of the military operation designed to keep the overland roads open had changed. Sully was detoured north up the Missouri River to Devil's Lake in Dakota Territory, and would not assist Connor, and Ford would not campaign southwestward along the Santa Fé road. The brunt of any proposed conflict would fall on Connor. Affairs in his District of the Plains remained volatile.

---

[39] *O.R.*, I, 48, pt. 2, pp. 707–8. McCook was a career officer and corps commander at Stone's River and elsewhere. Relieved of his command because of alleged failures at Chickamauga, he was on duty at the defenses of Washington when he temporarily was assigned to the Congressional committee.

CHAPTER TEN

Horse Creek Blunder; Moonlight's Mistake

Mrs. Lucinda Eubank and her infant son, Willie, captured by Cheyenne raiders along the Little Blue River the previous August, turned up at Fort Laramie the middle of May 1865. Two Face and Blackfoot, Sioux chiefs, had purchased the captives thinking they could be traded to the whites for ammunition or other wares. Two Face stole Mrs. Eubank and her child away from Blackfoot and raced to a Sioux village some ten miles from Fort Laramie, where peaceful Indians camped in an effort to avoid the trouble along the Platte. Collins had relocated the Oglala there during the winter. Charles Elston, who headed tribal police, arrested Two Face and took Mrs. Eubank, Willie, and the chief to Laramie. Mrs. Eubank, "ragged and weak, told of the brutality of the two chiefs." Just a few months earlier, Nancy Morton had been rescued, but in that short time things had changed at the fort. Colonel Moonlight lacked the calm temperment of Colonel Collins, and also his good sense.

Mrs. Eubank and Willie fortunately fell under the care of the wife of Captain Fouts (7th Iowa). She relayed her tale to both Colonel Moonlight and Lieutenant Colonel William

Baumer, of the 1st Nebraska Cavalry. They were incensed by what they heard and determined to act quickly. Two Face was already in hand, and Blackfoot was soon arrested as well. Colonel Moonlight reported to General Connor that he ordered the two Indians hanged "with a trace chain" after hearing Lucinda Eubank's story.[1]

William G. Bullock, the sutler's agent at Fort Laramie, vigorously protested the hanging because he knew that the peaceful Sioux camped nearby had become very uneasy. They had recently resented the hanging of Big Crow, who had distressed Nancy Morton and who had been saved from death by Colonel Collins. But Collins was now gone, and in the end Big Crow was hanged with a heavy weight attached to one leg. His body still dangled from the gallows, with the weighted leg now gone, when Two Face and Blackfoot met their fate next to him. The Sioux, some of whom had camped near Laramie for years, were ready to believe that peace with the whites could mean death as easily as war. Neither Colonel Collins nor General Mitchell were on hand to counsel otherwise. Moonlight, along with others, would all too soon pay for his ineptitude and anger.[2]

George Bent and his Cheyennes camped that spring on the Tongue River, west of the Powder River, both of which were tributaries of the Yellowstone. At that time Bent wrote, "the Indians lived just as they had in the old days, before the whites came. There were all kinds of ancient customs, ceremonies, and dances." Meeting in council, the chiefs felt the ponies were "nearly fat enough to be used," and raiding par-

---

[1] *O.R.*, I, 48, pt. 1, pp. 276–77; Ellenbecker, *Tragedy at the Little Blue*, 8–9; Becher, *Massacre Along the Medicine Road*, 370–72; Nadeau, *Fort Laramie*, 177–78; McDermott, *Frontier Crosswords*, 47–48. Colonel Moonlight asked no superiors for permission to execute the captured tribesmen.

[2] Agnes Wright Spring, "Old Letterbook Discloses Economic History of Fort Laramie, 1858–1871," *Annals of Wyoming* 13, no. 4 (October 1941): 243–44; Becher, *Massacre Along the Medicine Road*, 372–73.

ties could start out for the Platte. They were supposed to scout the best place for a "grand raid" to take place sometime in June. Bent noted that in addition to Cheyennes under Dull Knife, White Bull, and Roman Nose, the large village included Arapahos, Red Cloud's Oglala Sioux, Little Thunder's Brulé Sioux, and some Miniconjous and Sans Arc Sioux. Bent joined about a hundred Northern and Southern Cheyennes who intended to assault along the North Platte Road. Sioux raiders left at the same time, moving farther east.[3]

Bent's party struck the Platte River about thirty miles below Platte Bridge. On May 21, they approached the strongly stockaded and garrisoned Deer Creek station across the river. The raiders swam their horses across and attacked the station, firing at it all day. Bent said the soldiers stayed inside while the Indians ran off all the horses. According to Bent, the Cheyennes took no casualties. Bent noted there was a report that the raiders were led by Bill Comstock, the hunter, but Bent believed the soldiers mistook him for Comstock, though he wore paint and dressed like the other warriors. Bent denied that any troops came out and drove them across the river; since the river was in flood, the troopers would not follow tribesmen who swam across. "This is all fiction," Bent wrote.[4]

Next, the Cheyennes moved up to Platte Bridge and exchanged fire with the soldiers there. Along with "young Wolf Chief," Bent went up on the bluffs across the river and examined the post through field glasses taken in a previous raid. They saw a number of tents all around the stockade, and it appeared "quite a number of soldiers [were] stationed"

[3]Hyde, *George Bent*, 194–201.

[4]Ibid., 204–5; McDermott, *Frontier Crossroads*, 47; Hyde, *George Bent*, 205. Comstock could not have been involved. He was at Fort Halleck that May (see chapter 9) and also scouted for the 1st U.S. Volunteers. The Cheyenne killed him a year later; he was no friend of theirs. Brown, *Galvanized Yankees*, 201–3.

there. They decided Platte Bridge would be a good place "to make the big raid" the chiefs had in mind for June.[5]

Then they discovered a wagon train moving up toward Platte Bridge on the south side of the river. Hiding in a willow thicket, they watched as the teamsters corraled for the night and took their stock down to the river for a drink. At that point the tribesmen charged; the teamsters fled back to their wagons; their cavalry escort opened fire "but their shooting was poor and the range too great." The raiders stole the mules and took them across the river. "In five minutes the whole affair was over." The mules were "big strong fellows, many of them branded U.S." The next morning Bent and the Cheyennes rode back north, "having taken all the stock we could handle without difficulty."[6]

On Saturday, May 27, tribesmen "in considerable force" attacked Rocky Ridge station along the Sweetwater, ran off the stock, and cut the telegraph, reported Colonel Preston B. Plumb of the 11th Kansas. He heard nothing more until Wednesday, May 31, when a messenger from Sweetwater station told him that Lieutenant Caspar Collins and two others from the 11th Ohio had left Three Crossings earlier for Rocky Ridge. They found the station in flames and prudently returned to Three Crossings, not knowing the fate of the four or five men of the 11th Ohio who had been on duty there. Then, on Monday, May 29, "about 40 Indians" tried to stampede the herd at Sweetwater, getting four horses and six mules. On Wednesday, May 31, Plumb sent Lieutenant Henry C. Bretney and eight men of Company G, 11th Ohio, to Sweetwater, then to Rocky Ridge if Bretney thought it safe. He also sent Captain Louis F. Green with sixty men of the 11th Kansas to follow them to Rocky Ridge to replace the

[5]Hyde, *George Bent*, 205.

[6]Ibid., 205–7. See also Hervey Johnson's report in Unrau, *Tending the Talking Wire*, 247.

telegraph and rebuild the station. After an overnight ride, the Ohioans found that a company of the 1st Nevada, up from Fort Bridger, had just begun to rebuild the station. Plumb also ordered Captain A. Smith Lybe with five wagons and his company of the 3rd United States Volunteers to assist Green. He also sent rations for Bretney's 11th Ohio, "they being out." Plumb asked Fort Laramie to forward rations "at once" to the 11th Ohio and the 3rd United States Volunteers, reminding Colonel Moonlight at Fort Laramie it took twenty days to reach South Pass.[7]

Busy raiders stole stock from Sweetwater on May 28. They took others from Fort Laramie's sawmill at Laramie Peak. They hit a wagon train south of Platte Bridge on the 29th, and the next day attacked Three Crossings and tore down the telegraph. Those raiders harassing the Sweetwater River portion of the Oregon road moved south through Sage Creek Valley to hit the Overland road. Lieutenant James A. Brown, Company K, 11th Ohio, detailed his experience to Captain Humfreville. He reported he left Fort Halleck on June 2 with thirty-one troopers, following orders to reopen the mail route as far west as Fort Bridger in Utah Territory. The small party also included a member of General Connor's staff and an agent of the Overland Mail Company. They found Sage Creek station deserted, then four miles later the bodies of two emigrants, one scalped. The next two stations, Pine Ridge and Bridger's Pass, were also deserted. At the fourth station, Sulphur Spring, they discovered the herders and stage drivers, with the company's stock intact, but the Indians had gotten away with the animals from Bridger's Pass station. Brown learned that the stations further west

---

[7] *O.R.*, I, 48, pt. 2, pp. 724–25. See also Bretney's report, in pt. 1, p. 294; McDermott, *Frontier Crossroads*, 49. Both Caspar Collins and Henry Bretney were promoted May 1, Collins to 1st lieutenant, Bretney to captain. Their commissions had not reached them at this time; *Collins Family Papers*, item 85, also Reid, *Ohio in the War*, vol. 2, 818. Rocky Ridge station sometimes was called St. Mary's station.

were untouched, so he turned back east, dropping off four or five men to garrison the deserted posts. By then the troop had with them two mail coaches and enough stock to replenish the stations. Brown and the balance of the command returned to Fort Halleck. Meanwhile, Speaker Colfax and his party, with escort from Company F, arrived at Halleck June 6.

Two days later raiders attacked the Sage Creek station again. The tiny garrison of five 11th Ohio troopers fought for an hour, but ran out of ammunition. With two "civilians" they made a run for it through a gauntlet of Indians. The two who survived managed to reach Pine Ridge station, though they were wounded; two others were killed, and one was captured. The "citizens" went missing. Next, along with their fellows from Pine Ridge and Bridger's Pass, the soldiers retreated west to Sulphur Spring. On June 9 they started back east led by Sergeant William McFaddin, who happened to be on escort duty with ten men of Company K, 11th Ohio. They found the mutilated bodies of their dead with the corpse of one of the civilians; Sage Creek station had been burned to the ground. Brown reported "ten of the men have returned to" Fort Halleck, "the balance are doing all they can to keep open the road, but the force is inadequate to cope with the number of Indians" along the stage line. Reinforcements would not arrive until another week passed.[8]

Not all the raiders had moved south to the Overland road. Tribesmen also continued to trouble the Oregon road. First Sergeant Samuel B. White, Company G, 11th Ohio, reported to Colonel Moonlight at Fort Laramie that a few Indians appeared on the banks of the Platte River at Platte Bridge,

[8] *O.R.*, I, 48, pt. 1, pp. 295–96; Hull, "Soldiering on the High Plains," 38–39; McDermott, *Frontier Crossroads*, 49. McFaddin, a private, may have been a brevet or acting sergeant at the time, but in any event had charge of the escort. Lieutenant Brown formerly was a sergeant in Company A, 11th Ohio.

doubtless seeking to draw men out of the post. White dispatched a courier to Colonel Plumb, 11th Kansas, then ordered his soldiers to open fire on the Indians. A round from the twelve-pounder mountain howitzer sent the Indians scrambling over the bluffs. White next sent a corporal and ten men to the bluffs on the north side of the Platte to watch the Indians, and another corporal with another ten men on foot to guard the patrol's rear. Those on the bluffs saw an Indian attempting to cut the telegraph line, but drove him away. Plumb's detachment arrived early afternoon, and White's ten cavalrymen joined Plumb's troopers in pursuit of Indians. The soldiers returned to Platte Bridge early in the evening, having skirmished with tribesmen. One man of the 11th Ohio had been killed, but they returned with his body.

Plumb reported his version of this action too. He had been at Camp Dodge, "near Platte Bridge," and immediately mounted ten men, with another twenty to follow directly, from Companies A and F, 11th Kansas. While in pursuit they engaged in a running fight with the Indians, who subsequently turned and charged, then scattered when they got close. About sixty Indians tried to flank them, to cut them off from Platte Bridge, but at that point Plumb's other twenty troopers appeared and the Indians drew off. Plumb pursued them, but the Indians managed to ambush some of them, and two soldiers died: one from Company F, 11th Kansas, the other from Company G, 11th Ohio. The unfortunate Kansas trooper was scalped. The Indians drew off again, and Plumb called off the pursuit. He reported that the Indians were well armed, some with both rifles and revolvers, and had about twenty ponies in reserve.[9]

From the safety of division headquarters in St. Louis, General Pope acknowledged receipt of an order from Wash-

[9] *O.R.*, I, 48, pt. 1, pp. 296, 305–6; McDermott, *Frontier Crossroads*, 49–50.

ington that directed him to muster out the regiments recruited from rebel prisoners as soon as their places could be filled by other troops. Pope replied he could not "now replace them, as [he had] no infantry regiments in this division which [could] be spared." Those soldiers were all in "remote stations in the Indian country" and it would take "the whole summer to reach and relieve them." If the army wanted them mustered out, then he needed replacements "as soon as possible." If all the orders to muster troops out of service were enforced—not only the state volunteers whose terms of service either had elapsed or were about to, but also the United States Volunteers as well—his command would virtually be stripped of soldiers at a time when pressure was on to mount a campaign north into the heart of Indian country. The overland roads would be left undefended. Even though such discharges were in fact postponed for the time being, the future of the roads west looked bleak if the military forces all too soon melted away.[10]

If there was to be a campaign, it had to take place quickly. Pope, with this sense of urgency, told Dodge on June 3 that he "must deal" with the Indians and "establish the post at the Powder River." Pope would send more cavalry. "It is absolutely essential," Pope emphasized, "that this Indian force . . . be routed as soon as possible." Not just the specter of troops receiving discharges loomed large, but also other urgent matters too. Those parties sent out to construct the new wagon roads Congress had authorized "along the Niobrara and Little Cheyenne Rivers" would be unable to carry out their mission. "You know how important these roads are," Pope reminded Dodge, "and how deep the interest in Iowa in their completion." As projected, "these roads"—more properly, this road—would cut across country from east

[10] *O.R.*, I, 48, pt. 2, p. 751.

to west well north of the Platte but just south of the Black Hills, and would shorten the distance to the mines in Montana. Pope doubtless emphasized that project's importance since a month earlier Dodge had complained about furnishing escorts, that one included.[11]

Dodge heard from Connor on June 6. Connor urged him to send four regiments of cavalry and two of infantry, the cavalry to come west by forced marches. Connor would be at Fort Laramie by June 10, he said, and he would "move against the Indians" as soon as the cavalry arrived. Two days later Dodge replied that he had five regiments of cavalry that would leave Fort Leavenworth "this week," with two more to follow later. Infantry he would have to get "from the East," and made no promises about that. The cavalry, though, were "veterans from Sheridan's and Sherman's armies" and carried Spencer rifles. Such troops had no experience with western warfare and the hardships of western campaigns, obviously, but Dodge had high hopes. Besides, as Dodge reminded Connor, he wanted a force "in the Black Hills immediately." He asked, "Can you not send a good officer up there with 800 or 1,000 cavalry and get after" the hostile Indians now?[12]

By June 9, Dodge had responded to Pope's pressure to move quickly. Dodge assured Pope that he and Connor were "doing everything in our power to forward the expedition." Connor, ordered to "strip his line of cavalry," was doing just that. Dodge intended to replace those with other cavalry he had on the march. And with Sully's column out of the picture, Dodge planned to replace it with another column "which goes up Loup Fork, and thence north along east base of Black Hills. General Connor goes with other column along west base and up Powder River." Connor would command both columns. Dodge assured Pope adequate supplies were "well on their way."[13]

---

[11]Ibid., p. 756. [12]Ibid., pp. 799, 824. [13]Ibid., p. 846.

Dodge quickly put together the Sully replacement group. It included the 2nd Missouri Light Artillery, outfitted as cavalry, and eight companies of the 12th Missouri Volunteer Cavalry, all under the command of Colonel Nelson F. Cole. Their equipment included a train of 140 wagons and a section of three-inch rifled cannon. Dodge ordered them to leave from St. Louis for Omaha, Nebraska, "immediately." The directive went out June 10, and Dodge expected Cole's troops to reach Omaha on the 17th, where they would draw sixty days' rations. Though he had no choice, Dodge made a serious mistake by supplanting Sully, experienced in Plains Indian warfare, with the inexperienced Cole.[14]

Also on June 10 Connor, at Julesburg, assured Dodge he was "doing everything possible to hurry up the expedition." Yet many problems remained. "There is not a horse at Laramie [fit] for the service. No grass there." No corn had yet arrived. He had to cross the 16th Kansas Cavalry "over the Platte in a rickety scow." The 6th United States Volunteers were "100 miles east of here yet." The 16th Kansas needed clothing, as the "men are almost naked." But thankfully, his "two California companies have arrived at Laramie, horses in good order."[15]

That June, Dodge ordered the Sioux and Arapahos camped near Fort Laramie to be transferred to Fort Kearny. These tribesmen had not participated in the raids and were unable to hunt on the plains lest they be mistaken for hostiles. They depended on trade and handouts from the post for subsistence. Mitchell had called Dodge's attention to the problem in March. This group already was restless because of the hangings ordered by Moonlight. The move would get them away from the area that was under constant threat of

---

[14]Ibid., pp. 846–47, 849; Charles H. Springer, *Soldiering in Sioux Country: 1865*, Benjamin Franklin Cooling III, ed. (San Diego: Frontier Heritage Press, 1971), 2.
[15]*O.R.*, I, 48, pt. 2, p. 849.

hostile action, and perhaps keep them from joining their warlike brothers. Also, Dodge thought once they reached Kearny they might learn the rudiments of farming and save the government some money.[16]

Dodge failed to take into account the fact that these Sioux, already mistrustful of white intentions, would be apprehensive of a move that would bring their families so near the territory of their despised foe, the Pawnees. Dodge simply knew no better, nor apparently did any of his officers. Probably only Collins could have prevented such a blunder. Lieutenant Colonel Thomas L. Mackey, Collins's successor as leader of the 11th Ohio, for the moment in command at Fort Laramie, picked Captain William D. Fouts, 7th Iowa, veteran of the Mud Springs fight in February, to handle the move.[17]

So it was that Fouts's Company D, 7th Iowa, with detachments from Companies A and B, escorted 185 lodges of Sioux, numbering between 1,500 and 2,000 persons, eastward. Among the Sioux, Charles Elston's company of Indian police, uniformed by the government, kept order. The Sioux carried bows and arrows as well as some firearms. Supply wagons and ambulances accompanied the troops and tribesmen. Lucinda Eubank and her son Willie, as well as the families of Captain Fouts and Lieutenant Jeremiah H. Twiggs, rode in the ambulances. On June 12, empty wagons belonging to nearby traders James Bordeaux and George Beaubais joined the expedition, using the military escort to protect their resupply mission. The cavalry traveled in the van, the wagons and ambulances followed, and in the dust behind all came the Sioux. The Sioux considered that another indignity.[18]

---

[16]Ibid., p. 972; Hafen and Young, *Fort Laramie*, 333.

[17]Becher, *Massacre Along the Medicine Road*, 374; *O.R.*, I, 48, pt. 1, p. 322. Mackey had been promoted to lieutenant colonel May 1, and commanded the remainder of the 11th Ohio.

[18]Becher, *Massacre Along the Medicine Road*, 374; *O.R.*, I, 48, pt. 1, p. 322.

The Sioux carried arms partly because they would have to hunt while on the march. The army provided no rations for them. The troopers bore only empty guns, for Fouts had issued no cartridges to them. Just why that happened only Fouts knew. Perhaps the idea had been to prevent his soldiers from killing Sioux or perhaps to forestall unauthorized hunting on their part. Though at first the Sioux appeared to tolerate the move to Fort Kearny, their escort noted smoke signals from north of the Platte, and believed hostiles met with the ostensibly friendly Sioux at night. Some of the troopers also went into the Indian camp at night, especially to visit the young Sioux women. Such visits had not been unusual at Fort Laramie, but this time it seemed only to enrage the tribesmen. On Tuesday afternoon, June 13, Fouts and the escort pitched camp on the east bank of Horse Creek (where the ill-fated Treaty of 1851 had been concluded), the Sioux on the west bank. Captain John Wilcox, Company B, 7th Iowa, reported the Indians "had a dog feast, and 382 warriors sat in secret council."[19]

On Wednesday morning, Fouts ordered Wilcox to take the advance guard two miles east along the line of march, then halt to wait until the wagons closed up with the Indians behind, then resume the trek. The wagons no sooner came up than gunshots rang out in the rear. Wilcox, believing the Sioux had turned hostile, feared for the safety of the civilians, especially the officers' families and Lucinda Eubank and her child. He quickly corraled the wagons and issued cartridges to the soldiers. He learned by messenger that Fouts had crossed the creek to hurry the Sioux along, only to be shot and killed. Wilcox sent a cavalryman flying to Fort Mitchell, eighteen miles away, to report the incident and ask for help. Indians pursued the messenger.

---

[19]Becher, *Massacre Along the Medicine Road*, 374–75; *O.R.*, I, 48, pt. 1, p. 322.

When the remainder of the rear guard fell back to Wilcox's position, Wilcox supplied them with ammunition as well, and sent Lieutenants James G. Smith and Twiggs with sixty-five men to dig rifle pits. He and Lieutenant Dudley L. Haywood with seventy men "returned to the scene of the action." They found the body of Fouts, "stripped and mutilated." The Sioux fled to the Platte, "two or three miles away," and their women and children swam the river on ponies while warriors guarded the rear. Wilcox, through Elston, tried to get the help of any tribesmen who might still be friendly, but found none. Sioux charged the cavalrymen; dismounted, the troopers formed a skirmish line and repulsed the attackers. Other Indians flanked them and "closed on the rear." The cavalry mounted up and retreated "with desperate skirmishing back to the corral." The Indians drew off, and the "Battle of Horse Creek" was over.[20]

After replenishing their ammunition, Wilcox took a patrol of fifty men out toward the Platte to scout the Sioux, only to find they maneuvered to cut off the patrol. Wilcox returned again to the corral. Shortly after, Captain Jacob S. Shuman and a detachment of Company H, 11th Ohio, arrrived from Fort Mitchell. By then the Sioux were out of sight north of the Platte. They left behind their lodges and possessions, which Wilcox destroyed. Troopers repaired the telegraph line the Indians had disrupted, and carried Fouts's body, four dead 7th Iowa troopers, and four wounded men to Fort Mitchell.[21]

The column resumed its march. Though only a few Sioux remained, mostly elderly and orphans, it still had to convoy the civilians and the wagons to Julesburg. At Camp Rankin,

---

[20] *O.R.*, I, 48, pt. 1, pp. 322–23; Ware, *Indian War*, 457.

[21] *O.R.*, I, 48, pt. 1, p. 323; pt. 2, p. 895; McDermott, *Frontier Crossroads*, 51. Connor criticized his district commander, Moonlight, who was at Fort Laramie, for not dismounting the Indians before sending them on their way with Fouts.

just outside the settlement, they left Lucinda Eubank and her infant son with the only woman in the place, a laundress, Mrs. Noble Wade. Lucinda confided to her that she was pregnant by Blackfoot, but would never bear the child. While at Julesburg, Lucinda Eubank put down the story of her captivity, actually written by Lieutenant Twiggs, because she was illiterate. The statement was witnessed by the district's judge advocate. On June 22, she and little Willie took an eastbound stage, perhaps feeling finally free.[22]

George Bent also heard of the the battle at Horse Creek. According to his sources among the Indians, the Sioux at Fort Laramie were in fact "uneasy" about the move to Fort Kearny because it "was in the country of their bitterest foes, the Pawnees." Then, on the march, "the soldiers of the escort began to ill-treat the Sioux" by selecting "a number of young Sioux girls" and taking them "to their own tents for the night. . . . This made the Sioux furious," and that precipitated the uprising.[23]

Upon receiving a telegraphic message about Horse Creek, Moonlight, at Fort Laramie, reacted in anger again. He "mounted every cavalryman" he could and galloped out of Fort Laramie to intercept the tribesmen who had killed Fouts. He had 234 cavalrymen initially, but 103 turned back as their horses gave out. The remainder rode down river about nine miles, then crossed to the north side of the Platte. On June 18, the column halted at Dead Man's Fork, about 120 miles east-northeast of Fort Laramie to rest the horses and troopers. At ten the next morning the Indians attacked Moonlight's camp and stampeded his horses. Moonlight could not continue the pursuit on foot. He estimated that of 131 horses, the Indians ran off 74, 51 from the 2nd California alone, 12 from the 11th Kansas, 8 from the 11th Ohio, and 3 belonging to the 16th

[22]Becher, *Massacre Along the Medicine Road*, 375–76.
[23]Hyde, *George Bent*, 209–10.

Kansas. In disgrace, Moonlight claimed the march back to Laramie was "tedious."[24] He certainly knew how serious was the loss of so many cavalry horses, considering the plans afoot for the expedition into Indian territory.

George Bent recorded that the fugitive Horse Creek Sioux had been joined by a hostile raiding party, and they had shadowed Moonlight's column. In camp, Moonlight had turned the horses out to graze, a mistake that sealed his fate. The tribesmen sent two hundred warriors to Dead Man's Fork to seize Moonlight's horses, and they got about two-thirds of them. Bent noted that these "Indian fighters" had to walk back to Laramie carrying their saddles and equipment, with virtually no rations. This "savage and footsore band" of troopers "finally straggled into Fort Laramie, and neither men nor officers forgave Moonlight for what he had led them into."[25]

The fugitive Horse Creek Sioux continued north to the Black Hills, but did not join the others gathering on the Powder River. They still rejected war with the whites, and in July they returned to Fort Laramie and surrendered. Fortunately for them, Moonlight was gone. These were mostly Brulé Sioux, a few Oglala, and some Northern Arapahos, united against war for a long time. They were among those who had parleyed with Mitchell and who Collins had nurtured at Laramie.[26]

Moonlight's ineptness brought a swift reaction from Dodge and Connor. Connor relieved Moonlight of command June 20, telling Dodge that Moonlight had "been unfortunate in his dealings with Indians" and he fully intended to "further investigate his conduct." Connor was doubly furious with Moonlight since the California horses he had brought east "were the

[24]*O.R.*, I, 48, pt. 1, pp. 325–26; McDermott, *Frontier Crossroads*, 51–52. Included in Moonlight's force were 87 troopers of the 2nd California, 20 of the 11th Kansas, 17 from the 11th Ohio, and 7 of the 16th Kansas.

[25]Hyde, *George Bent*, 211–12.

[26]Ibid., 208–9, 212.

best horses I had for the present service." Dodge went even further. Moonlight would not just be relieved and investigated, Dodge ordered him "mustered out of service."[27]

Moonlight's stupidity was trouble enough, but Connor had other problems too. Not only was he scratching to put his expedition together, but also he had to keep open transportation and communication routes in the face of constant Indian raids. Colonel Carrol H. Potter, commander of the 6th United States Volunteers, reported from Fort Halleck that he had ordered a company of the 1st Colorado to garrison stations along the Overland Stage Line east of Halleck with at least eight men each. He said Captain Humfreville, Company K, 11th Ohio, had scouted west of Halleck and had found large numbers of Indians near Sulphur Springs. All the stock had been driven from stage stations for a hundred miles west of Halleck, and while Humfreville was at Sulphur Springs, raiders drove off forty-seven more animals owned by the stage company. Humfreville could not catch them. He returned to Halleck with a stage drawn by cavalry horses carrying mail from the west. Potter thought even if he opened the road west as far as he could, there would not be, even with expected reinforcements, enough troops to make the road safe for both mail and travel. The reinforcements that he expected consisted of three companies of the 11th Kansas Cavalry under Lieutenant Colonel Preston B. Plumb. A fourth 11th Kansas company was ordered to Camp Collins. They had been told to be in place "as soon as possible."[28]

Within ten days Potter could report that there had been no

---

[27] *O.R.*, I, 48, pt. 1, p. 332; pt. 2, p. 951.

[28] Ibid., pt. 1, p. 328; pt. 2, pp. 921, 951–52; Walker, "Eleventh Kansas Cavalry," 335. Colonel Potter had been breveted brigadier general for meritorious service in the Civil War. Reverted to his permanent rank of colonel, he took command of the 6th U.S. Volunteers and had trained and equipped its ten companies; they arrived at Fort Kearny May 31, then garrisoned posts at Kearny, Cottonwood, and west. Three companies went on to Fort Laramie; Brown, *Galvanized Yankees*, 143–45. Potter commanded the South Sub-District under Connor, with his headquarters at Denver.

more depredations along the line and he did not anticipate any more trouble. Inspecting Camp Collins he "found the post in very poor condition; the [11th Kansas] troops not well disciplined." Potter also thought the "stock tenders" for the Overland Mail Company should corral their stock at night, in order to keep them from straying or being taken by Indians. Sometimes, including once from his own "eyesight," stock had strayed, been reported stolen, then afterward found unnmolested.[29]

Meanwhile up north at Sweetwater station, Corporal Johnson, Company G, 11th Ohio, wrote his sister in Ohio that a company of the 3rd United States Volunteers "came up, 14 of whom would stay at Sweetwater," while the remainder moved up the line farther west. He expected to be relieved, and by June 15 he wound up at Platte Bridge. He repeated a rumor—and that's all it was—that "most of the officers belonging to the 11th are going to resign," and wondered what would become of the enlisted men if they did. A few days later Johnson noted the "musketo" season was in full swing, and he had never encountered anything like it. He thought the 3rd United States Volunteers "a quiet civil set of fellows." Except for hearing of some Indian trouble at Sweetwater, all was quiet at Platte Bridge—for the moment, anyway.[30]

On June 19 another problem arose for Pope, Dodge, and Connor, who were still trying to put together the expeditions, keep the roads open, and handle expiring enlistments. The army's commander, General Grant, wired Pope that "the cost of keeping the amount of cavalry called for on the prairies is so enormous I wish you would cut down the expeditions all you can and direct that the animals be grazed as far as possible." Pope replied he would keep expenses down "as far as possible," but, obviously worried, he told Grant "the

[29] *O.R.*, I, 48, pt. 2, pp. 1010–11.

[30] Unrau, *Tending the Talking Wire*, 254, 259, 261–62.

Government will find it true economy to finish the Indian war this season so that it will stay finished." Pope's reply made some sense to Grant, who responded the next day "push out your expeditions . . . in your own way." The problem, Grant said, "was the difficulty and expense of procuring forage for so large a force" as Pope had on the plains.[31] With the eastern war finished, military budgets began to shrink. The troops on the plains would feel the result.

At the same time, Dodge kept pushing units west. On June 19 he told Connor "another brigade of cavalry (2,000) men" who were "fully equipped in every particular" was on the way. He meant Brigadier General Peter Stagg's Michigan brigade, the 1st, 5th, 6th, and 7th Michigan Volunteer Cavalry. A few days later Dodge mentioned yet another brigade was "arming at Leavenworth, and will get off to you next week." Connor wired Dodge that he was moving troops to Fort Laramie as fast as he could for the expedition. He mentioned the 16th Kansas was en route there, and four companies of the 6th United States Volunteers would depart Julesburg for Laramie "tomorrow." He also noted that a part of Cole's command had reached Omaha. On the 24th Connor himself left Julesburg for Laramie.[32]

When three companies of the 11th Kansas arrived at Fort Halleck on the 26th, Sergeant Hull and Company K, 11th Ohio, turned the post over to the Kansans and left for Fort Laramie on June 29. They would become a part of the expedition that Connor was then assembling. With snow still in banks along the way, they arrived at Laramie five days later, just in time for Independence Day festivities. But aside from the "national salute" fired at noon and music from Company I's band, the celebration appeared to consist of a "big drunk."[33]

[31] *O.R.*, I, 48, pt. 2, pp. 933, 946.

[32] Ibid., pp. 735, 938, 950–51, 961, 989. The Michigan troops were those veterans Dodge had mentioned previously.

[33] Hull, "Soldiering on the High Plains," 41.

To expedite travel on the roads west, Dodge, always the engineer, proposed to bridge some streams, especially the Platte. Lack of bridges, Dodge told Pope, "retarded the movement of troops very greatly." He asked for, and got, pontoon bridges to cross the Loup Fork near Columbus, Nebraska Territory, and the Platte, near Fort Kearny. He expected twenty million pounds of freight to pass along the Oregon road "this year." He also suggested the need for a bridge over the South Platte near Julesburg, as treacherous fords and high water caused many delays there. He thought the government ought to build permanent bridges, since "wooden pontoons" probably would last only a year. Of course Connor supported Dodge.[34]

During the last days of June, Dodge struggled to get Colonel Cole's column in place for the campaign, and succeeded by July 1. On June 27, the War Department once again reorganized administrative divisions. The military Division of the Mississippi came under Major General William T. Sherman's command, and included the military Departments of Ohio, Missouri, and Arkansas. Pope now commanded the Department of the Missouri, which included the states of Wisconsin, Minnesota, Iowa, Missouri, and Kansas, plus the territories of Nebraska, Dakota, and Montana. Sherman's headquarters would be in St. Louis, Pope's at Fort Leavenworth. Dodge remained in command of Kansas, Colorado, Nebraska, Montana, and Dakota west of the Missouri River. His headquarters were to be "in the field." This new military administration had few immediate consequences for the units on the plains, but Connor's command would be sorely tested in the summer and fall of 1865.[35]

---

[34] *O.R.*, I, 48, pt. 1, pp. 333–34; pt. 2, pp. 982–83, 993.

[35] Ibid., pt. 2, pp. 1003–4, 1024, 1030–31, 1112.

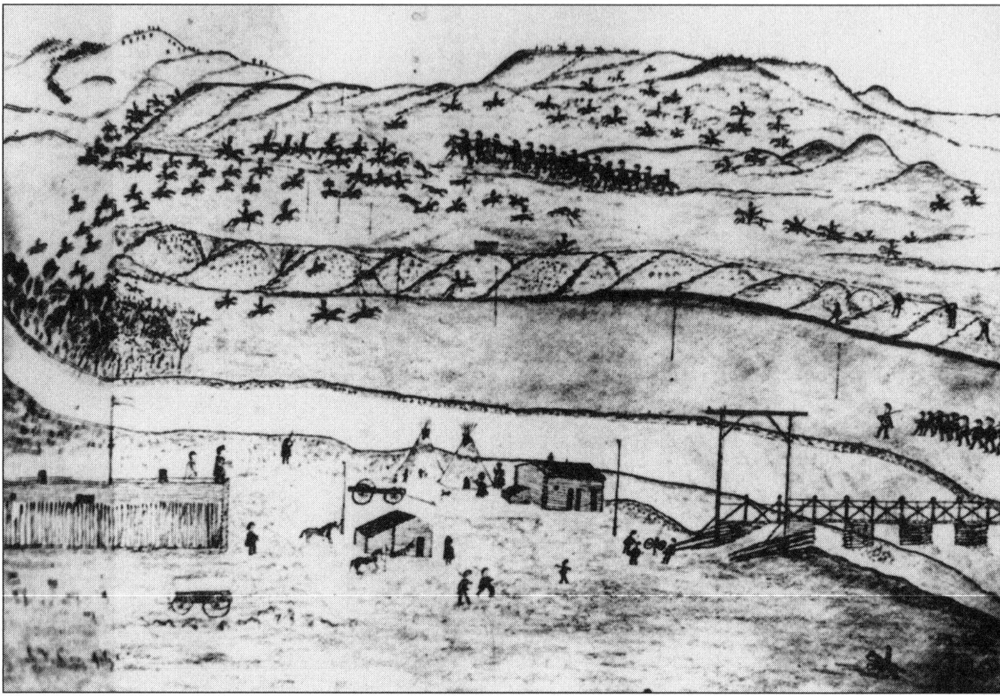

Beginning of the battle at Platte Bridge, July 26, 1865. Sketch by an unidentified soldier of the 11th Kansas Cavalry who was present. The small post, palisaded, is at the lower left, with Platte Bridge at lower right. Between the fortified post and the bridge are two tepees, where the extended families of Shoshoni and Cheyenne traders lived, the Lajeunesse and Boyds. A mountain howitzer is at the foot of the bridge. The group of horsemen on close order, shown very dark in the sketch, at the top center are Lieutenant Collins and the men of the 11th Kansas sent out to escort an incoming wagon train. Indians on horseback are shown swarming all around them. At the lower right is a squad of men with Captain Bretney to keep open a means of retreat for Collins's troop. *Photo courtesy of the Wyoming State Archives.*

CHAPTER ELEVEN

Death at Platte Bridge

Troopers from Kansas, Iowa, and California, along with regiments of galvanized Yankees, rendezvoused with the 11th Ohio at Fort Laramie in June 1865. Other units marched toward them as quickly as Dodge could move them west. Haste mattered, for any expedition into the heart of hostile Indian country had to be launched forthwith. The end of the Civil War in the East meant military manpower would melt away as volunteer enlistments expired, as would federal funds to support any offensive, with the government struggling to return to a peacetime economy. Dodge, especially, had wanted such a campaign to begin in early spring, but difficulties of weather, distance, supply, and availablity of troops postponed offensive activity.

Dodge and Connor planned to have Colonel Nelson F. Cole lead the right wing northwest from Omaha to the Black Hills, then west to meet the center and left wings near the Powder River. Lieutenant Colonel Samuel Walker would take his center column north from Fort Laramie, and General Connor would march his left wing from Laramie up the Bozeman Trail and eventually join the other campaigners on or near the Powder River. The three forces would then destroy the hostile Indians in the heart of their own country. By successfully doing so, Connor and Dodge believed they could assure the safety of the Oregon and Overland communication routes.

Connor, in whose hands the expedition's fate rested, faced great pressure to get underway. Ever since he took command of the department in January, Dodge impatiently sought to wage a punative campaign against hostile tribesmen, and, along with his commander, Pope, the two relentlessly urged Connor to take the field. Availability of troops and supplies on one hand, and high plains weather on the other, constantly frustrated them. The tribesmen proved merciless as well, continually disrupting both the Overland Mail road and the Oregon road with its telegraph. In June conditions on the Overland road proved as fragile as the discipline among some of the Kansas troops posted there. On the Oregon road, Sweetwater, Platte Bridge, Deer Creek, and other posts squirmed under constant threat. The Indians pinned down cavalry that Connor needed for his expedition and stole their animals whenever possible.

Fresh troops arrived, though much later than all the generals preferred, but difficulties with supply and forage remained. Companies E and K, 11th Ohio, gathered at Laramie by Connor's order, and waited for the expedition to begin. June 1865 passed, and still much remained to be done before Connor could mount his campaign. On July 1, Cole reported that his command departed Omaha that morning. Along with Cole's 2nd Missouri Light Artillery (equipped as cavalry) went eight companies of the 12th Missouri Volunteer Cavalry, with a section of artillery and 140 wagons to support the 1,400 men. But Cole was not happy. He complained to Dodge that his men had not been paid, some for six or eight months. He knew a paymaster was at Fort Kearny "with plenty of funds" and asked that he meet his troops at the Loup Fork of the Platte so his men could send money home to support their families. Dodge agreed.[1]

---

[1]*O.R.*, I, 48, pt. 2, pp. 1039–40; Springer, *Soldiering in Sioux Country*, 2.

On July 4, Connor directed Cole not to "receive overtures of peace or submission from Indians, but . . . attack and kill every male Indian over twelve years of age." That order applied not only to Cole. The day before, Connor told Dodge that no Indians could be trusted. "They must be hunted like wolves. The severest punishment is necessary before we can have any peace with them." Connor also instructed Colonel Carroll H. Potter, 6th United States Volunteers, who commanded his southern district from Denver, to "show no quarter to male Indians over twelve years of age." Perhaps continuing depredations on the mail and telegraph lines frustrated Connor at a time when he sought to get his expedition under way, but his activities in Utah and Idaho in 1863 had previously demonstrated his attutude toward tribesmen. His orders to kill male Indians over the age of twelve would return to haunt him.[2]

The remainder of Cole's orders from Connor laid out his route. He would go up the east base of the Black Hills to a place called Bear Butte, where he might encounter "a large force of hostile Indians," then turn around the north base of the Black Hills to "Three Peaks," and then northwest to Panther Mountain, where he might link up with Connor's force. Connor advised Cole to use caution, keep flankers out, even hire "a number of guides and scouts from among the Pawnee" if possible. Cole had by far the longest march of any column in the expedition.[3]

At Fort Laramie, Connor struggled to get his other two columns ready, and at the same time try to keep open the Overland Mail route. He fussed about supplies that failed to arrive. He learned of 11th Kansas troops who nearly mutinied at Fort Collins. On July 15, Connor reported the 11th Kansas as "insubordinate and disobedient." They acted that way

---

[2] *O.R.*, I, 48, pt. 2, pp. 1045, 1048–49.

[3] Ibid., pp. 1048–49.

because Colonel Moonlight had told them "they were entitled to muster out." Previously sent to Fort Kearny to be mustered out himself, Moonlight refused to cooperate with the "commissary of musters," but Connor ordered him mustered out anyway. Connor's best news was the arrival of his wife, Johanna, in mid-July. She would remain at Laramie until they both left in October. Dodge, meanwhile, continued to forward troops as fast as he could. He also told Connor that the Loup Fork and the Platte would be bridged "in a few days," and believed that such would help speed both supplies and reinforcements.[4]

Connor reported to Dodge that five Indians who had been with the group that murdered Captain Fouts "escaped" from that band and had fled to Fort Laramie. They told Connor that Indians at Bear Butte, along with others, planned to move to the Powder River. They also provided information concerning the tribesmen gathered along the Powder and Tongue Rivers. In return for their information and honesty, Connor threw the five in the guardhouse. A few days later Connor complained that not only the 11th Kansas but also part of the 1st Nebraska at Fort Kearny had mutinied. Connor ordered them suppressed "with grape and cannister" and their leaders tried by court-martial. On July 21, Dodge noted similar mutiny problems at Fort Leavenworth, but claimed he solved such with "new reorganization of commands." Dodge assured Connor "all troops going to the plains have one and two years yet to serve."[5]

By July 25, Connor reported that heavy rains had delayed subsistence trains. He complained that the 6th Michigan had arrived at Laramie, but only half were armed, and he had no spare weapons for them. Both the 6th Michigan and the

---

[4]Ibid., pp. 1051, 1059, 1060–61, 1063, 1064, 1067, 1072, 1077, 1084; Madsen, *Glory Hunter*, 133n. 43. Johanna had been with him at Salt Lake and Denver, and left there July 10 for Fort Laramie.

[5]Ibid., pp. 1086, 1112–13.

16th Kansas "demand their discharge," Connor said, but "I will manage them." The mutiny of the 1st Nebraska "subsided," and this time Colonel Livingston, who "was the cause of it," was mustered out as Moonlight had been before him. Dodge replied, "none of those troops can get out of service until we settle the Indian troubles," after which "their case will be considered." Dodge understood their "dissatisfaction," but they had to understand "they must cheerfully obey orders." They might grudgingly obey orders, but certainly would not do so "cheerfully." There were no difficulties with the 2nd California Cavalry that Connor ordered to Laramie from Utah. He replaced the Californians with three companies of the 6th United States Volunteers, with Colonel Potter to make headquarters at Camp Douglas, Utah.[6]

As Connor and Dodge discussed their problems, violence erupted northwest of Fort Laramie at Platte Bridge. Early in 1865, Colonel Collins had ordered the place stockaded. The station, though small, was "solidly built" and included warehouses, a telegraph station, a blacksmith shop, and barracks capable of housing about a hundred men—all surrounded by a pine log stockade from twelve to fourteen feet high "with heavy gates." Between the stockade and the bridge were a couple of tepees housing Indian traders, and a few yards north of the stockade a howitzer covered the bridge. The station had earned its name early from the permanent bridge across the Platte. Built of cedar logs resting on twenty-eight cribs filled with stones, all in all about nine hundred feet long and thirteen feet wide, the toll bridge charged from one to six dollars per team for wagons and stage coaches, depending on the condition of water in the river. The bridge had been built

[6]Ibid., pp. 1122–23, 1124–25; Brown, *Galvanized Yankees*, 146. Connor had built a model, comfortable post, Camp Douglas, overlooking Salt Lake City. In contrast to the adobe and log garrisons on the overland roads, duty at Camp Douglas was very pleasant.

in 1859 by Louis Guinard at a cost estimated well over thirty thousand dollars.[7]

When George Bent had earlier returned to Powder River, he found many other raiding parties had arrived laden with plunder. He claimed that at least one thousand soldier society warriors joined in a "Shield Dance." The chiefs, who decided their big raid would be against Platte Bridge, forbid any additional war parties from leaving camp. "Everyone," Bent wrote, "was busy preparing for war; all the charms worn in battle were being repaired, new eagle feathers were put in the war bonnets and on the shields." He continued: "Even the war ponies were painted and their tails tied up and ornamented with eagle feathers. The march to Platte Bridge was conducted just as the expeditions of olden times were." The soldier societies acted as police, leading the march and keeping order. When they drew near the bridge, a few scouts went out to survey the scene, while the others went into camp out of sight of the post. Bent claimed three thousand warriors were ready, "the biggest war party that I ever saw, and perfectly organized."[8]

Major Martin Anderson, 11th Kansas, commanded at Platte Bridge and had ninety-six officers and men on hand. Seventy belonged to the 11th Kansas; others included small detachments of the 11th Ohio, the 3rd United States Volunteers, and twenty-three transients on their way to other

---

[7]Hebard and Brininstool, *The Bozeman Trail*, vol. 1, 157–58; Brown, *Galvanized Yankees*, 35–36; Merrill, *Bound for Idaho*, 175; J. W. Vaughn, *The Battle of Platte Bridge* (Norman: University of Oklahoma Press, 1963), 10–11 (Vaughn also noted that Louis Guinard built and operated a toll bridge across the Sweetwater River just below Independence Rock in 1857); McDermott, *Frontier Crossroads*, 23–24, 42–43; Todd Guenther, "Pioneers Extraordinaire: A Most Unusual Wagon Train," *Overland Journal* 18, no. 4 (Winter 2000/2001): 4; Unruh, *The Plains Across*, 299, 493n. 128; Mokler, *Fort Caspar*, 10, 11, 15. Platte Bridge Station was built of adobe "sun-dried bricks" in 1858, stockaded in 1865, and rebuilt and enlarged, according to plans drafted earlier by Lieutenant Collins, in the summer of 1866 minus the stockade, then abandoned in October 1867.

[8]Hyde, *George Bent*, 213–15; McDermott, *Frontier Crossroads*, pp, 56–57.

posts. Lieutenant Caspar Collins, Company G, 11th Ohio, was among the transients, having brought mail up from Fort Laramie on the way to rejoin his men at Sweetwater. A few Indians tried to lure the soldiers out of the stockade on July 25, but prudent troopers fired a howitzer at them and they scattered. Next, some warriors swam the river and charged a party of soldiers about two miles east en route to the stockade. They were rescued by other troopers, who galloped out of the fort to aid them. An Indian, identified as High Backed Wolf, was killed as his compatriots fled back across the river. Warriors tried to stampede the cattle herd, but managed only to kill one steer, which soldiers dragged back to the stockade. High Backed Wolf was scalped.[9]

Meanwhile, fourteen men of the 3rd United States Volunteers, under Captain A. Smith Lybee, and Captain Bretney and six men of Company G, 11th Ohio, had encountered numerous Indians on the 25th while checking the telegraph line from Sweetwater to Platte Bridge. They took a defensive position nine miles west of Platte Bridge, near Red Buttes, waiting for nightfall to continue. They had overtaken a small wagon train—five empty wagons escorted by twenty-five men of the 11th Kansas led by Sergeant Amos Custard. The Ohioans warned the Kansans of Indians ahead and recommended Custard follow them to Platte Bridge after dark. But Custard was determined to rest his animals and claimed he had no fear of the Indians. He told the Ohioans that he and his men had fought in the South, and that was the real war. He implied that the Ohioans were too reluctant to engage

[9]Utley, *Frontiersmen in Blue*, 319; Grinnell, *Fighting Cheyennes*, 221–22; Hebard and Brininstool, *The Bozeman Trail*, vol. 1, 167; Nadeau, *Fort Laramie*, 189–90; Mokler, *Fort Caspar*, 19. High Backed Wolf was killed by Mich Lajeunesse, son of Charles Lajeunesse, a trader at Platte Bridge. Mich's sister, a Shoshone woman, celebrated High Backed Wolf's death as revenge for the death of her father, who was killed by hostiles a few weeks earlier; Guenther, "Pioneers Extraordinaire," 5; McDermott, *Frontier Crossroads*, 58, has a slightly different account of the death of High Backed Wolf.

the enemy. Having had much more experience with Indian warriors, the Buckeyes knew better, but Custard would learn the hard way. He intended to move out in the morning. During the night, Captains Bretney and Lybee and their troopers made it into Platte Bridge to alert the garrison of the presence of the Indians and the location of the wagon train.[10]

After dawn on July 26, the tribesmen decided on their strategy; as yet they had not discovered Custard's wagon train. They divided into three parties. While one group went downstream, another, with George Bent, hid behind the hills north of Platte Bridge, and the third formation, the largest, rode to the hilltops northwest of the bridge. Aware of the Indians but not of their overwhelming numbers, Major Anderson decided to send out a detachment of troops to bolster the small 11th Kansas wagon train escort. A bitter controversy followed over who would lead the detachment.[11]

In the end, Major Anderson chose Lieutenant Collins. He would take twenty-five men of Companies I and K, 11th Kansas. The question as to why a transient officer of the 11th Ohio should command Kansas troopers with whom he had not served and did not know failed to bother the major. Apparently there simply were not any Kansas officers to do the job. Kansas captain James E. Greer had been involved in a skirmish the day before, and three lieutenants, George M. Walker, William Drew, and James J. Clancy, complained of illness or thought of other reasons why they were not available.[12]

As far as the Kansas officers were concerned, their time of service was over. They were certain they would be mustered out soon, and wanted to return home alive. They had fought

[10]Vaughn, *Battle of Platte Bridge*, 33–34; Utley, *Frontiersmen in Blue*, 319; Hebard and Brininstool, *The Bozeman Trail*, vol. 1, 167, 183; McDermott, *Frontier Crossroads*, 59; Nadeau, *Fort Laramie*, 190; Mokler, *Fort Caspar*, 26.

[11]Hyde, *George Bent*, 217; Utley, *Frontiersmen in Blue*, 319.

[12]Vaughn, *Battle of Platte Bridge*, 55–56; Walker, "Eleventh Kansas Cavalry," 336.

well in Arkansas and Kansas since 1862 and arrived at Fort Laramie on April 9, where they learned of Lee's surrender. In addition, bad feelings existed between the Kansans and Ohioans. These were soldiers from the same Kansas regiment that had nearly mutinied at Fort Collins, and had refused to relieve other members of the 11th Ohio. Also, just two weeks earlier Captain Bretney and Captain Greer had disagreed over the command at Platte Bridge, at which time 11th Ohio troopers drew guns on some of Greer's soldiers. Kansans also believed ex-Confederates among the 11th Ohio had encouraged and cooperated with hostile Indians. On the other hand, Lieutenant Collins was familiar with area tribesmen, having been in the area since 1862.[13]

Captain Bretney believed Collins was chosen because he belonged to the 11th Ohio, so despised by the Kansans. As Collins's superior officer, Bretney advised him to disobey the order. But Bretney had not the rank to countermand it. Bretney did protest vigorously to Major Anderson using "very strong language," and also quarreled again with Captain Greer, giving him "a sound thrashing." Consequently Bretney spent a few hours under arrest. Not quite twenty-one years old and boyish in appearance, Collins had been teased about being afraid to fight Indians. Some thought he was determined to prove he was not a coward.[14]

First Sergeant Isaac B. Pennick, 11th Kansas, wrote in his diary that Captain Greer first received the order to take a detachment to meet Custard's wagons, and he, Pennick, took charge at Greer's request. When he reported to Major Anderson, Pennick learned that Lieutenant Collins "was going out alone," but Greer thought it best for Pennick's

[13]McDermott, *Frontier Crossroads*, has an excellent account of the Platte Bridge battle, 61–66; Utley, *Frontiersmen in Blue*, 320; Nadeau, *Fort Laramie*, 305–6.

[14]Vaughn, *Battle of Platte Bridge*, 57, 71; Brown, *Galvanized Yankees*, 37; Hebard and Brininstool, *The Bozeman Trail*, vol. 1, 172, quoting from the diary of First Sergeant Isaac B. Pennick, 11th Kansas Cavalry.

detachment to go along. That may have been the cause of Bretney's attack on Greer, who apparently dodged the assignment, and Bretney's argument with Anderson. Everyone else appeared to believe Anderson ordered Collins to take charge of the detachment, and it would seem that in fact he did, especially if Greer previously refused to lead it.[15]

About nine in the morning on Wednesday, July 26, Collins led twenty-five Kansas troopers out of the Platte Bridge stockade. Riding a large, borrowed gray horse, attired in a new dress uniform, and carrying two pistols borrowed from Bretney, Collins led the little detachment across the bridge and rode west for half a mile when the warriors executed their ambush. The soldiers apparently had not noticed tribesmen on the hills. When they came opposite a large party of Indians, "a couple thousand mounted warriors" swept "down into the valley." The troopers then wheeled around, and Bent's party dashed in to cut the troopers off from the bridge as the group of warriors from the east did the same.[16]

The Indians came "from the northeast and southwest, and every point of the compass," Pennick wrote in his diary. "It appeared as though they sprung out of the ground. They completely surrounded us." With no alternative, "we turned and charged into the thickest of them, drawing our pistols. . . . It was really running the gauntlet for dear life." Bent said "they had no time to stop and face us. As we rushed in among them, the air was thick with dust and powder smoke; you could not see a dozen yards and the shots and yells deafened the ears." Then, "as we went onto the troops, I saw an officer [Lieu-

[15]Pennick's diary, as quoted in Hebard and Brininstool, *The Bozeman Trail*, vol. 1, 167–68. Also see Service, *Life and Letters of Caspar Collins*, 16–22, Nadeau, *Fort Laramie*, 305–6, and Mokler, *Fort Caspar*, 27–29, for thorough discussions of the Collins situation.

[16]Vaughn, *Battle of Platte Bridge*, 56, 57; Utley, *Frontiersmen in Blue*, 320; Hyde, *George Bent*, 217; Nadeau, *Fort Laramie*, 191–93; Walker, "Eleventh Kansas Cavalry," 336–37; Ayres, *Hills of Highland*, 450–51.

tenant Collins] on a big bay horse rush past me. . . . His horse was running away with him." Collins "had an arrow sticking in his forehead and his face was streaming with blood."[17]

Captains Bretney and Lybee obtained Anderson's permission to support Collins with their small group and desperately tried to keep open an escape path. They used the howitzer as best they could. Young Collins had shouted a command to return to the bridge, and his troops, more or less in a column of twos, charged right through the fighting warriors. It was said that Collins, wounded in the hip, had paused to aid a fallen soldier when the arrow struck him in the forehead, and his horse apparently bolted. Pennick wrote "the Indians suffered dreadfully, as our pistols were pushed right against their bodies and fired, doing great execution." Bent remembered "the road for a mile or more was dotted with dead bodies, and at the point where our party struck the troops the bodies of men and dead horses lay in groups."[18]

Miraculously only five of the soldiers were killed, including Collins. Eight others had serious wounds, and all of the other twelve were hurt. Nearly every horse was wounded, and four were killed. Some warriors tried to rush the bridge, but the howitzer with Lybee and Bretney's force kept them away. The Indians retired to the hills, and as they did so their compatriots signalled that more soldiers were coming from the west. Sergeant Custard, with his wagon train, had heard the firing, and sent four of his men to investigate. They ran into warriors riding at top speed in their direction, but even so, three lucky ones made it to the stockade. Custard corraled his wagons as best he could. By the time Bent reached the wagons, "they were being attacked by hundreds of warriors,

---

[17]Pennick's diary in Hebard and Brininstool, *The Bozeman Trail*, vol. 1, 168; Brown, *Galvanized Yankees*, 38; Hyde, *George Bent*, 218–19.

[18]Utley, *Frontiersmen in Blue*, 320; Pennick's diary in Hebard and Brininstool, *The Bozeman Trail*, vol. 1, 168; Hyde, *George Bent*, 219.

who ran off the mules." The Indians charged in "swarms," while Custard's men "rolled volley after volley into them." Bent said the soldiers "stood off a thousand warriors for at least half an hour." Inevitably, far outnumbered, Custard and his men perished and their wagons were burned. Bent counted twenty-two white bodies, claimed only eight Indians died with "many more . . . wounded."[19]

Almost simultaneously, warriors cut the telegraph east of Platte Bridge. Lieutenant George M. Walker took thirty men of the 11th Kansas out to repair the line, but lost one dead and two wounded as they fled back into the stockade—their mission unsuccessful. With the telegraph down, Major Anderson sent brothers Mich and Noel Lajeunesse, the "two friendly Snake Indian scouts," to alert Deer Creek. Under cover of darkness, they made the twenty-eight-mile trek safely. On the morning of July 27, "hundreds" of warriors "were in sight on all the hills." The "Indians are very mad," Pennick wrote. They told some friendly Snake Indians that just as they wiped out the wagon train the day before, and because the soldiers "had killed and wounded heaps of Indians," they were going to kill "more white men today." But the garrison at Platte Bridge remained steadfast.[20]

Pennick described some "papers found on the battle ground yesterday." According to the sergeant, they read in part, "Blackfeet, Cheyennes, Arapahoes, Sioux, and a few Comanches are here now. They want to fight four days more. I was taken prisoner down on the Platte River. You killed a chief yesterday evening." The note continued, "they say they do not want to have peace. . . . They want your stock and want to fight. They are moving to battle." Just who might

[19]Utley, *Frontiersmen in Blue*, 320–21; Hyde, *George Bent*, 219–21; Pennick, in Hebard and Brininstool, *The Bozeman Trail*, vol. 1, 169; McDermott, *Frontier Crossroads*, 67–70; Brown, *Galvanized Yankees*, 38; Nadeau, *Fort Laramie*, 194–96.

[20]Pennick, in Hebard and Brininstool, *The Bozeman Trail*, vol. 1, 168–70; Hafen and Young, *Fort Laramie*, 335; Guenther, "Pioneers Extraordinaire," 5.

have left this warning on the field is unknown, but it probably was "written in a female hand." Those "papers" doubtless were found by troopers who went out in the late afternoon on Thursday, July 27, to try to bring in "some of the dead." Pennick and that detail found Collins and two others "in a dreadfully-mangled and cut-up condition." They counted twenty-four arrows in Collins, fifty-eight in another body. By sundown they safely brought in all five of their dead. Some fifty 11th Kansas troopers arrived from Deer Creek that same afternoon as reinforcement.[21]

How many tribesmen died in the Platte Bridge attack on Wednesday, July 26, is uncertain. Bent mentioned how the road was "dotted with dead bodies," and where his group "struck the troops the bodies of men and dead horses lay in groups." Later he claimed there was almost "no loss to the Indians." As just five soldiers were killed, one can wonder what Bent meant by "practically no loss" with so many bodies about. In the wagon train fight he noted "eight Indians were killed." Lieutenant William Y. Drew, 11th Kansas, wrote in his diary that he "heard" the tribesmen lost "over sixty killed and about one hundred and thirty badly wounded." He saw first hand the scalps warriors left on the ground, "which was a sure sign that their loss had been so heavy they did not think they had cause to exult over their victory." He counted "about forty lodge-pole trails," which tribesmen used as stretchers to carry off their wounded.[22]

Connor heard of the Platte Bridge attack on Thursday, July 27. He directed Colonel James H. Kidd to take four squadrons of his 6th Michigan Cavalry and another five squadrons under

[21]Pennick, in Hebard and Brininstool, *The Bozeman Trail*, vol. 1, 170; Brown, *Galvanized Yankees*, 41; *O.R.*, I, 48, pt. 1, p. 357, pt. 2, p. 1132; Walker, "Eleventh Kansas Cavalry," 339–40. See diary of B. F. Rockafellow, in LeRoy R. Hafen and Ann W. Hafen, *Powder River Campaigns and Sawyers Expedition of 1865* (Glendale, Calif.: The Arthur H. Clark Company, 1961), 169.

[22]Hyde, *George Bent*, 219, 221–22; Drew's diary in Hebard and Brininstool, *The Bozeman Trail*, vol. 1, 199; *O.R.*, I, 48, pt. 1, p. 358.

Captain William Crevy "by forced marches to Platte Bridge for the relief and assistance of that garrison." Most of these soldiers would make up part of Connor's "left" column in the expedition north, and Platte Bridge was on the way. Connor planned to move two days later with the rest of his column.[23]

By then, the attackers were gone. They had ridden north "excited about their day." While some "broke up into small war parties" and took off "in different directions to raid the roads," most, including Bent, returned to their village on the Powder River. They did so "to hold the usual summer medicine ceremonies." Some famous, or soon-to-be famous, warriors had been at Platte Bridge. Red Cloud and Crazy Horse had been among the Sioux, the fearsome Roman Nose with the Cheyenne. Certainly, Bent knew them all.[24]

From Platte Bridge, Pennick wrote on Monday, July 31, "our rations are out today. . . . things begin to look serious. If nothing turns up we will have to begin butchering and jerking beef for our subsistence. . . . Succor must come soon; this suspense is terrible." Late on Tuesday Pennick reported that the telegraph finally had been repaired; on Wednesday some of the 6th Michigan arrived, along with rations and ammunition, Pennick hoped, as the garrison was down to ten carbine rounds a man. Finally, on August 3, the disgruntled 11th Kansas left for Fort Laramie and home.[25]

---

[23]*O.R.*, I, 48, pt. 1, p. 357; pt. 2, p. 1127.

[24]Hyde, *George Bent*, 216, 221–22; James C. Olson, *Red Cloud and the Sioux Problem* (Lincoln: University of Nebraska Press, 1965), 25–26; Robert W. Larsen, "Red Cloud, Part I: The Warrior Years," *Montana: The Magazine of Western History* 47, no. 1 (Spring 1997): 30.

[25]Pennick in Hebard and Brininstool, *The Bozeman Trail*, vol. 1, 171–72. Colonel Kidd and the main body of the 6th Michigan had been ordered to halt at LaBonte station, to await the rest of Connor's force on August 1, and did not go on to Platte Bridge until August 3; James H. Kidd, *One of Custer's Wolverines: The Civil War Letters of Brevet Brigadier General James H. Kidd, 6th Michigan Cavalry*, Eric J. Wittenberg, ed., (Kent, Ohio: Kent State University Press, 2000), 153, 155. The "west" column, Brown and the Californians, departed for Platte Bridge from La Bonte August 4; Rockafellow's diary in Hafen and Hafen, *Powder River Campaigns*, 171.

CHAPTER TWELVE

Powder River

Connor's relief of Platte Bridge coincided with the beginning of the Powder River Campaign for the left and center columns. The right column, commanded by Colonel Nelson Cole, had already taken the field. The center column, led by Lieutenant Colonel Samuel Walker, comprised 600 officers and men of the 16th Kansas Volunteer Cavalry. Walker received his orders to leave Fort Laramie on July 28, the same time Connor expected to depart with the left column. Connor reported that his left column, under the nominal command of Colonel James H. Kidd, 6th Michigan, included 90 officers and men of the 11th Ohio, another 90 officers and men of the 7th Iowa, 200 officers and men of the 6th Michigan, and 95 Pawnee Scouts—or 475 troops in all. In addition, Connor mentioned a "west" column under Captain Albert Brown, 2nd California Cavalry. Brown had 116 officers and men from his 2nd California, and 84 Omaha scouts under Captain E. W. Nash, for a total of 200. Connor's numbers are suspect. He claimed Cole's right column had 1,108 officers and men, when in fact it had about 1,400; he mentioned 90 men of the 11th Ohio, when it numbered 130. Also along were 7 experienced guides, including Jim Bridger.[1]

[1] *O.R.*, I, 48, pt. 2, pp. 1129–30; Springer, *Soldiering in Sioux Country*, 2; Robrock, "The Eleventh Ohio," 45; H. D. Hampton, "The Powder River Expedition of 1865," *Montana: The Magazine of Western History* 14, no. 4 (October 1964): 12; (*continued*)

Connor "supplied" each column "with artillery." Walker's 16th Kansas, the center group, had "forty days' supplies on pack mules," to insure their mobility. The supply and equipment wagons, all 184 of them, followed Connor's column. Even so, by whatever count, 2,500 to 2,700 men, Connor and Dodge mounted the largest expedition of volunteer soldiers to fight Indians ever put in the field.[2]

Connor ordered Walker on July 28 to take his regiment through the Black Hills, cross the headwaters of the Little Missouri moving northwest to the Powder River, follow it to the north end of Panther Mountain, and then west "to the general rendezvous of the four columns of the expedition on the Rosebud River." Connor warned Walker to always have scouts out, to march with caution, to protect his stock, as the Indians would try to stampede them, and not to accept any peace overtures from Indians. He instructed Walker to "attack and kill every male Indian over twelve years of age," just as he had told Cole. Although Connor ordered Walker's center column to depart on its mission right away, it did not happen.[3]

Cole's right-hand column had left Omaha July 1 and was making its way much as Connor had directed. Part of Connor's left column, the 6th Michigan, actually got underway on July 28, ahead of the remainder, as it went to the relief of Platte Bridge, 120 miles away. By July 30, the remainder of

---

Brown, *Galvanized Yankees*, 186. Robrock notes that Marshall, promoted to major May 1, commanded the 11th when Lieutnant Colonel Mackey returned to Ohio on leave; *Collins Family Papers*, item 89. Brown claimed that in Connor's column "were the best cavalrymen then soldiering in the west." Palmer ("History of the Powder River Expedition," 204–5) provided slightly different numbers for both the center and left columns combined: 67, E Company, 7th Iowa; 60, E Company, 11th Ohio; 70, K Company, 11th Ohio; another 57, E Company, 11th Ohio; 61, M Company, 2nd California; 14, 2nd Missouri Artillery; 15, U.S. Signal Corps; 15, 11th Ohio as quartermasters; 75 Pawnee Scouts; 70 Omaha Scouts; 250, 6th Michigan; and 195 teamsters, for a total of 799, not counting the teamsters.

[2] *O.R.*, I, 48, pt. 2, p. 1130; Utley, *Frontiersmen in Blue*, 324. Varley, in *Brigham and the Brigadier*, 221–54, provides an excellent narrative of the Powder River campaign.

[3] *O.R.*, I, 48, pt. 2, pp. 1130–31.

the left and west columns were en route as well. But the center column, the 16th Kansas, balked. Many of its troopers demanded their discharge. On July 30 Walker asked for assistance to put down a mutiny, receiving it in the form of "two howitzers, double shotted" so that he could talk to his disgruntled men and threaten them "with grape and cannister." Detachments of the 11th Ohio and the 2nd California, with loaded weapons, assisted Walker and the howitzers. The men of the 16th gave in, and enough backed Walker "to maintain discipline." Seven leaders of the mutiny were put in irons pending court-martial. The center column left Fort Laramie at last on August 5.[4]

Connor led the left column north and west more or less along the Bozeman Trail, while the west column essentially covered his left flank. Connor left the overland roads largely in the hands of elements of the 3rd, 5th, and 6th United States Volunteers. Meeting no resistance, but finding many Indian trails, some recent, the force went into camp on the Powder River on August 11. Three days later the 6th Michigan began erecting the stockade that became Fort Connor, close to where the Bozeman Trail crossed the river. Connor and Kidd had selected its location, and Connor put Kidd in command. Kidd said of Connor, "he appears to be a strict disciplinarian and not an unpleasant man to be with although not sociable at all." Sergeant Hull and the wagon train, with Company K, 11th Ohio, and some Michigan troops as escort, arrived August 19.[5]

While the 6th Michigan built the new post, Connor sent patrols to search the vicinity. They fought several times with small parties of warriors, some doubtless returning from the

---

[4]Ibid., p. 1145; Springer, *Soldiering in Sioux Country*, 2, 5–22 passim; Utley, *Frontiersmen in Blue*, 324; Robrock, "The Eleventh Ohio," 44.

[5]Kidd, *One of Custer's Wolverines*, 158, 160–61; Hull, "Soldiering on the High Plains," 45. Connor kept tight control of his column on the march, revealing "shrewd understanding of cavalry requirements" and "the strengths and weaknesses of horses and men." Brown, *Galvanized Yankees*, 186.

Platte Bridge fight after raiding along the Overland and Oregon roads. In one of these fights Pawnee scouts ambushed a group of twenty-four Cheyennes, killing them all. They captured nineteen animals, mules and horses, ten of which belonged to the "Government," and some from the Overland Stage Line. They also found "white women's and children's clothing and 2 of the infantry coats issued by Colonel Moonlight last spring to the Indians who subsequently killed Captain Fouts and 4 soldiers of the 7th Iowa." The Pawnees claimed to have found white scalps among Cheyenne belongings, as well as both men's and women's clothing and a number of Ben Holladay's horses (branded "BH"). In another skirmish on August 21, Major Marshall and Company E, 11th Ohio, killed two tribesmen and recovered "twenty horses and mules . . . most of which are Government animals, together with several packs of plunder" that included "papers addressed to men of the Seventh Michigan, which show that the Indians" came "directly from the [Overland] road."[6]

Kidd met Major Levi G. Marshall, 11th Ohio Cavalry, and could not refrain from describing him, as he did not want to "forget him entirely." Here was

> a company of 80 good well-armed men commanded by a certain Marshall whose surname is Capt a man with a great deal of whiskers very little sense and no brains who says, "I ken jest take that air company o men . . . [and] jest lick any number o men you ken bring agin em." One of those meddlesome officers, self-conceited, ignorant men who are always successful in making themselves ridiculous—and their neighbors uncomfortable.

Kidd, who had attended the University of Michigan and rose from captain to colonel in spit-and-polish eastern armies—

[6]Hafen and Young, *Fort Laramie*, 338; Utley, *Frontiersmen in Blue*, 325; Grinnell, *Fighting Cheyennes*, 206–7; Fred B. Rogers, *Soldiers of the Overland: Being Some Account of the Services of General Patrick Edward Connor and his Volunteers in the Old West* (San Francisco: The Grabhorn Press, 1938), 180–81; Brown, *Galvanized Yankees*, 187; *O.R.*, I, 48, pt. 1, p. 358. The 7th Michigan was on the Overland road.

those of the Shenandoah and Potomac—fell for Marshall's own brand of humor. Previously, Marshall had commanded Company E, 11th Ohio. Promoted to major May 1, 1865, everyone still called him "Captain," a sign that he did not wear insignia of his rank. He was not the only 11th Ohio soldier who liked to poke fun at those they thought were greenhorns in the West: "stringing the Greeners," as one western writer put it.[7]

George Bent recorded that Pawnee scouts caught "several of our small raiding parties returning from the Platte and punished them severely." With a Cheyenne party ambushed by the Pawnees was Bent's stepmother, Yellow Woman (the younger sister of his birth mother, Owl Woman). The Pawnees killed her and four others, wrote Bent. "They may have killed twenty-four Indians in some other fight about this time," but not Cheyennes. The Pawnees knew otherwise. Bent also claimed the main body of Indians failed to realize Connor's force was on the Powder River at that time, and wondered why Connor had not followed one of the large trails north and surprised them.[8]

Cole's column, meanwhile, faced a number of problems along their march, but fought no Indians. Lieutenant Charles H. Springer, 12th Missouri Volunteer Cavalry, had fought Confederate guerrillas in Missouri and served in Tennessee, Alabama, and Mississippi. He and others spent a fair amount of time on the march hunting game. Along with other members of his regiment, he had no love for Colonel Cole. Nor did he like the July heat. "It was insufferable hot," he wrote in his diary July 13, and the men like him "who faced death in many hard contested battles in Dixie, and would sooner do it again, than suffer so intensely . . . in this inhos-

[7]Kidd, *One of Custer's Wolverines*, 157. Editor Wittenberg identified the company as Company F, when in fact the two 11th Ohio companies with the expedition were E and K. Marshall, commander of the 11th, was in the field with these two companies and was the former captain of Company E. For "stringing the Greeners," see Brown, *Woundrous Tales*, 87–105.

[8]Hyde, *George Bent*, 227–28.

pitable country." Once, their horses stampeded in a thunderstorm, but most were recovered. Then four days later, the weather was "exceedingly cold," and he was "not prepared for a winter march." First hot weather, then cold followed, next more stampedes of horses. Springer accused the men of the 2nd Missouri Artillery of "maliciously and willfully" fomenting some of the stampedes because they wanted to end the march and return home. By July 29 it was hot again. What with lost and worn-out animals, they burned some wagons, as there were no teams to pull them. Even so, Springer kept his "black servant 'Sam'" busy. August 4 arrived, rations were largely exhausted, and the column was living on game. By the time Connor reached the Tongue River on August 11, Cole's column camped on the north bank of the Cheyenne River, several days' march from the Tongue.[9]

On August 19, Colonel Walker and fourteen men of the 16th Kansas met up with Cole's column at Pine Creek, a tributary of the North Cheyenne (or Belle Fourche) River. Walker's center column then was almost two weeks out of Laramie, the main force occupying Cole's camp of the previous night. They carried mail for Cole's men. From that time on, the two columns moved more or less in tandem. They marched northwest to the Little Missouri River and continued on through rough country and "intensely hot" weather toward Powder River and Panther Mountain. On August 29, Cole sent a scouting party of twenty men and an officer west to find Connor's command. On August 30 the column reached the Powder River and went into camp. Cole's scouts returned September 1 not having found any "depot of supplies" or any trace of Connor on the Powder or Tongue Rivers.[10]

---

[9]Springer, *Soldiering in Sioux Country*, 3, 10–12, 21, 23, 25, 28, 30. Although Springer does not say, this was the South Fork of the Cheyenne River; see *O.R.*, I, 48, pt. 1, 369–72, 381.

[10]Springer, *Soldiering in Sioux Country*, 34, 43, 45, and 78n. 36; *O.R.*, I, 48, pt. 1, pp. 369–72, 381. Colonel Walker's report is reproduced in Hafen and Hafen, *Powder River Campaigns*, 92–100.

Meanwhile, on August 22, leaving the 6th Michigan behind to finish the fort, Connor took his western cavalry of experienced Indian fighters and set off northwest to the Tongue River, then north along that stream expecting to rendezvous with Cole and Walker. They marched through beautiful country: "hills are all covered with a fine growth of grass, in every valley there is . . . a stream or . . . brook of pure clear snow water, filled with trout" and along the banks, the trees, "wild cherry, quaking asp, some birch, willow and cottonwood." Soldiers found "the eastern slope of the Big Horn mountains" very "picturesque."

Late on the 28th Connor discovered an Indian camp ahead of him. Deciding to surprise it, Connor took elements of Companies E and K, 11th Ohio, with Major Marshall and Captain Humfreville, along with Company E, 7th Iowa, ninety Indian scouts, and two six-pounder guns, forward cautiously, poised to strike in the morning. The rest of his column remained behind with the wagons. About 9:00 A.M. Connor charged into the Indian camp. Though the tribesmen outnumbered them, Connor had surprise on his side. They fought almost hand-to-hand and put the Indians on the run at first. Soldiers "destroyed an immense amount of property—fully two hundred and fifty Indian lodges and contents." In early afternoon the Indians, Arapahos of Black Bear's band, counterattacked, and Connor's cavalry prudently withdrew. They took with them about 1,100 ponies and eight Arapaho women with thirteen children.[11]

Black Bear's Arapahos pursued Connor's cavalry even after dark and tried, but failed, to recapture their ponies. Connor reached his main camp about 2:00 A.M. on August 30, and

[11]Utley, *Frontiersmen in Blue*, 325–26; Brown, *Galvanized Yankees*, 187; Rogers, *Soldiers of the Overland*, 192–96. Quotation from Captain Henry E. Palmer's diary. Palmer, 11th Kansas, had not been mustered out with his unit: he was on detached service as quartermaster. See Palmer, "History of the Powder River Indian Expedition," 210–11; and also Robrock, "The Eleventh Ohio," 45; Madsen, *Glory Road*, 147–48.

the Arapahos withdrew. Connor's cavalry had ridden about a hundred miles, fought a battle, and returned in about forty hours. His troopers carried back seven wounded men; Arapahos killed one Pawnee scout. Palmer noted in his diary that along with Black Bear's son, sixty-three warriors had been killed, though Connor claimed only thirty-five Indian dead. Later, Connor released the captive women and children, but kept the ponies. Captain Humfreville, Company K, 11th Ohio, claimed never had he witnessed troopers facing "such hardships as we experienced during the forty hours of this march and battle." Two of Humfreville's men were wounded, one of whom was Ed Ward. The twenty-year-old private, "who enlisted in the Eleventh Ohio under the alias John Johnson," was formerly one of Confederate raider Morgan's men. For the next week, through rain and even snow, his column traveled both north and south along the Tongue, in the vain hope it would find Cole or Walker or both.[12]

On September 1, troopers at the head of the column heard a cannon shot, but could not pinpoint the direction of the sound. Connor sent Marshall and thirty men of Company E, 11th Ohio, with twenty Pawnee scouts to search toward the Rosebud for Cole and Walker. Out four days, they found nothing. On September 4, other scouts discovered that a road-building party had been attacked west of the Tongue River. This party had been looking for a way to connect Sioux City, Iowa, and the Bozeman Trail. Congress had appropriated fifty thousand dollars for the project. James A. Sawyers of Sioux City had assembled this expedition in June. Sawyers led the party of 53 men and 15 wagons, along with 5 emigrant wagons and another 36 belonging to the Sioux City firm of

[12]Brown, *Galvanized Yankees*, 188–89; Utley, *Frontiersmen in Blue*, 325–26; Rogers, *Soldiers of the Overland*, 196–99; Robrock, "The Eleventh Ohio," 45–46; Humfreville, quoted in Hafen and Hafen, *Powder River Campaigns*, 369–70; Sergeant Hull wrote in his diary, "Arapahoes that we fed at [Fort] Halleck [are] now fighting [us]." Hull, "Soldiering on the High Plains," 47. Hull remained behind with the wagons.

C. E. Hedges and Company. The escort of 161 men included Companies C and D, 137 men of the 5th United States Volunteers commanded by Captain George W. Williford, and 24 troopers of Company B, 1st Dakota Volunteer Cavalry, led by Lieutenant John R. Wood. The soldiers had 25 more wagons. They began their survey June 13 and encountered no openly hostile Indians until the second week in August. Then, between the Belle Fourche and Powder Rivers, Cheyenne and Red Cloud's Oglala Sioux harassed the expedition.[13]

George Bent was there. After noting that Connor made "a sort of peace" with the Arapahos by returning their women and children—but not the ponies since the Pawnees claimed them—he mentioned that he was among the Cheyennes who took on Sawyers train. Though the Cheyennes "did not see any of Connor's troops," they had found Sawyers and kept his train corraled for four days, fighting some, but really looking for plunder. Speaking for the Cheyennes, George and his brother Charles met with Captain Williford, who commanded the escort. During the parley, Cheyennes heard for the first time how Connor was building a fort on the Powder River, and became "very angry when they heard the news," for the fort would be in the heart of their hunting grounds. George, wearing an army officer's uniform he had captured at Julesburg, said the Cheyennes accepted a wagon load of goods—three thousand pounds, including flour, sugar, coffee, and tobacco—as a bribe to call off the fight. But another band came up and, angry they had not shared the loot, kept up the fight for another two days. Then the Cheyennes drew off, and Sawyers's train went on to Fort Connor. On August 29, Williford reported his command lost two soldiers of Company B,

[13]Utley, *Frontiersmen in Blue*, 326–27; Brown, *Galvanized Yankees*, 121–25; Hafen and Young, *Fort Laramie*, 339; Lass, *Overland Freighting*, 167; *O.R.*, I, 48, pt. 1, p. 388. Williford, a Civil War veteran, had seen hard action with the 9th Illinois Volunteer Infantry.

1st Dakota, and two civilians perished as well. He claimed there were "many killed and wounded braves." Bent made no mention of Indian casualties.[14]

The Cole and Walker columns on the Powder River encountered "about 50 Sioux warriors" on September 1. They "gathered about 20 horses and fled among the hills and mountains." Some troopers went out after them "and some of our men [who] were out hunting had quite a tussel with the Indians. 5 of our men were killed . . . and one of them scalped, two were wounded." The next day the column headed north (downstream), as they saw smoke columns in that direction and thought it might have been a signal from Connor. After a twenty-five–mile march in "intense heat" with very little forage available, the column turned about and retraced its steps south in the general direction of Fort Laramie. As they did so, the unpredictable high plains weather changed to a cold drizzle. Over September 2 and 3 Cole and Walker lost 225 horses and mules "from excessive heat, exhaustion, starvation, and extreme cold." From necessity, they destroyed wagons and other equipment.[15]

George Bent recalled learning that the soldiers with Cole and Walker were new to the plains and had no experience with conditions there. "From the very beginning" they "mismanaged" everything. "From the lower Platte to the Black Hills the column's trail could have been followed by the carcasses of dead horses and mules." Also, "they had no good guides." Bent knew Missouri River Sioux attacked the columns after following "the trail of the column to the Powder, and on September 1 stampeded part of the cavalry herd." With more horses and mules dying every day on the column's slow move south, the Sioux, six hundred strong, attacked the camp on September 4, but could not overrun it "and left at

---

[14]Hyde, *George Bent*, 231–33; Grinnell, *Fighting Cheyennes*, 208; Brown, *Galvanized Yankees*, 129–32; *O.R.*, I, 48, pt. 1, pp. 388–89.

[15]Springer, *Soldiering in Sioux Country*, 44–46; *O.R.*, I, 48, pt. 1, p. 373.

nightfall." With still another group of Sioux and Cheyennes, Bent joined in another attack on September 5.[16]

The Sioux and Cheyenne struck that morning with "more than a thousand" warriors. Only artillery kept the Indians at bay. By 9:00 A.M. tribesmen tired of the fight, apparently awed by the shells that burst among them and the rapid fire of the trooper's carbines. A cold north wind chilled the embattled soldiers. Bent wrote that the Indians captured many worn-out cavalry horses with their equipment, but could not overcome the soldiers as the tribesmen had "very few guns" (small arms) and "did not like the big guns" (howitzers) the soldiers used against them. After this fight, the Cheyennes broke off and headed east to the Black Hills, leaving the Sioux to deal with Cole and Walker. The troopers resumed their slow march south.[17]

Charles Springer wrote on September 6: "the Idaho Militia did not show themselves today." He complained that his "wardrobe needs a new supply . . . everything is fearfully dilapidated . . . the whole command is in the same plight." September 8 "dawned cold and rainy." They marched about twenty miles before 1:00 P.M., with Walker's 16th Kansas in the lead. But Walker ran into Indians "unaware" of their presence. An orderly of the 16th Kansas estimated three thousand warriors then moved to attack, but Springer thought it "a devilish rough guess." The "big guns" again kept the Indians at bay, and the columns resumed their march. When they camped that night, the wind blew hard and it was "as cold as if it came direct from the north pole, and the icebergs of Greenland." At dawn the troopers discovered many of the remaining animals had perished, so many that Springer called the place "Dead Horse Camp." Animals continued to die as the march resumed. "The mules are dying in

[16]Hyde, *George Bent*, 233–38

[17]*O.R.*, I, 48, pt. 1, pp. 373–74; Springer, *Soldiering in Sioux Country*, 47–49; Utley, *Frontiersmen in Blue*, 329.

the harness, the horses are falling down dead from under their riders." They only made five miles that day, and had lost at least "350 heads of animals since last night, and will lose a good many more tonight" because of the continued cold. On September 10, they burned more wagons and equipment, fought off Indians again, and made about twelve miles. The next day they marched about fifteen miles, with no trouble from the "Idaho Militia." The horses that were still alive were consolidated so that a few companies could remain saddled. Lieutenant Springer was allowed to keep a horse, but he chose to walk as his men had to, and "most of them have no boots. . . . I can and will share their misfortune." He kept the horse "for sick men to ride."[18]

At Fort Connor, Dodge and his escort of about a hundred troopers of the 14th Pennsylvania Cavalry arrived on September 7. He visited with Colonel Kidd and inspected the post. When some of his officers inquired of Captain Williford about Sawyers's wagon road, he told them "it would be a good route if one half of the hills were inverted and dumped into the ravines." Dodge experienced the storms and cold of that part of the world before he left for Fort Laramie on September 10.[19]

Meanwhile, up north on the Tongue River, Connor still worried about Cole and Walker. On September 8 he sent two parties out: Major Frank North and his Pawnees scouted in the direction of the Powder River, and Humfreville and K Company, 11th Ohio, went north to the Rosebud. Humfreville marched through rain and snow, but when he returned on September 11, he reported he found no sign of the missing columns. But later North had something. His Pawnees found five hundred or more dead horses and mules and intentionally destroyed wagons and equipment, but not the missing columns. Connor now feared the worst and sent out

[18]Springer, *Soldiering in Sioux Country*, 50–56.

[19]Rockafellow's diary in Hafen and Hafen, *Powder River Campaigns*, 190–91.

more scouting parties, including Sergeant Charles L. Thomas, Company E, 11th Ohio, and five Pawnee scouts. They found Cole and Walker on September 15. The next day, Cole sent a detachment of the 2nd Missouri to accompany Connor's scouts back to the general, and to tell him they were on their way to Fort Connor, now that they knew where to go, a distance of perhaps forty miles.[20]

The Cole-Walker column straggled on, subsisting on "horse and mule meat," some elk, and once a bear, but "no coffee, salt bread, or other necessities of life." The bedraggled troops reached Fort Connor on September 19 and 20. Destitute soldiers, barefoot and tattered, received welcome rations at Fort Connor, but not clothes or boots and shoes. As Connor headed back to the fort on September 22, Major Marshall and a detachment of the 11th Ohio, coming from that post, brought the general news that he had been relieved of command of the District of the Plains. Connor also learned that the Cole-Walker group had arrived at Fort Connor in very poor condition, without rations, and without most of their horses and equipment. They were no longer a fighting force. When Connor arrived at the fort September 24, Cole reported he had lost twelve killed, two missing, and an officer wounded. He optimistically estimated Indian loss "from 200 to 500 killed and wounded."[21]

After Sawyers's train had reached Fort Connor on August 24 following its engagement with the Cheyennes, Connor ordered Captain Williford and his 5th United States Volunteers to remain at the fort. The same order required Colonel

---

[20]Grinnell, *Fighting Cheyennes*, 212; Brown, *Galvanized Yankees*, 189–90; Robrock, "The Eleventh Ohio," 46; *O.R.*, I, 48, pt. 1, pp. 377, 379, 382, pt. 2, p. 1224; Utley, *Frontiersmen in Blue*, 330. According to Springer, Connor's scouts made contact on the 15th (*Soldiering in Sioux Country*, 57); Cole's September 25 report also says September 15, but a later report of his makes it September 13 (cited above). Sergeant Thomas subsequently was awarded the Congressional Medal of Honor "for rescuing the lost commands."

[21]Springer, *Soldiering in Sioux Country*, 57–61; Rogers, *Soldiers of the Overland*, 239.

Kidd, 6th Michigan Cavalry, to escort the party when it moved on. But Sawyers ran into more trouble along the Bozeman Trail. On August 31, Indians killed Captain Osmer F. Cole, 6th Michigan, who had been scouting ahead. Again the wagons were corraled. The attackers were Northern Arapahos, upset and angry over the encounter with Connor's troops just two days earlier. Sawyers sent for help, and a company of the 2nd California with Omaha scouts rode to the rescue. The Arapahoes moved off, and the 2nd California escorted the train as far as the Bighorn River. With no hostiles ahead, the escort returned safely to Fort Connor and Sawyers's party continued unmolested to Virginia City.[22]

Connor failed to meet his goal of punishing the Sioux and Cheyennes enough to make them eager for peace. The effort to conduct successfully a complex and closely timed operation in a vast and virtually unmapped region frustrated Connor and his commanders. Neither Cole nor Walker had experience with this unfamiliar country and its hostile climate, and, inadequately supplied and poorly guided, they had little chance of success. Even so, the Powder River affair kept the tribes off the Oregon and Overland roads as long as the army was in the field. Beyond that, it publicized the Bozeman Trail and the area through which it passed. By doing so, it "insured that the road [Bozeman Trail] would attract mounting emigrant travel in 1866." When that materialized, there ensued "fresh demands from the army to finish the job begun by Connor."[23]

While Connor's expedition toiled in the field, a great deal of activity took place at the various headquarters: Washington, St. Louis, and Fort Leavenworth, all directly affecting the expedition, Connor, and the future of the roads across the high plains.

[22] *O.R.*, I, 48, pt. 1, pp. 388–89; Utley, *Frontiersmen in Blue*, 327–28; Hyde, *George Bent*, 233; Kidd, *One of Custer's Wolverines*, 163–64.

[23] Utley, *Frontiersmen in Blue*, 331–32.

CHAPTER THIRTEEN

Phase Down

From his headquarters in Washington, General Grant complained to General Pope in St. Louis, on July 29, 1865, that both the Quartermaster and Commissary departments were alarmed by "requisitions of such magnitude coming from Leavenworth." He ordered Pope to investigate and "stop all unnecessary expenditures." Grant also thought the cavalry force in Pope's department "might be materially reduced." Army expenditures and manpower had to be reduced, since the Civil War had ended.[1]

Pope relayed Grant's concerns to General Dodge at Fort Leavenworth. Dodge replied on August 2: "it seems the Government does not appreciate the magnitude of the difficulties . . . that we have had to overcome." He had to remount all the cavalrymen since the horses they had on the plains were not serviceable. They were nearly "out of stores of all kinds." His troops were "dismounted, dissatisfied, and mutinous." Nearly "one-fourth have deserted." It might have seemed that they had a lot of cavalry, "but it is very small in the field when you contemplate the ground it has to cover and the work it has to do." Dodge continued, "the Government" has to "understand that it has either got to abandon the country west entirely to the Indians or meet the war issue

[1] *O.R.*, I, 48, pt. 1, p. 364.

presented." Dodge had to mount expeditions "strong enough to take care of themselves" and also "hold troops enough to guard 3500 miles of overland route[s]." In addition, every mail coach and every wagon train "must be guarded." If we fail to deliver the mail we get complaints "that we are not protecting the mail line." Grant knew that he, Dodge, never asked for troops or incurred any expense except what was necessary. "Never before have we had so extensive a war on the plains. Never before have we had" so much of the country "to protect." Dodge thought he carried out the "instructions and intentions of the Government." He then noted that he was going to Fort Laramie "tomorrow" to personally supervise affairs. "All I ask is that the Government be patient with us, not ask us to do too much in too short a time." On August 4, General Sherman wrote Grant that Dodge was "fully competent" to handle operations on the plains.[2]

As if Dodge did not have enough to cope with, Pope sent him an indictment of Connor. "I have just received copies of instructions from General Connor to the commanders of his expedition" that included the following statement: "'You will not receive overtures of peace or submission from Indians, but will attack and kill every male Indian over twelve years of age.'" Pope found this "atrocious, and . . . in direct violation of my repeated orders." He told Dodge to countermand them immediately. If Connor's orders were carried out, such would "cost him his commission, if not worse." Pope was furious with Connor, who had only himself to blame.[3]

Dodge tried to shield Connor as best he could. He replied to Pope immediately. "I have seen no instructions of Connor's. I see . . . he instructs them that they must follow a trail

[2]Ibid., pt. 2, pp. 1144, 1156–58. Cavalry horses in frontier posts were often rendered unserviceable for lack of a proper diet. They were larger animals than Indian ponies and had different nutritional requirements. But Indian ponies suffered in the winter also for lack of forage.

[3]Ibid., pt. 1, p. 356.

whenever they find it until the Indians are caught; and also instructs them that they must not be guilty of any outrage of any kind on women and children." Dodge failed to see how he could relieve Connor, "as he is now far north of Laramie," and he had no one else to put in command. But Pope came down hard on Connor again. He proclaimed, "Connor is ignoring the quartermaster and commissaries, and violating law and regulations in making contracts himself and forcing officers to pay public money on them. Stop all this business at once, and order all officers to conform to law and regulations." Dodge replied that he had never heard of Connor "letting any contracts with officers on the plains," and "never received the orders you spoke of in relation to contracts."[4]

Dodge forwarded Pope's correspondence to Connor, but it had to be sent by courier from Fort Laramie, and with the reply returned the same way, it took Connor nine days to respond. From "Headquarters . . . Near Fort Connor," he acknowledged Pope's dispatches "in reference to instructions to column commanders and contracts in Utah." He conveniently omitted mention of any instructions to column commanders such as Cole and Walker. The contract dispute, he said, took place before he assumed command on the plains. "I hope on my return to give such explanations as will be deemed satisfactory." Connor appeared untroubled by Pope's accusations. If so, he underestimated the general.[5]

Word of Connor's campaign bothered President Andrew Johnson as well. Secretary of War Stanton informed Grant, who still commanded all United States forces, that Johnson was "much concerned about the Indian expedition." Not only that, Stanton continued, but the treasury secretary claimed to be unable "to meet [the cost of] an expedition so large and

---

[4]Ibid., pt. 1, p. 356, pt. 2, p. 1177. Connor may have been guilty of Pope's accusations; Madsen, *Glory Road*, 128, 137–38, 152.

[5]*O.R.*, I, 48, pt. 1, pp. 356–57.

unexpected, not sanctioned by the Government." Stanton asked Grant, "who planned it?" Grant answered that Pope planned it, but he was not "posted as to the necessity" of it. He told Stanton he would go to St. Louis "in a few days and look into this matter myself." He thought "extraordinary requisitions should be disapproved."[6]

Clearly, those in Washington assigned a low priority to affairs in the West. New in his job, Johnson's understanding of Lincoln's desire to keep the western communication routes open was limited at best. Buried under details of the demobilization of the volunteer army, in the midst of a reorganization of the regular army, and with a need to keep alert to the activities of the French in Mexico, Grant was distracted. He welcomed the opportunity to travel to St. Louis and confer with his old friends Sherman and Pope.

As Grant left for St. Louis, Dodge headed west from Council Bluffs. "I get off today," he wired Pope at St. Louis, to "straighten matters on the plains." Besides the Connor expedition, other affairs troubled him. "It seems all the rascals in the West are combined to swindle the Government." His staff officers reported many irregularities. Those included "stealing Government stock . . . in every conceivable way." He had recovered "over 100 stolen horses and mules" at Council Bluffs, and claimed "there appears to be a fearful organization extending clear to Denver and Missouri. They entice men to desert, sell the Government property, and then assist them in" escaping.[7] Dodge implied many requisitions would not be necessary were it not for the lawlessness.

It mattered little to those on the overland roads what their leaders in Washington knew or thought they knew. On August 7, while Connor was in the field, his adjutant at Fort Laramie reported to Dodge, then at Fort Leavenworth, that

---

[6]Ibid., pt. 2, pp. 1178–79.

[7]Ibid., p. 1179.

two hundred "Cheyenne Indians attacked [the] station near Big Laramie," killing five and making prisoner of a fifteen-year-old young woman and a two-year-old baby, "a fate worse than death." The tribesmen also stole thirteen government horses and killed four more people at another nearby station. He assumed these were the same Indians that fought at Platte Bridge "a few days ago." He reported, "Michigan horses jaded so as to be worthless for pursuit." He noted also that on the Overland road, a non-commissioned officer and thirteen men had been posted at each station from Fort Collins to Sulphur Springs, a distance of 275 miles. The adjutant complained that the stage company refused to operate, but government teams carried the mail three times a week. "It is a shame," he wrote, "when emigrants and freighters travel the road daily without escorts, the stage company, when afforded all the protection necessary, is afraid to run their stock."[8]

Pope learned all of this. The expedition in the field, even if commanded by someone in whom he had lost confidence, required attention as did the roads. On August 15, he told Sherman "it is essential that early steps be taken to furnish this department with the . . . regiments needed for the protection of the overland routes to New Mexico and Utah." He told Sherman about volunteers so unhappy and plagued with desertion "that they are nearly altogether inefficient." Matters would only "be much worse" when his planned reduction in force went into effect on October 15, leaving only five infantry and two cavalry regiments west of Leavenworth. Right now, he argued, his "only reliable troops" were the United States Volunteers, enlisted from rebels. He asked for Sherman's "attention to the subject in time to prevent embarrassment and trouble." Pope wanted Sherman to have a clear

[8]Ibid., pt. 1, p. 357.

idea of the situation on the plains when he spoke with Grant.[9]

Dodge had reached Fort Kearny by August 15, on his westward tour of inspection. From there he wired Connor's adjutant at Fort Laramie to learn the strength of Connor's command, not only the expedition but the whole of the District of the Plains. He discovered that Connor had 7,700 cavalry and 2,100 infantry overall, but about 1,200 cavalry and 1,000 infantry would be discharged by Christmas. About 2,500 cavalry were with Connor in the Powder River Expedition. He included in his account the 21st New York, 6th West Virginia, and 7th Kansas, then en route, but with them he calculated there would be only four officers and men to each mile of the 2,650 miles of mail and telegraph roads. "To have any less force is to offer a premium for Indian attacks," he added. In another report, he told Dodge that Connor wanted a regiment of infantry with "more than one year to serve," with four of its companies placed at Fort Connor and four at Laramie and along the telegraph line, with the remaining two at Julesburg. He relayed Connor's word that the expedition "is in excellent health. Plenty buffalo, wood, bunch grass, and water, but no hay." Connor needed clothing for 500 cavalry, as well as building tools and a sawmill "more than anything else."[10]

Still at Kearny on August 16, Dodge reported to Pope that the post, a supply depot, was "in excellent condition," but discipline among the troops "scattered along the road guarding the overland coaches" was poor. The stage company would not move its coaches "unless we guard it over every mile," which was very hard on the cavalry horses. Dodge included with this report another from Connor's adjutant at Fort Laramie. "There are only 100 infantry and 430 cavalry in

---

[9]Ibid., pt. 2, pp. 1183–84.

[10]Ibid., p. 1184.

Utah," and half the infantry would be discharged by Christmas. "Not enough troops there to protect the posts in the districts, and what few we have are scattered on the mail line [the Overland road] as far west as Washakie Station, just the other side of the Rocky Mountains. In case of any Indian troubles in Utah [we] could do absolutely nothing." He also mentioned that "cavalry overtook Indians who committed depredations at Big Laramie several days ago, whipped them badly," and still pursued them. Quartermaster and commissary supplies were arriving regularly, but the shortage of troops remained the big problem. "We can hardly obtain men to do the necessary camp and post duties, so great is the demand for escort and scouting duty."[11] Pope had no shortage of information about what it took to protect the mail and telegraph lines and the roads they followed.

Pope also knew all about the Powder River Expedition, as Captain George F. Price, Connor's adjutant at Fort Laramie, kept Dodge informed, and Dodge passed the news on to Pope. Yet Pope remained determined to get rid of Connor. On August 22, a week before Connor fought Black Bear's Arapahos, Pope issued General Orders Number 20, which abolished Connor's District of the Plains. Instead, it set up the District of Nebraska (including the Territories of Nebraska and Montana, and part of Dakota) with headquarters at Fort Laramie. Brevet Major General Frank Wheaton replaced Connor. A District of Colorado (the entire territory) went to Brevet Major General Emory Upton, headquarters to be at Denver. Dodge continued in "general command west and south of the Missouri River." Pope banished Connor back to the District of Utah, headquartered at Salt Lake.[12]

A civil engineer from Rhode Island, Wheaton had a distinguished career throughout the Civil War, rising from regi-

[11] Ibid., pp. 1187–88.

[12] Ibid., pt. 2, p. 1201, 1205.

mental command at First Bull Run to division command with Major General Philip H. Sheridan. Before the Civil War, he had served in the West as an officer with the 1st Cavalry and as a staff officer with both generals Edwin V. Sumner and William S. Harney. Pope advised Wheaton that the permanent military posts in his new command were Fort Kearny, Cottonwood, Julesburg, Fort Laramie, and Platte Bridge. Pope ordered each post to be garrisoned by three infantry and two cavalry companies. He thought Wheaton might need some "intermediate small posts . . . but I think not," except perhaps for a post "in the valley of the Sweetwater." The fort that Connor built on the Powder River would be under Wheaton's charge also, to be supplied from Fort Laramie. Apparently Pope gave little thought to protection of the telegraph and stage stations.

"In any event," Pope continued, "it is the purpose to return to a purely defensive arrangement for the security of the overland routes to Salt Lake." Pope decided "one cavalry and two infantry regiments will be sufficient force." He admonished Wheaton to be very frugal, and "return without delay to a peace basis, and to the economical arrangements which obtained before the rebellion." When Wheaton chose the troops allotted him, all the others should be sent to Leavenworth to be mustered out. This included Connor's Powder River Expedition troops when they returned to Fort Laramie. Wheaton would report to Dodge. Largely due to peacetime finances, the strategy for protection of the overland routes of communication changed again, back to the defensive.

Pope left orders for Connor to return to Utah as soon as he could. There he would have one regiment of cavalry and one of infantry, "no more . . . under any circumstances." He ordered Connor not to interfere with paymasters or make contracts on his own. "I make these remarks," Pope said, "because there has been much complaint of you in this direction." Connor, too, would report to Dodge.[13]

Pope sent his plans on to Sherman. Including those troops he assigned to Wheaton and Connor, he needed seven regiments plus a battalion of infantry and four regiments of cavalry. He confided,

> this is the least force, in my opinion, which can perform the service required. West of Fort Leavenworth there are 3,500 miles of overland routes to California and New Mexico to protect. The whole distance traversed is through Indian country, and the overland routes . . . will for some time be infested by wandering parties of lawless white men,

army deserters, bushwackers, and former "rebel" soldiers. He thought these more "dangerous to travelers than the Indians themselves." Yet Indians always are blamed for "all outrages," so "it requires great vigilance" that innocent tribesmen not be retaliated against. Pope concluded,

> a much larger force is required on the plains than has hitherto been considered necessary. . . . As there seems to be great anxiety and some misapprehension in Washington concerning the condition of the troops in this department, I . . . request that copies of this letter be furnished to the General-in-Chief [Grant] and the Secretary of War [Stanton].[14]

Also on August 25, Captain Price reported to Connor from Fort Laramie that the 7th Michigan, on the Overland road, had found that 400 Indians had crossed the road between Big Laramie and Virginia Dale stations "traveling [north] very rapidly for their villages. They have heard of you." Almost two weeks earlier, 150 Indians had attacked Willow Springs station and stampeded the stock, but Michigan cavalry recovered part of them and drove off the Indians. Price men-

[13]Ibid., pp. 1206–9.

[14]Ibid., pp. 1210–11.

tioned that the 21st New York would soon be at Fort Collins. Happily, he noted that because the Indians were all fleeing north, the [Overland] road was open and the mail could move.[15]

Dodge had reached Fort Laramie by August 31, and from there he wired Pope at St. Louis: "I consider the Indian matters here of so much importance, and knowing no one can judge them so well as when he is on the ground," that he had a "proposition" to make to "the Government." He asked to keep Connor in the field with two thousand men in addition to the forces "you have designated to garrison the posts on the plains," and wrote, "I will settle these Indian difficulties before spring . . . and bring about a peace that will be lasting." This might take a month or more. All it would cost the government would be the pay for those troops. Dodge needed no more supplies because those were either already on hand or on the way. Then as soon as "we settle" with the Indians, we can muster out those troops and two thousand more. If "we will allow him [Connor] time he will settle the matter before he returns. Should he come back by our orders" before the Indians are defeated, "entire Indian tribes will be down on our lines and we will have our hands full, and more too." Dodge's "proposition" fell on deaf ears.[16]

Pope replied that orders already had been sent to Wheaton and Connor, and made it clear that he had no intention of changing them. "The pressure on me about expenses on the plains is tremendous. Whether reasonable or not, the demands of the Government must be complied with," Pope explained. "Whatever the result of Connor's expedition" so far, it made no difference, in light of concern about numbers of troops and expenses. All soldiers other than those Pope allowed to Wheaton and Connor had to be hurried back to Leavenworth to be mustered out.[17]

---

[15]Ibid., p. 1212. [16]Ibid., pp. 1220–21. [17]Ibid., pt. 1, pp. 355–56.

By September 15, Dodge had visited Fort Connor on the Powder River and was on his way back south when he sent his impressions to Pope. Fort Connor, he said, was "well located; right in the heart of Indian country, and it is an important post." Dodge thought it would be very useful "holding in check Indians." They still needed quartermaster stores though, since those earmarked for Fort Connor had yet to reach Fort Laramie. He mentioned that the road from Fort Laramie via Fort Connor to Virginia City "is an excellent wagon road; good grass, water, wood all the way" and quite direct, since "it saves over 450 miles" to the Montana mines. He expected "immense" travel next season.

Dodge noted that when the Indians had attacked Sawyers's party, "Colonel [William] Bent's sons . . . appeared on part of the Indians." He told Pope that George Bent said there was one condition that would lead the Cheyennes to agree to a peace treaty: "the hanging by the Government of Colonel Chivington." Bent was also supposed to have said that he believed not only were the Cheyennes "strong enough to fight the Government; they preferred to do it." The Cheyennes knew the "Government would withdraw troops in the fall; then they would have it all their own way again." Dodge claimed the Cheyennes "expressed great fear about Connor" and were getting ready to concentrate against him, "which is true." Indians moved north for that reason, which explained why, with Connor in the field, there had been no trouble on the mail or telegraph line. Of the Bent brothers, Dodge reported they "were educated in St. Louis. One [George] has been with [Major General Sterling] Price in the rebel army." After being captured "his father got him released" but he shortly joined the Cheyennes. "He was dressed in one of our staff officer's uniforms" when he parleyed with Sawyers. This was a lot of information for Pope, but if Dodge thought any of it would change

Pope's mind about Connor's usefulness, or Dodge's desire to keep him in the field, he was mistaken.[18]

As Connor marched south along the Powder River toward the post named for him, he learned that he had been relieved as commander of the District of the Plains. Connor also heard that Cole and his Missourians, along with Walker and his Kansans, had arrived at Fort Connor "in a very destitute condition, half the men barefoot," and that they had lost most of their trains, stock, and camp equipage. Then on September 17, the 6th Michigan received notice of their muster-out, and Kidd wasted no time putting his men on the march for Fort Laramie. No longer in command, with the manpower of Cole, Walker, and Kidd effectively lost to him, Connor knew the Powder River Expedition was over.[19]

Hervey Johnson, now a corporal in Company G, 11th Ohio Cavalry, had been on garrison duty at Sweetwater station since November 1864, but by July 8, 1865, had been rotated back to Fort Laramie. There he witnessed the excitement of "an expedition fitting out for the Powder River." From time to time Johnson served on escort duty of one sort or another. On a trip back to Sweetwater in early August, he wrote his sister about the battle of Platte Bridge and the death of Caspar Collins. Johnson had been safe at Fort Laramie at that time. On the way back from Sweetwater in August, he wrote to his sister again, this time from Platte Bridge. He had been in the company of Captain Bretney and about thirty men of Companies I and L, 11th Ohio, repairing the telegraph as they went. While doing so, he learned Connor's expedition already was on the Powder River. Johnson had missed that adventure as well.[20]

That detachment of the 11th Ohio ran into Indians tearing

[18]Ibid., pt. 2, p. 1229.

[19]Rogers, *Soldiers of the Overland*, 239–40; Kidd, *One of Custer's Wolverines*, 167.

[20]Unrau, *Tending the Talking Wire*, 269, 271, 281.

down telegraph wire and burning poles near Platte Bridge, but they managed to get the line working without getting into a fight. Johnson heard about Washington wanting to make peace with the tribes, but could not see "any use" in so doing "while they are carrying on as they are out here." Those eastern peacemakers "howling about the condition of the '*poor indian*'" would quickly find out, if they came out west, "that the only medicine needed for the indians is plenty of powder and lead and good strong wills to use it." Unknowingly, he agreed with both Connor and Dodge.[21]

On September 19, Lieutenant Springer, 12th Missouri Cavalry, a member of Cole's ill-fated right column of the Powder River Expedition, stumbled into the stockade of Fort Connor. His regiment straggled in after him. The garrison took him "without much ceremony" to their mess, "and for the first time in 4 weeks, I sat down with good grace at a well supplied table, and how the biscuits and coffee disappeared." Then his men "came rolling in," the rank and file of two regiments being treated the same as he. "We gave our most heartfelt thanks. . . . Our command soon felt in better spirits." That evening Major North's Pawnee scouts treated the newcomers to a scalp dance, while they consumed "cherry-brandy and cigars."[22]

In the evening of September 24, Connor's column also arrived at the post. Springer learned that his regiment would depart for Fort Laramie the next morning. Then Connor, also heading there as ordered and riding in an ambulance as ranking officers often did, saw Springer's troops marching largely barefoot. Connor "gave the boots from his own feet to our men," Springer reported. When they camped at Buffalo Creek after making thirteen miles, Connor ordered Cole's men to wait for forty wagons he had sent for to transport the

[21]Ibid., 281.

[22]Springer, *Soldiering in Sioux Country*, 61.

barefoot column. Even so, many of Springer's men continued walking to Laramie barefoot.[23]

Along with a detachment of the 11th Ohio, Corporal Johnson made a twenty-three-day round trip to Fort Connor, meeting Connor's expedition, including E and K Companies of the 11th Ohio, returning to Fort Laramie. They herded cattle, horses, and mules to the post on the Powder River. Captain Williford took command of Fort Connor as Kidd's 6th Michigan had departed. Only C and D Companies, 5th United States Volunteers, remained. Though Connor reached Fort Laramie on October 1, Springer and his regiment, still on foot, did not arrive until October 4. Not only the Missourians, but also Ohioans of Company K "mixed up clear to Fort," wrote Sergeant Hull. "Have marched nearly 800 miles over all kinds of country. We started out with twenty-two extra horses and came back with nearly twenty dismounted men." By then Dodge had left Laramie on his western tour, departing September 18 for Denver. He took Pallady along for a guide with a few Pawnee scouts. Indians stampeded his horses on the first night out, and Crow Indians attacked his party later. Along the way, Dodge, always the railway engineer, located an easy pass through the foothills, which the Union Pacific would use later.[24]

From Central City, Colorado Territory, on the way to Denver, Dodge conveyed to Pope his favorable impression of the Powder River affair. He told how Connor surprised some Arapahos, captured their village and took all their winter provisions and six hundred horses from them. He claimed that Cole and Walker had defeated the Indians they faced,

[23]Ibid., 63–65; *O.R.*, I, 48, pt. 1, p. 378.

[24]Unrau, *Tending the Talking Wire*, 292; Springer, *Soldiering in Sioux Country*, 66; Brown, *Galvanized Yankees*, 133, 190; Hull, "Soldiering on the High Plains," 52–53; J. R. Perkins, *Trails, Rails, and War: The Life of General G. M. Dodge* (Indianapolis: The Bobbs-Merrill Company, 1929), 1897.

"totally" routing them, "driving them in every direction with great loss." He mentioned the "severe snow storm" of September 9, "in which 400 of Colonel Cole's horses perished." Dodge noted that the storm reached him at Fort Connor, and he lost "several animals" himself. Then at Denver, he wired Pope again on October 1. He knew that Connor reached Fort Laramie that day, with his columns either at Fort Connor or on the way to Laramie. Connor reported to Dodge he had chastized the Indians, but not severely enough "to compel them to behave." Connor believed he should have continued the campaign for forty more days had his orders not prevented it. Connor told Dodge fifteen hundred troops should remain at Fort Connor "to make a winter campaign to insure a final settlement." That same day, Dodge congratulated Connor and thanked him "for the success you have met with." He also commended Connor's command for the "success and fortitude" it exhibited "under such trying circumstances and hardships."[25]

General Wheaton arrived at Fort Laramie while Connor was still in the field, but on Dodge's orders, he later met with the former commander. Dodge thought perhaps a chance still existed to make peace with the Indians, and proposed to send Indian emissaries, "Big Ribs and some of his head Sioux," out to the Cheyennes and Sioux proposing that they come into Fort Connor or Laramie to talk of peace. Dodge advised Wheaton that he should tell the Indians that if they failed to come in and make peace, "what they have had is only a taste of what they will get this winter," for "you will give them no rest. You and General Connor can fix this." But do it, Dodge said, "before they discover our force on the plains." Our dwindling force, he must have meant. Dodge warned Wheaton to run a bluff with the tribesmen, for certainly

[25] *O.R.*, I, 48, pt. 2, pp. 1236–37.

there would be no winter campaign, and no Connor, either, in the face of Pope's direct orders.[26]

With Connor out of the picture, Wheaton turned to Colonel Henry E. Maynadier of the 5th United States Volunteers, now in command at Fort Laramie and also of the newly-created West Sub-District of Nebraska as a field commander. A West Pointer and a Virginian, Maynadier had served in the West before the Civil War and had some experience with the Oregon road. As early as April 4, 1861, Secretary of War Simon Cameron had ordered Maynadier, then a captain of the 10th Infantry, to organize a "protective corps" of fifty to a hundred men to escort emigrants from the Missouri River to the California, Oregon, and Washington frontier. Captain Maynadier then served with the provost-marshal-general, and later with the 12th Infantry as a major. In August 1865 he assumed command of the 5th United States Volunteers as their colonel. In August 1865, he left Fort Riley, Kansas, with much of his regiment once again for the Oregon road. He took command at Fort Laramie in time to meet Wheaton, and was on hand when Connor returned to the post. Wheaton entrusted Maynadier with carrying out Dodge's orders originally directed to him and to Connor.[27]

It would have been difficult to find many of the Cheyennes, regardless. According to George Bent, the Southern Cheyennes had, after their conflict with Cole and Walker, moved east into the Black Hills in search of buffalo. The Northern Cheyennes, including Roman Nose, remained in the north that winter. Some of the Sioux headed east for the Missouri

[26]Ibid., p. 1229; pt. 1, p. 364. Also, the two companies of the 3rd U.S. Volunteers stationed on the road west of Laramie pulled out in October, their enlistments nearly up. They marched for Fort Kearny; Brown, *Galvanized Yankees*, 44.

[27]Olson, *Red Cloud and the Sioux Problem*, 28; *O.R.*, I, 48, pt. 2, p. 1217; 50, pt. 1, pp. 460–61; III, 5, pp. 601, 712–13.

River. By mid-October the Southern Cheyennes left the Black Hills and headed south, "anxious to return home." Bent wrote that they crossed the Platte about October 20 and "made some raids along the road, capturing trains loaded with goods for Denver."[28]

Raids continued along the Oregon road that fall. John J. Pattison, Company B, 7th Iowa Cavalry, noted in his sketchy diary on September 25 that a "train of 200 mountain pilgrims" was attacked at Pole Creek and "107 horses and mules [were] stampeded and stolen." Another train met hostiles on September 30, as did others on October 21 and October 28, all between Fort Kearny and the vicinity of Julesburg. On October 22 Alkali station came under attack, and Pattison noted "twenty-five soldiers killed (First Nebraska)." When a detachment of the 7th Iowa and the 3rd United States Volunteers went to the aid of Alkali station, it encountered Indians, but unfortunately on the 28th a train was burned nearby, "oxen ham-stringed; four men killed and burned." Forty-eight men went in pursuit, and on October 30 they overtook the raiders, killing twenty-five of them and losing but one pursuer. Trouble in the vicinity of Alkali continued until November 9. Doubtless George Bent's Cheyennes made the late October raids.[29]

Connor remained at Fort Laramie until October 4. Then he and his wife departed for Denver, arriving there October 15. He failed to leave for Utah immediately, as his orders implied he should. Connor received a warm welcome in Denver, complete with "a large and enthusiastic reception." Meanwhile, on October 6, four hundred of Cole's soldiers received orders to work on fortifications around Laramie, and, as Cole reported, these "ragged, barefooted men, emaci-

[28]Hyde, *George Bent*, 242–43; *O.R.*, I, 48, pt. 2, p. 1243.

[29]John J. Pattison, "With the U. S. Army Along the Oregon Trail, 1863–66," *Nebraska History Magazine* 15 (June 1934): 86–87.

ated with fatigue" worked "without a murmur of discontent" as Laramie's "well-appointed idle troops," including some of the 11th Ohio, watched. Not involved, Springer's 12th Missouri received their necessary, and very welcome, clothing issue that day.[30]

Wheaton then ordered Cole to take the 2nd Missouri to Fort Leavenworth to be mustered out, along with Walker's 16th Kansas and the 6th Michigan. But not all of the 6th: only those whose enlistments expired before February 1, 1866. The others, in fact, would be sent to Utah. Springer's companies of the 12th Missouri were not included in the trek to Leavenworth; they remained at Fort Laramie. Other volunteers melting away from Dodge's command included the 1st Colorado Cavalry and the 2nd and 3rd United States Volunteers. But Dodge kept the 11th Ohio Cavalry (considered to be at battalion strength), the 7th Iowa Cavalry, Springer's 12th Missouri Cavalry, the 1st Michigan Cavalry (newly constituted from among the 1st, 6th, and 7th Michigan—to form one regiment), a battalion of the 21st New York Cavalry, the 5th and 6th United States Volunteers, a battalion of the 1st Nebraska Cavalry, the 6th West Virginia Cavalry, the 13th Missouri Cavalry, the 1st Battalion Nevada Cavalry, the 3rd Battalion California Veteran Infantry, 48th Wisconsin Infantry, the 17th Illinois Cavalry (though ordered to be mustered out), and the 1st Battalion, 13th United States Infantry (regulars). Some of these units stationed posts in Utah, Missouri, Kansas, Dakota Territory, and Colorado Territory, protecting the route to Santa Fé as well as the Oregon and Overland roads. Dodge reported the aggregate would total about 9,311, but many were absent (on leave, ill, or deserted), and he estimated his "real strength" at 6,990.[31]

---

[30]Rogers, *Soldiers of the Overland*, 241; *O.R.*, I, 48, pt. 1, p. 378; Springer, *Soldiering in Sioux Country*, 67; Madsen, *Glory Hunter*, 155; Hull, "Soldiering on the High Plains," 53.

[31]*O.R.*, I, 48, pt. 1, p. 347; Kidd, *One of Custer's Wolverines*, 167–68.

In a lengthy response November 1 to communications from both Grant and Pope, Dodge worried "that an erroneous impression prevailed at Washington as to the number of troops, supplies, expenses" and "the condition of things generally on the plains." He claimed that a large part of this misapprehension was due to the number of troops hastened to the frontier by requests from both Pope and himself in the spring, when they planned their campaigns, and prior to orders for the mustering out of volunteers. Three regiments of infantry and six of cavalry had been forwarded west, a total of 4,056 men, but they were discharged before they could be used. This contributed to the frustration that Dodge felt as he struggled to send additional troops to Connor, who had tried to ready his expedition in the spring and early summer.[32]

Dodge also reported to Pope his belief that it was "probable" that peace commissioners could successfully make a treaty with Native Americans on the plains. But he continued to hold the "opinion that any peace made with them before they are severely punished will not carry with it that assurance of perpetuity and good faith it would had we first chastized them" for the "outrages they have committed" in the last eighteen months. Dodge noted that during the last month they had attacked a train on the Santa Fé road, killed five men and destroyed the wagons, and assaulted a station on the Smoky Hill route, where they "burned stages, and carried off stock." As he returned to Leavenworth via that route, Dodge "had personal knowledge of these acts of hostility and treachery." These acts were committed by tribes, "portions of whom" were even then "sitting in council" with peace commissioners. He repeated his effort to get the northern tribes to come in and talk, but he heard nothing from them. "While

---

[32]*O.R.*, I, 48, pt. 1, p. 346. All of these regiments were far below full strength. Many men were either on leave and not expected to return, or had deserted, or, in some cases, died.

the old men and some of the principal chiefs are anxious for peace, the young men (dog soldiers), . . . get beyond their control" and continue attacks. "The Cheyenne are even now continuing their work on the North Platte, and I fear when they reach the Arkansas . . . they will induce many of the young men of the southern tribes to join them." Where treaties had been made, Dodge instructed his officers to "rigidly and faithfully" observe them, but to come down hard on those who remain hostile.[33]

Dodge added that he considered "it the duty of the Government to . . . effectually protect these overland routes and render them at all times safe and secure." After all, the "telegraph, mail, and express lines" are on the Oregon and Overland roads, "the best natural road from the Missouri River to the Pacific Coast." Most of the emigration followed along those routes. In a little over five months from March to early August 1865, "9,386 teams and 11,885 persons" passed Fort Kearny going west. A "vast amount of trade, travel, and capital . . . [is] flowing to the great mineral regions of Colorado, Utah, Montana, and Idaho." It also took a lot of commerce "to supply the hundreds of thousands now there," and with "immense yearly emigration" there is developing "an empire rich in mineral resources, and destined . . . to form the future basis of our financial system." In other words, the need to protect the overland routes was overwhelming.[34]

These routes could be secured, Dodge asserted, by confining Native Americans "north of the North Platte and south of the Arkansas River." And the "Government" should act now while troops were out there, even though "it would cost us thousands." If left to the future, it would "cost hundreds of thousands." Dodge claimed that "while all departments of the Government are disposed to do justice to the Indian,"

[33]Ibid., pp. 338–40. [34]Ibid., pp. 342–43.

desiring "to make him friendly," it made no sense to be making peace with some Native Americans in one place and fighting them in another. "They have watched our vacillating course . . . until they have lost all confidence in us" and no longer "respect us." They told my officers:

> War . . . has been a benefit to us. We have never been so well fed, have helped ourselves from your trains, ridden your mules and horses, had white women for wives, and went with plenty of white scalps from the routes to our villages, and make peace when you come to fight us.

Dodge recommended letting the army "have full and entire control" of "Indian matters" where the military have responsibility. Such would avoid conflicts between Indian superintendents and agents on one hand, and the military on the other. "Responsibility to both makes responsibility to neither," the authority of neither is respected, "and the Indians are wronged and robbed." His conclusions, he urged, "are the result of much personal experience and careful study, and they also reflect the opinions of the most experienced residents of the plains," people who have lived on the frontier and dealt with "Indians all their lives." Dodge's eloquent pleas and advice came to grief on the rocks of politics, financial retrenchment, and demobilization. Pope held similar views and had made them known earlier. Even Grant had agreed, but all to no avail.[35]

Dispatches flew back and forth among the commanders. On October 10, Pope wrote Grant: "All the volunteer regiments on the plains are dissatisfied and mutinous, and . . . rapidly deserting." Pope feared posts on the plains would be abandoned unless "reliable" troops could be found for replacement. "It is now too late in the season to send regular

---

[35]Ibid., pp. 344–46; pt. 2, pp. 480, 565–68, 879–82; Richard N. Ellis, "Civilians, The Army and the Indian Problem on the Northern Plains, 1862–66," *North Dakota History* 37, no. 1 (Winter 1970): 34–35.

regiments to the remote posts." He wanted to consolidate and re-enlist the 2nd and 3rd United States Volunteers. A few days later Grant replied that he would send "four regiments of colored infantry, or more" if Pope could use them to replace "white" volunteers. Sherman supported Pope by telling Grant "we need more regulars out on the plains. Volunteers are all discontented and unreliable." Pope then warned Grant: "it is too late in the season to get troops farther out than Fort Kearny," but two regiments of United States Colored Troops could be used between Leavenworth and Kearny to replace two regiments of white soldiers. When Grant inquired of Major General Philip H. Sheridan, then in New Orleans, about the availability of African-American regiments for Pope, Sheridan recommended against it. They would be better off in New Mexico, he said.[36] Whatever Sheridan's reasons, he failed to convince Grant.

Pope asked Grant if he was required to furnish mounted escorts for the overland stages, since it was "enormously expensive, as it kills up both horses and men at a fearful rate, and requires very large force, more than the Government is willing to allow." If the military must furnish escorts, it might as well carry the mail itself. The stage company threatened to stop the mail without escorts.

So far as Native Americans were concerned, Pope echoed Dodge and claimed some of them wanted peace, but were unable to restrain young warriors. As a result, "our troops must therefore continue on the plains and be on alert." He noted that young "Cheyennes are committing some depredations on the Platte route on their way south." Grant replied that Pope "need not furnish escorts . . . except when it can be done without much inconvenience or expense." Pope should do the best he could "with the means at your disposal." Then

---

[36] *O.R.*, I, 48, pt. 2, pp. 1239–40, 1241–42.

Grant asked, "with the colored and regular troops sent to you can you not now muster out of service all the volunteers remaining?"[37]

Pope patiently replied to the last question. Grant had forgotten about the treacherous climate on the plains. Pope agreed he could use the troops that Grant proposed to send, but repeated that it was impossible to get them on the plains this winter. No way could he "relieve troops farther west than Kearny . . . without enormous cost . . . and great suffering to men." New troops could "relieve all volunteer troops east of . . . Fort Kearny." Sherman told Grant he would send Pope the 2nd United States Cavalry and the 3rd and 10th United States Infantry. That sounded good, but Pope discovered the 10th Infantry had just 250 troops, and the 3rd only 90 men, "eighty of whom will be discharged this winter. I cannot relieve many volunteer regiments with these two regular regiments." When he told Grant he could relieve the volunteers east of Kearny, Pope had "supposed" the regular regiments would be "at least two-thirds full."[38]

Grant advised Sherman on October 31 to be certain to give "the best protection to the overland lines of travel" as well as the "frontier and mountain settlements." Because he believed railroads were making "rapid progress" westward, Sherman need not "establish many permanent posts" or spend "more money than is absolutely necessary." Grant believed railroads would solve the transportation problems, and military posts along the overland roads would become redundant. He also mentioned that he had ordered four regiments of United States Colored Troops dispatched to Pope to be placed as far out on the plains as he could. He would send more soldiers if they could be used. Grant thought "these troops will do very well on the plains . . . and may also furnish labor hereafter for

[37]Ibid., pp. 1243–44.

[38]Ibid., pp. 1244–45.

our railroads and mining interests." Also, Pope should not worry, since "recruits will be sent to you rapidly to fill up the regular organizations." With winter at hand, he wondered if Sherman could not "anticipate this increase and discharge volunteers accordingly." Pope had already answered that question.[39]

Pressure mounted for the government to discharge the volunteer soldiers. Governor Charles Anderson of Ohio wrote Secretary of War Stanton as early as September 16, offering a strong case for mustering out all Ohio volunteers. Then on October 27 he wrote Stanton again. This time he specifically requested the discharge of the 11th Ohio Cavalry, and enclosed an "application" from Major Marshall for mustering out. Anderson protested "the detention of volunteers in a service not contemplated by themselves when they enlisted, nor yet authorized by the acts of Congress." The governor noted that "having failed apparently in procuring an assent to my demand for the prompt discharge" of Ohio volunteers, all he could do, unfortunately, was "forward" the applications of the troops themselves. Equally unfortunately for the governor, Marshall's 11th Ohio Cavalry was too far out on the plains to be relieved at this time. They still had months to serve.[40]

---

[39]Ibid., p. 1250.

[40]Ibid., III, 5, pp. 115–16, 161. Governor Anderson stretched a point or two in his arguments. Men of the 11th who had enlisted in 1863 and 1864 did in fact do so to fight in the West. Even so, Anderson was only one among many governors who wanted the boys home. So did their constituents, and the governors knew it. When Governor John Brough died in office, Anderson filled the remainder of his term.

CHAPTER FOURTEEN

Goodbye

The winter of 1865–66 at Fort Laramie settled in with its usual harsh weather, accompanied by dreary routine duty for the troops. From Fort Laramie, on October 19, 1865, Corporal Johnson wrote to his sister in Ohio that Companies F, G, and K, 11th Ohio, along with Company G, 6th United States Volunteers, and Company F, 7th Iowa, garrisoned the post. Johnson, whose duties included office work and guard duty, neglected to mention that the 12th Missouri camped a mile or two "below" the fort. Springer, with his company of the 12th Missouri, met a "former companion" of his, dating back to brief service in the 1st Cavalry in 1860–61, who had "bought a squaw" from the Sioux. The friend and his wife had produced a child, about whom Springer said "the boy is white and no Indian blood is visible in him." About the same time, Springer encountered another "great chum," also "married" to a Sioux woman who served as an interpreter. They, too, tried to convince Springer to stay in the West and marry, but Springer said the Powder River Expedition knocked any notion of living there out of his head.[1]

Springer went wolf hunting on October 20, and though he winged one, it got away. In the next few days the temperature

[1]Unrau, *Tending the Talking Wire*, 298; Springer, *Soldiering in Sioux Country*, 68. The 6th U.S. Volunteers replaced the 3rd U.S. Volunteers.

fell, rain changed to sleet, then snow, and the 12th Missouri held a massive snowball fight on the 24th. Springer confided to his diary the good news that orders had come for his regiment to return home, but then he followed with the bad news that Companies B and C and Springer were not included. Most of his regiment actually left on the 30th, but Springer then had "to do post and garrison duty." Meanwhile, the 6th West Virginia Veteran Volunteers finally arrived in the vicinity, relieving the departing 6th Michigan. Two companies pushed on to Platte Bridge. The 21st New York Volunteer Cavalry made it to Fort Collins, to take up duty on the Overland Road. Even as these events unfolded, George Bent's Cheyennes had crossed and raided along the Platte, then camped with Cheyenne Dog Soldiers on Solomon's Fork of the Kansas River. As they next moved on south they attacked the new stage line on the Smoky Hill route to Denver, as Dodge had witnessed, went on to cross the Arkansas River in December, and arrived on the Cimmaron late that month. They camped with Black Kettle's followers, where Kiowas, Comanches, and Apaches located also.[2]

November 1865 proved cold and windy, with some snow. Garrison duty at Fort Laramie settled into a boring routine, only occasionally relieved by action. On November 1, eleven men of the 12th Missouri began to convoy a mule train to Platte Bridge. Three miles from the fort, Indians attacked them, then fled when "troops turned out" from the garrison. When General Wheaton left Fort Laramie for Omaha, where he intended to establish his headquarters, a detail from Company F, 11th Ohio, served as his escort. Corporal Johnson asserted that Wheaton had pledged to Major Marshall that the 11th Ohio would be relieved in four months.[3]

---

[2]Springer, *Soldiering in Sioux Country*, 69–71; Hyde, *George Bent*, 243; *O.R.*, I, 48, pt. 2, pp. 1178, 1185, 1212, 1222; McDermott, *Frontier Crossroads*, 79–80.

[3]Unrau, *Tending the Talking Wire*, 303; Springer, *Soldiering in Sioux Country*, 71; Hyde, *George Bent*, 243.

In his diary a bored Springer constantly confided his "blues" concerning his duty. Sometimes he acted as officer of the day; he and his companions played a lot of baseball in the gloomy, chilly November weather. By November's end "life at the Fort got so monotonous" that he discontinued his "daily journal." Companies I and L, 11th Ohio, at Platte Bridge and other units from Fort Laramie served as escorts and on scout duty, their only breaks from monotony. General Pope issued General Order Number 49 on November 21, renaming Platte Bridge as Fort Caspar, in honor of Lieutenant Caspar Collins. The post office apparently spelled the name incorrectly, and today the community is Casper, Wyoming.[4]

If the troopers found their duty dull, at least they could be thankful that the winter of 1865–66 proved quiet along the Oregon and Overland roads. Native Americans in the north huddled in their winter camps, while many of the Sioux had gone east, and the Southern Cheyennes lodged far away, south of the Arkansas River. Though Indian marauders were few that snowy winter, they killed soldiers and civilians at Fort Laramie's sawmill by Laramie Peak in November, took stock from Horseshoe Station, and in December stole the horses from Camp Marshall. Given the aggression and determination of the tribesmen following the Sand Creek Massacre and the failure of the military to master the situation in 1865, fear of a repetition in the new year troubled the troopers on duty and their commanders as well.

The safety of the roads and the conflicting views on Native American affairs worried Pope enough that in February 1866, he prepared a lengthy and thoughtful report for Sherman. Agreeing with Pope's recommendations, Sherman sent the recommendations on to Grant. Diplomatically, Grant called

[4]Springer, *Soldiering in Sioux Country*, 70–73; *Collins Family Papers*, item 98; Spring, "An Army Wife Comes West," 241n. 2. For part of the following paragraph, see McDermott, *Frontier Crossroads*, 82.

it a "very admirable report." Pope noted that protection of communications across the "broad and desolate plains, infected by hostile Indians" was "essential," especially since "people in incredible numbers . . . continue to throng across the great plains" regardless of seasons, hardships, or the "constant and relentless hostility" of the Indians.

Pope urged completion of the Pacific railroad, which would "diminish the cost and hazard of transportation." It would also cost less in the long run and be more beneficial for Native Americans if the government would just buy their lands outright, locate them on decent reservations, and protect them from "dishonest agents" and "lawless white men," rather than concluding peace treaties that were followed by Indian wars. As it was now, Pope wrote, the Native American "is forced to protect himself" as whites simply "seize" whatever Indian property they want. His views on that subject had been previously stated, as both Sherman and Grant well knew.

Under the present unsatisfactory circumstances, Pope had calculated the number of troops that would be necessary to carry out his assignment. He required a total of twelve regiments of infantry and six of cavalry, or 9,000 troops (not counting the volunteers, of whom he he had 3,650 on hand). Then, "for contingencies about one-third should be added to the force." Moreover, new troops should arrive at Fort Leavenworth "as early as April 10" in order for them to "reach remote posts and relieve the volunteers in time [for them] . . . to reach Fort Leavenworth before cold weather." Pope based his estimate, he said, "upon the understanding that the government means to give protection to the frontiers, to trains and emigrants" and the miners. Pope asked what "the general-in-chief" concluded from his report. While Grant may have agreed with Pope, he had not the means, financially or politically, to implement it, with unfortunate results for the future.[5]

[5]Richard N. Ellis, ed., "General Pope's Report on the West, 1866," *The Kansas Historical Quarterly* 35, no. 4 (Winter, 1969): 345–72.

As the volunteers gradually departed for discharge, hope for security along the roads increasingly rested on the nearly impossible task of convincing tribesmen to keep the peace. This view was in keeping with the thinking of President Johnson's administration in Washington. While Connor had been in the field, Governor Newton Edmunds of Dakota Territory, along with General Henry H. Sibley of Minnesota and others, comprised a peace commission that visited the Sioux along the upper Missouri River. They persuaded many lesser chiefs to sign nine separate peace treaties, but although they sent runners into the Black Hills and the Powder River country, they were unsuccessful in attracting any who were occupied in resisting Connor. Even so, optimistic authorities in Washington considered the treaties as a sign that hostilities were at an end, and that million-dollar expeditions such as Connor's would be unnecessary in the future. Those actually present with Edmund's commission and other westerners knew the treaties were meaningless without the compliance of the Powder River war chiefs.

It also appeared certain that 1866 would bring even larger numbers of gold seekers to Montana. That meant the Bozeman Trail, the shortest route from Fort Laramie to Fort Connor (soon to be renamed Fort Reno) and on to the mines in Montana, would be very busy. Though a good road and relatively easy to travel, it ran through the heart of Sioux country. It proved to be a very dangerous road. The water route, up the Missouri River, was secure enough, but much longer; the Oregon and Overland roads into Utah and then north to Montana were more difficult and many miles longer than the Bozeman, but considerably safer. Colonel Maynadier at Fort Laramie understood all this very well.

Following Wheaton's order in October, Maynadier sent Big Ribs and four other friendly Sioux to convince Red Cloud and others to come to Fort Laramie and talk of peace. These emmisaries, sometimes called the "Laramie Loafers," as they were among those who habitually camped near the fort, were in fact clever Native American traders who also had much to gain from peace. Maynadier heard nothing from them until mid-January, when they turned up with two needy bands of Brulés led by Standing Elk and Swift Bear. Corporal Johnson, Company G, 11th Ohio, reported to his brother that Indian chiefs were coming in and spending time talking with the officers.[6]

An optimistic Maynadier thought that peace could be made with the tribesmen, not only the Sioux, but also the Northern Cheyennes and Arapahos, though it would be spring before he could communicate with all of them, he told the commissioner of Indian affairs. The United States readied a commission to negotiate with the tribes sometime in late spring at Fort Laramie. Maynadier proved to be something of a diplomat, as Colonel Collins had been before him. He arranged a spectacular funeral for Fleet Foot, daughter of Brulé chief Spotted Tail, who died as her father brought her to Fort Laramie for treatment by the post physician. Later, when the redoubtable Red Cloud appeared, Maynadier escorted him into camp with military pomp and circumstance.[7]

Life at Fort Laramie continued with only occasional excitement for Corporal Johnson and the men of the 11th Ohio. He noted that two men from each regiment—the 11th Ohio, the 12th Missouri, and the 6th United States Volunteers—had deserted, and the detachment sent to find them returned empty-handed. A soldier from Company E, 11th Ohio, was killed by another trooper. The man who died was, at the time, serving at hard labor with ball and chain for trying to kill his captain. Johnson thought it was no loss, as the

[6]Brown, *Bury My Heart at Wounded Knee*, 123–24; Olson, *Red Cloud and the Sioux Problem*, 28–29; Unrau, *Tending the Talking Wire*, 315.

[7]Olson, *Red Cloud and the Sioux Problem*, 29; Brown, *Bury My Heart at Wounded Knee*, 124–25; McDermott, *Frontier Crossroads*, 83–84.

man was a hard case at best. He reported that Lieutenant Collins's remains had been brought to Laramie, and he attended the funeral.[8]

The troopers at Laramie witnessed larger and larger numbers of tribesmen gathering in the vicinity that spring, awaiting the arrival of the peace commissioners. Johnson noted that the soldiers were cautiously alert. In the midst of this, he described for his sister the unusual ceremony of drumming a soldier out of service (akin to a dishonorable discharge). One of the "galvanized yankees" of the 6th United States Volunteers, formerly a British army officer, then a lieutenant in Confederate service, was court-martialed (for an offense Johnson neglected to explain). The man was brought out on the parade ground in front of the assembled garrison. After having his sentence read and his uniform stripped of insignia, fifers and drummers played the "Rogue's March" and soldiers with fixed bayonets marched the culprit out of the garrison. Once outside, he was on his own.[9]

In March 1866 the remaining two companies of Springer's 12th Missouri finally received orders to return to Fort Leavenworth and were separated from service there on April 9. On April 1, the 7th Iowa received orders for their muster out. The seven companies still in the field, now under the command of Major John Wilcox, rendezvoused at Fort McPherson (formerly Fort Cottonwood) and marched east. They arrived at Fort Leavenworth early in May and were mustered out on the 17th. Meanwhile, the 11th Ohio had been melting away. Some thirty-three had been discharged in 1865 (a third of those in Company F); between January and April 1866 another twenty-seven left; in May 1866, forty-five more were

---

[8]Unrau, *Tending the Talking Wire*, 315, 319, 325.

[9]Ibid., 338. Editor Unrau notes this man ultimately found his way to Denver, and became a mining engineer and businessman. Hull witnessed a similar event at Fort Laramie, July 8, 1865; Hull, "Soldiering on the High Plains," 41.

discharged, including thirty from Company F, men who had accompanied General Wheaton from Laramie to Omaha the previous November. Orders for the remainder came to Fort Laramie in May. The two companies at Fort Caspar, I and L, came in to Laramie and joined the remainder of Companies E, F, G, and K. They united with Company H at Fort Mitchell and reached Fort Leavenworth in early July. On the 14th all 327 were sent home. But some members of the 11th Ohio remained behind. Eighty-four more were discharged at Laramie on July 21, with 2 more on July 26, and 2 others in September. The total number mustered out between January and September 1866 was 529.[10]

As the volunteer presence faded away, the peace commissioners arrived at Fort Laramie on May 30. Corporal Johnson was not optimistic that they would meet with success. Replacements began to arrive in June. Three companies of the 18th United States Infantry, with a cavalry company due shortly, along with another company of the 6th United States Volunteers arrived to replace those who had been sent home.[11]

Although Corporal Hervey Johnson could not have known it, the arrival of the replacements broke up the peace conference. The troops were led by Colonel Henry B. Carrington, commander of the 18th United States Infantry. He was a

---

[10]Springer, *Soldiering in Sioux Country*, 4, 73; Pattison, "With the U.S. Army along the Oregon Trail," *Nebraska History Magazine* 15 (1934): 91–93; *Official Roster of the Soldiers of the State of Ohio*, 560–82. Captain Bretney, perhaps still upset over the way in which Caspar Collins died, faced a court-martial September 28, 1865, for conduct unbecoming an officer. Convicted, he was dismissed from service November 1. Still at Fort Laramie, he spent part of the winter of 1866 in hospital with pneumonia before returning to Ohio in the spring; see McDermott, *Frontier Crossroads*, 79.

[11]Unrau, *Tending the Talking Wire*, 340, 343. On July 26, 1866, Companies C and D, 5th U.S. Volunteers, left Fort Connor, replaced by elements of the 18th Infantry. But Captain Williford was not among them: he died at Fort Casper, April 29, 1866; Brown, *Galvanized Yankees*, 133–37. The peace commissioners were E. B. Taylor, head of the Northern [Indian] Superintendency as president, Colonel Maynadier, R. N. McLaren of Minnesota, and Thomas Wistar of Philadelphia. Charles E. Bowles from the Department of the Interior was secretary.

lawyer who had practiced in Columbus, Ohio, with William Dennison. When Dennison became governor in 1861, he made Carrington Ohio's adjutant general. While in that position, he received a commission as colonel of the 18th Infantry. Carrington never saw field duty, serving Ohio and Indiana as a brigadier general of volunteers in an effort to root out subversives such as the Knights of the Golden Circle and the Sons of Liberty. In 1866 he returned to the regular army as a colonel.[12]

When Carrington and three hundred men of the 18th Infantry camped four miles east of Fort Laramie on the 13th, Standing Elk, one of the Brulé chiefs who had been at Laramie since January, rode out and spoke with Carrington to ascertain his destination. Carrington bluntly told him that he was on his way to the Powder River country to protect the route to Montana. Standing Elk warned Carrington if that were so, he would have to fight the Sioux. Red Cloud and his Oglalas would not allow white men in that country. It made no difference when Carrington said he would not fight the Sioux, only guard the road. News of Carrington's intentions quickly spread among the tribesmen. On June 14, the peace commissioners formally introduced Carrington to the chiefs and let it be known that the United States intended to open a road to Montana through their territory. Indignant with the commissioners and considering a road through the Powder River country not negotiable, Red Cloud and the Oglalas stormed out and were gone by morning.[13]

As Red Cloud left Laramie, so did six companies of the 11th Ohio. They camped a mile downstream to make room for Carrington's 18th Infantry, and to prepare for their march to Fort Leavenworth. Johnson observed that no peace treaty

---

[12]John T. Hubbell and James S. Geary, eds., *Biographical Dictionary of the Union: Northern Leaders of the Civil War* (Westport, Conn.: Greenwood Press, 1995), 86–87.

[13]Brown, *Bury My Heart at Wounded Knee*, 128–30; Olson, *Red Cloud amd the Sioux Problem*, 35–37; McDermott, *Frontier Crossroads*, 85.

had materialized, and he frevently hoped the tribesmen would remain calm until he was east of Fort Kearny. "I wont feel safe this side of there," he wrote. Fortunately for Johnson, those tribesmen who were hostile focused on Carrington and his movement north into the Powder River country, and not on the Oregon road to the south. Meanwhile, the peace commissioners signed a treaty with those Indians whose interest in the Powder River area was marginal and who were unconcerned with any road through it. That treaty brought no peace to Laramie.[14]

The companies of the 11th Ohio leaving Fort Laramie joined the remaining company, H, at Fort (formerly Camp) Mitchell, a few miles west of Scotts Bluff. The 327 men were the second-largest assemblage of the 11th Ohio: the only larger group were the 384 who had crossed west to Fort Laramie in May 1862. At Fort Sedgwick, near the crossing of the South Platte by Julesburg, the post commander ordered them to surrender their horses, but Major Marshall refused. He told the officer he had orders to take them to Fort Leavenworth. If the colonel at Sedgwick persisted, Johnson reported, "we wouldnt leave enough of his men to tell the tale." The troopers of the 11th were told "to shoot the first man to come after our horses." Sedgwick's commander told Marshall he would issue no rations without the horses. Marshall believed the 11th had enough rations of its own for a day or two; certainly no cavalryman would walk all the way to Leavenworth. Even so, they almost lost their mounts when they stampeded in a terrific hailstorm, but the 11th recovered the horses the next morning.[15]

---

[14]Unrau, *Tending the Talking Wire*, 345; Brown, *Bury My Heart at Wounded Knee*, 130–31; Olson, *Red Cloud and the Sioux Problem*, 37–38; McDermott, *Frontier Crossroads*, 85–86.

[15]Unrau, *Tending the Talking Wire*, 351–52; Robrock, "The Eleventh Ohio," 47. Not just the 11th Ohio left for muster out, but also the 6th West Virginia, the 21st New York, and other volunteer troops as well.

The remainder of the 11th Ohio's journey east was uneventful, at least so far as hostile tribesmen were concerned. Following the south bank of the Platte River, they picked up necessary provisions at Fort McPherson. Surveyors and graders for the Union Pacific Railroad were working on the north bank, but at that time the tracks stretched only a few miles from Omaha. The troopers passed damaged and burnt road ranches, as well as some that had somehow survived the depredations of 1864. At Plum Creek, about halfway between Julesburg and Fort Kearny, they rode by the scene of the 1864 massacre where thirteen civilians had perished, the grass barely beginning to grow over the mass grave. That was also the place where young Nancy Morton, whom some of the troopers of the 11th had met after her release, had been captured and her husband slain.

After Fort Kearny, they followed the road down the valley of the Little Blue River, also a scene of carnage in August 1864. As they passed Kiowa Station, a few of the men could remember Lucinda Eubank, who had been taken near there and whose tormentors, Two Face and Blackfoot, had been hanged at Laramie by Colonel Moonlight following her release from captivity. Others could remember the butchery they saw there while on their way to Fort Kearny in August 1864. When the seven companies of the 11th reached Fort Leavenworth, they turned in their horses and equipment and were mustered out of service on July 14, 1866. They returned to Columbus, Ohio, by rail and received their final pay. They were the last volunteer troops from Ohio to return from the field.

Guarding the Overland and Oregon roads fell to the regular army again, as it had before the outbreak of the Civil War. Within a few years, the roads would be largely supplanted by the railroad, and places such as Fort Kearny became redundant. The railroad reached there in late August 1867. Four years later, Kearny, unneeded, was abandoned. So were other posts near the rail line, such as Fort Halleck. Fort Laramie survived until the 1890s, as it was not on the railroad. The Union Pacific Railroad transported goods and supplies at a fraction of the cost of overland wagon freight, saving the United States government millions of dollars as it supported regular troops in the field. The railroad also moved troops quickly from place to place, reducing the need for and number of military posts. The railroad also created many new towns peopled by emigrants and others who came at relatively low cost in both time and money. The railroad accelerated agricultural settlement and mineral exploration across the region. The plains would never be the same as it had been when the Ohioans and other volunteers arrived in the early 1860s.

Much unfinished business remained after the volunteers turned over protection of the Overland and Oregon roads, the telegraph, and the mail to the regulars. Connor's Powder River Expedition had ended in controversy. Even though Dodge backed Connor and believed he accomplished a great deal, others disagreed. Connor's work in the field kept the tribesmen occupied, and for that brief window in time commerce on the roads remained relatively free from interference. Once Connor and his men left the Powder River, leaving only a small garrison at Fort Connor, the tribesmen were free again to harass the roads. The expedition failed to bring the permanent peace to the roads that both Connor and Dodge sought. Both men believed it necessary to keep a significant force in the field, but were thwarted by fiscal necessity and the desire of the government to send the volunteers home. In March 1866, Connor traveled to Washington, D.C., to confer with Grant, and on April 19, with Dodge's recommendation approved by Grant, Connor was brevetted major-general of volunteers retroactive to March 13, 1865, for "gallant and meritorious service." Grant offered him a commission as a colonel in the regular army's cavalry, but Connor declined, desiring to return to his business activities.[16]

Connor never felt any disgrace attached to his abrupt removal and exile back to Utah. His reputation among Westerners remained undiminished. Samuel Clemens, the redoubtable Mark Twain, who had traveled the Oregon road and worked in the West, wrote in 1867: "I am waiting patiently to hear they have ordered General Connor out to polish off those Indians, but the news never comes." He knew how "to fight the kind of Indian that God made, but I suppose the humanitarians want somebody to fight the Indians that J. Fenimore Cooper made." That was the problem. "The Cooper Indians are dead—died with their creator." Those remaining are "altogether a different breed, and cannot be successfully fought with poetry, and sentiment, and soft soap, and magnanimity." Today Twain would not win a "politically correct" award with such prose, but he reflected western white sentiment at the time.[17]

Even before Twain wrote, news of the Fetterman Massacre of December 21, 1866, in which eighty-one troopers of Carrington's command were slain, spread across the nation. This was in the heart of the country Connor had traversed along the Bozeman Trail. Sioux, Cheyennes, and Arapahos continued to plague the trail, harassing newly-created forts Reno, Phil Kearny, and C. F. Smith until the United States abandoned those posts in July and August 1868, leaving the country to the tribesmen and shutting down the trail. For

[16]Rogers, *Soldiers of the Overland*, 248; Madsen, *Glory Hunter*, 161–62.

[17]*Alta California*, August 11, 1867, letter dated New York, June 5, 1867, quoted in Rogers, *Soldiers of the Overland*, 246; Mattes, *The Great Platte River Road*, 19; Hafen and Young, *Fort Laramie*, 304.

this, Twain chided the peacemakers, who were unable to handle Red Cloud and his allied warriors any more than the army could. If they had continued another phase of the Powder River affair in 1866, would Connor and his volunteers have so chastized those intrepid northern tribesmen that the Bozeman Trail would have remained open and the other roads made safe? Questionable, at best, but a hypothesis both Dodge and Connor—and Twain—believed. In less than two years, the Union Pacific Railroad largely superseded the Overland and Oregon roads, making the question moot.

★ ★ ★

The men who comprised the 11th Ohio Volunteer Cavalry provided a vital service to the United States. From the president down, government leaders stressed the importance of communication with the states of California and Oregon to the embattled Union. The Far West held great wealth, both immediate and potential, and was urgently needed to help finance an unprecedentedly expensive war effort. The Pacific Rim was important politically as well. Yet the lengthy communications link faced a threat far more serious than the government recognized, as powerful combinations of misunderstood and often mistreated Native Americans determined to disrupt it.

The Overland roads needed protection. By the summer of 1862, fewer than 350 Ohioans, with a handful of others, guarded some thousand miles of the Oregon road with its telegraph and the Overland road with its mail service. Other small volunteer units provided some assistance over the next two years, but not until the debacle at Sand Creek and the months of bloody revenge that followed did reinforcements in any number arrive to help protect the vulnerable stretch of road from Julesburg west to the Continental Divide.

Not only did these few face duty that stretched their thin blue line over vast distances, but also they confronted the vicissitudes of a hostile climate as well as increasingly violent Native Americans. Yet in spite of the hardships and bloody confrontations, emigrants, the mail, and telegraphic messages continued to flow westward with only brief interruptions.

Whitelaw Reid, the intrepid war correspondent from Ohio whose reporting from Shiloh and Gettysburg was widely reprinted, by 1865 had become editor of the *New York Tribune*, following Horace Greeley. He wrote: "It is impossible to give even an outline of the services of the Eleventh Ohio Cavalry" out in the Far West "from 1862 to 1865. A complete history would be full of startling incidents and hair-breadth escapes." Their losses "fully equalled the average loss in other cavalry regiments from Ohio. In addition, . . . many men were frozen to death. The skirmishes were almost innumerable." Distances traveled by "scouting and escorting parties was probably not paralleled in any other service during the war." Reid emphasized the "occasional severity of the weather," but "with the hardships and dangers" were "a few pleasures," such as the bands, the library at Fort Laramie of "about 800 volumes . . . obtained . . . by donation and purchase" and circulated "to distant posts." He mentioned that "even a theater was improvised" for the troops, and it seemed "some . . . had faced the footlights before." Reid could not let these Ohioans be very easily dismissed even though their Civil War service differed from most others in Union volunteer armies.[18]

In 1869, with the coast-to-coast rail completed, the overland roads declined in importance. Fort Laramie survived for another three decades, however, as it took the military until the 1890s to bring peace to the high plains, subduing proud Native Americans who lost their tribal homelands and their

[18]Reprinted in Mokler, *Fort Caspar*, 52, 54.

way of life. In their place, towns, cities, ranches, and farms appeared even as the tribesmen, buffalo, and other game disappeared. By the turn of the century, the high plains and intermountain region that once-vital overland roads had traversed had changed radically, and the troopers of the 11th Ohio were virtually forgotten.

APPENDIX

Author's Notes and Statistics

The Forts

Readers may think of a "fort" as an enclosed and defensible position. But west of the Mississippi River in the 1860s few "forts" were fortified. Fort Laramie was a major military post and supply base built around a sizeable square of parade ground, in the center of which was a flagpole. Around the sides of the parade ground were barracks, officer's quarters, a headquarters building, a military jail, and scattered about were a large stable, kitchens, a hospital, the sutler's store and dwelling, laundry facilities, and other structures. Some were frame buildings, built of lumber supplied from the post's own sawmill; others were constructed from logs or adobe. There were no breastworks or stockade for defense. The same held true for other "forts" in this story, such as forts Kearny, Larned, Halleck, Leavenworth, and so on.

Smaller positions the soldiers occupied along the Oregon and Overland roads were fortified. Camp Rankin, close by Julesburg, Colorado Territory, where the Oregon and Denver roads converged, had a sod wall about three feet thick and five feet high around its adobe buildings. After it became Fort Sedgwick in September 1865, the wall was removed to permit the post to be enlarged. Camp, later Fort Mitchell, just northwest of Scotts Bluff and close to the North Platte River, also was built of adobe enclosed by a defensive wall.

Of the smaller stations the military occupied, those that served primarily as stage stations or telegraph relay stations or both usually had corrals that were stockaded. In the winter of 1864–65 many of those along the Oregon road west and north of Fort Laramie such as Platte Bridge and Deer Creek were ordered enclosed with stockades. At Platte Bridge a sturdy stockade was built—fortunately for the battle there in July 1865—but it was removed when the post was renovated and enlarged in 1866.

Uniforms and Clothing

The uniforms of A, B, C, and D Companies of the 11th Ohio were initially provided by the state of Ohio. When the Civil War broke out, it fell to the states to equip soldiers with uniforms and supplies, then bill the federal government for them. Later enlistees, especially in 1863 and after, were outfitted by the United States. The government's clothing allowance for privates was $3.50 a month or $42 a year. A soldier could outfit himself for about $28. This meant the trooper had to take good care of what he had, since any additional clothing the soldier had to buy himself out of his regular pay of $13 a month. Officers had to purchase their own uniforms. Troopers hoarded their good uniforms, wearing them only on dress occasions or when ordered to do so. Everyday appearance depended upon the strictness of the officers, with soldiers often being allowed to wear whatever they had on hand. Soldiers in garrison usually were uniformed, but a cavalryman in the West on scout or escort duty seldom wore more uniform than a coat or jacket, with the remainder of their clothing of their own choosing. Cavalrymen were issued greatcoats for winter wear, but there was no lightweight summer uniform for any soldier.

Discipline and Morale in the 11th Ohio

Generally, troopers operating west of the Mississippi believed they were citizens first and soldiers second. Often they obeyed those orders from officers they deemed reasonable, not because they were orders. Private Hervey Johnson had trouble from thè first with military authority, beginning early in his career on the march west. He never ceased to ridicule officers. Sergeant Hull, more experienced, expressed displeasure with some activities of the soldiers, especially their drinking to excess. At one time or another the men served in tiny posts with just a few others, more or less left to their own devices. They faced the danger of hostile Indians together and coped as best they could with loneliness. Military discipline may have been lax at such times, still they had to be alert to the hazards of their duty. They depended on their comrades.

While on garrison duty at Fort Laramie more rigorous discipline applied. Regular daily military forms were followed, from roll call and reveille to taps and lights out, with drill and training in between. For many the routine seemed monotonous compared with being in the saddle in the field. To those rotated back to the fort after weeks or months of service largely on their own at small posts, garrison work at the fort seemed welcome.

Morale rose and fell depending on circumstances. It usually was high at enlistment. For the companies enlisted in 1861 and 1862, disappointment touched them all when they discovered they were ordered west, away from the war with Confederates. But adventure followed with the trek west into country they had never seen or experienced before, with their future unknown. There was excitement present, and they overcame their disappointment with their new assignment.

Those who enlisted from 1863 on knew they were going

west from the outset. Many had signed up for the adventure of it; others were pleased to escape the draft and at the same time be saved from fighting relatives and friends in Southern armies; some joined up to elude the pain of prisoner-of-war camps; and there were those who planned to desert when they arrived in the West to seek their fortune in gold fields. For all of them, morale was high at enlistment.

When the time came to staff the new companies, many non-commissioned officers expected to become officers in them. Most were disappointed. Those who were held after their enlistments expired also faced disillusion. Lack of mail service from time to time displeased others. Morale, or the lack of it, was usually an individual phenomena. While at Fort Laramie, and to some extent at other posts, the troops were permitted various entertainments and celebrations that doubtless boosted morale.

Overall, the troopers did what was required of them. There may have been individual gripes and concerns, but anyone who has been in military service knows this was standard procedure. When they faced battle, the troopers did not flinch. Indian warriors gave no quarter, offered no surrender even to wounded troopers.

Native Americans of the Plains

Those Native American nations, or tribes, that primarily involved the 11th Ohio and the other units that patroled the Oregon and Overland roads were the Sioux, Cheyennes, and Arapahos. The economy of these nations, perhaps as much as 80 percent of it, depended upon the buffalo. Any threat to that animal could be devastating to the tribes who sought to protect themselves from that menace by any means available.

The political organization of these plains tribes was common to each. Each of the nations was subdivided into an array of kinship bands. These bands gathered together as a nation once a year, usually in the spring, for a communal hunt and religious observances such as a Sun Dance. After that, the numerous bands went their own way for the remainder of the year. Leadership was limited to the band level, which explained the number of "chiefs." In times of peace, the chief of a band usually was a respected elder, such as Black Kettle of the Cheyennes. But with hostilities, the warriors chose a respected and fearless fellow combatant to lead them, like the Sioux Red Cloud. The only authority that either war or peace chiefs had rested on the consensus among those in the particular band. Overall tribal leaders could be appointed for collective activities such as the communal hunt each spring, but often such was the business of a council of band chieftans.

Neither the nation as a whole nor any of its bands bore any responsibility for the actions of any single band, something white people, especially the white military, never understood. If Shaking Leaf's band stole horses from whites, for example, and the whites punished Lone Eagle's band for it, Lone Eagle's people considered that wholly undeserved and unjust treatment. While some whites could distinguish Cheyennes from Sioux or Arapahos (and not all could), few (if any) could tell one band from another. This single fact led to many serious misunderstandings and caused great Native American resentment of whites.

The Cheyenne and Arapaho belonged to the Algonquian language group, the Sioux to the Siouan language classification. Yet these plains tribes had been in contact with one another for many years, they had intermarried, and communication between them was not a problem. All were male-dominated societies.

Ages of Troopers in the 11th Ohio at Enlistment

Average age of all officers was just over 26 (26.1); the range of ages varied from 18 to 64. The average age of all sergeants was 24 (23.8); the age range was also 18 to 64. The average age of privates and corporals was also 24 (23.6); their ages ranged from 15 to 50.

Average age of privates in Companies A, B, C, and D who enlisted in 1861 and 1862 was 25 (24.5). Of privates in E, F, G, and H Companies enlisted in 1863 and 1864 it was 23 (23.0). The average age of privates in Companies I, K, and L who enlisted in 1864 or transferred from other companies was also 23 (22.5).

Those who enlisted in 1863 and 1864 were younger than those who enlisted earlier.

The army had no companies with the designation J.

Further Statistics Concerning the 11th Ohio

These were assembled from the *Official Roster of the Soldiers of the State of Ohio in the War of the Rebellion, 1861–1866*, vol. XI, pp. 549–82.

Number arriving at Fort Laramie, May 30, 1862: 369 officers and men from four companies, plus 15 field and staff, officers and non-commissioned officers, total 384.

Co. A, 104 men accepted for duty.

1 died January 7, 1862, in Ohio
1 died at Fort Kearny, May 27, 1862
6 discharged for one reason or another prior to march west
96 officers and men arrived at Fort Laramie.

Co. B, 89 men accepted for duty.

3 died at Fort Kearny, May 11, 19, and 23, 1862
2 discharged before march west
84 officers and men arrived at Fort Laramie.

Co. C, 99 men accepted for duty.
2 left in Ohio March 15, 1862
1 enlisted elsewhere February 28, 1862
1 deserted after February 28, 1862
95 officers and men arrived at Fort Laramie.

Co. D, 107 men accepted for duty.
1 died in Ohio, December 20, 1861
1 discharged November 30, 1861
1 became recruiter, December 19, 1861
1 died at Fort Kearny, May 13, 1862
2 discharged at Camp Dennison, Ohio, March 26, 1862
2 transferred to infantry
3 others discharged in March, 1862
1 left sick in Ohio, March 15, 1862
1 discharged near Fort Leavenworth, April 17, 1862
94 men arrived at Fort Laramie.

Replacements for Companies A, B, C, D enlisted in 1863: 104
Field and Staff: 14
Co. A, 19; Co. B, 15; Co. C, 16; Co. D, 40.

Dead of Companies A, B, C, D, while on duty in West: 17
Co. A, 5; Co. B, 7; Co. C, 2; Co. D, 3.

Total discharged and enlisted in Company F, 4th U.S. Cavalry in January 1863: 10 from Company A, 1 from Company C, and probably 1 from Co. D, total 12

Companies A, B, C, and D:
Total discharged, after arrival at Fort Laramie, most on surgeon's certificate of disability, 35
Total resigned (officers), after arrival at Fort Laramie, 6
Total disappeared or deserted, after arrival at Fort Laramie, 53

Total that reenlisted and transferred to Companies E, F, G, H, I, K, and L, and did not return home with Companies A, B, C, and D: 123
Most joined Co. L: 73; 17 to Co. H

Total Companies A, B, C, D discharged April 1, 1865: 204 in the 4 companies, plus 12 field and staff, total 216

Companies E, F, G, H, I, K, and L formed in June and July 1863, and January to July 1864.
By June 1, 1865, Companies E, F, G, H, I, K, L, numbered 665 officers and men in the 7 companies, plus 6 field and staff, total 671

Company E: original strength, officers and men, 169
unknown, probably deserted, 51
discharged, died, or transfered (outside regiment), 21
joined from Co. A, 2; Co. B, 16; Co. D, 3, total 21
Certain on hand June 1, 1865: 97
Company F: original strength, officers and men, 130
unknown, probably deserted, 22
discharged, died, or transfered (outside regiment) 12
joined from Co. A, 3; Co. B, 3; total 6
Certain on hand June 1, 1865: 96
Company G: original strength, officers and men, 117
unknown, probably deserted, 6
discharged, died, or transfered, 3
joined from Co. A, 1; Co. D, 1; total 2
Certain of hand June 1, 1865, 108
Company H: original strength, officers and men, 144
unknown, probably deserted, 32
discharged, died, or transfered, 17
joined from Co. A, 2; Co. B, 14; Co. D, 1; total 17
Certain on hand June 1, 1865, 95
Company I: original strength, officers and men, 92
unknown, probably deserted, 1

discharged, died, or transfered, 3
joined from Co. B, 1; Co. D, 1; total 2
Certain on hand June 1, 1865: 88
Company K: original strength, officers and men, 96
unknown, probably deserted, 6
discharged, died, or transfered, 7
joined from Co. A, 2; total 2
Certain on hand June 1, 1865, 83
Company L: original strength, officers and men, 90
unknown, probably deserted, 1
discharged, died, or transfered, 1
joined from Co. A, 16; Co. B, 6; Co. C, 13; Co. D, 38; total 73
Certain on hand June 1, 1865, 88

Unassigned recruits: listed, 112
10 mustered in July, 1863
1 mustered in October, 1863
101 mustered in in 1864
unknown, probably deserted, 11
no further record found, 49
forwarded to depot, no further record found, 40
mustered out: 6 at Fort Leavenworth, 2 in Ohio, total, 8
died: 2, 1 at St. Louis, 1 at Fort Leavenworth
discharged, 2 in Ohio

Discharges, other than for disability or sickness (surgeon's certificate):
In 1865: 33. Largest numbers: Co. F, 11; Co. I, 9; Co. E, 6
In 1866: January–April, 27. 6 in Co. I; 5 in Co. E; 4 in Co. F.
May 1866: 45. 30 in Co. F, at Omaha.
June 1866: 42. 17 in Co. F, 12 in Co. E, 7 in Co. G.
July 14, 1866, general muster-out at Fort Leavenworth: 327. Largest numbers: Co. G, 69; Cos. I and K, 54

July 21, 1866, at Fort Laramie: 84. Largest number, Co. L, 20

July 26, 1866, at Fort Laramie: 2, Co. F.

August-September, 1866: 2, 1 in Co. E, 1 in Co. L.

Total discharged January–September 1866: 529.

Deaths, from killed in action, died of wounds, died of illness: total, 76

1861: total, 1

December 20, 1861, Latham, Ohio, while on leave, Co. D

1862: total, 11

January 7, 1862, Camp Crittendon, Ohio, Co. A

May 11, 1862, Fort Kearny, Co. B

May 13, 1862, Fort Kearny, Co. D

May 19, 1862, Fort Kearny, Co. B

May 23, 1862, Fort Kearny, Co. B

May 27, 1862, Fort Kearny, Co. A

September 20, 1862, Fort Halleck, Co. A

October 3, 1862, Fort Halleck, Co. A

November 24, 1862, South Pass, Co. B, known killed in action

December 10, 1862, Three Crossings, Co. B

December 31, 1862, Fort Halleck, Co. A

1863: total, 11

February 28, 1863, place not listed, Co. C, frozen

February 28, 1863, place not listed, Co. C, frozen

March 31, 1863, Sweetwater Bridge, Co. B

April 6, 1863, Sweetwater Bridge, Co. B, wounded on April 3, 1863

August 7, 1863, Camp Dennison, Ohio

August 21, 1863, in pursuit of Quantrill, sunstroke, Co. E

September 16, 1863, Platte Bridge, Co. D

November 7, 1863, Sweetwater Bridge, Co. D
November 28, 1863, Camp Dennison, Ohio, Co. G
December 13, 1863, Fort Laramie, Co. E
December 27, 1863, Fort Laramie, Co. A

1864: total, 14

March 4, 1864, Fort Laramie, Co. G
May 12, 1864, South Pass, Co. E
May 12, 1864, South Pass, Co. E
May 17, 1864, died of wounds at Fort Laramie, Co. E
June 16, 1864, Fort Halleck, Co. F
July 20, 1864, North Platte, killed in action, Co. E
September 15, 1864, South Pass, Co. A
October 5, 1864, Fort Halleck, Co. D
October 13, 1864, Camp Collins, Co. B
October 19, 1864, La Bonte, Co. E
October 29, 1864, Fort Kearny, Co. E
November 7, 1864, Deer Creek, Co. G
December 2, 1864, Fort Laramie, Co. E
December 20, 1864, Fort Laramie, Co. L

1865: total, 29

February 8, 1865, Fort Collins, Co. F
February 8, 1865, Rush Creek, Co. C, killed in action
February 13, 1865, Laprelle Creek, Co. G, killed in action
February 17, 1865, Bear Creek, frozen, Co. K
February 24, 1865, Fort Laramie, wounded at Mud Springs, Co. B
March 2, 1865, Fort Halleck, Co. K
March 8, 1865, Poison Creek, Co. G
March 19, 1865, no location, Co. H
March 20, 1865, Cincinnati, Ohio, Co. G
March 23, 1865, Fort Laramie, Co. A
March 28, 1865, Fort Marshall, Co. E

April 21, 1865, Laprelle, Co. E
May 19, 1865, Fort Laramie, Co. H
May 28, 1865, Elkhorn, Co. E, killed in action
June 3, 1865, Deer Creek, Co. G, killed in action
June 4, 1865, Fort Laramie, Co. E
June 8, 1865, Sage Creek, Co. K, killed in action
June 8, 1865, Sage Creek, Co. K, killed in action
June 22, 1865, Sweetwater Bridge, Co. E, killed in action
July 26, 1865, Platte Bridge, Co. G
July 26, 1865, (Fort Caspar) Platte Bridge, Co. I, killed
July 27, 1865, Fort Laramie, Co. F
July 22, 1865, Pole Creek, Co. H
July 2, 1865, Denver, Co. L
September 14, 1865, Fort Laramie, Co. G
September 27, 1865, Fort Laramie, Co. L, killed in action
October 27, 1865, Fort Laramie, Co. G
November 20, 1865, Fort Laramie, Co. K

1866: total, 10

January 7, 1866, Fort Mitchell, Co. H
January 10, 1866, Fort Marshall, Co. L
January 14, 1866, La Bonte, Co. G
January 25, 1866, Fort Casper (Platte Bridge), Co. I
February 20, 1866, Fort Laramie, Co. E
March 22, 1866, Deer Creek, Co. I
March 24, 1866, Fort Laramie, Co. K
April 27, 1866, Fort Laramie, Co. E
May 31, 1866, Mud Springs, Co. H
June 2, 1866, Fort Laramie, Co. K

Disappeared or Deserted

The *Official Roster* does not distinguish between those who simply disappeared, such as missing in action, or those who deserted. A number did in fact desert, as various diaries assert, but the exact number may never be known. These numbers of "Disappeared or Deserted" are those who are listed in the *Official Roster* as never having been mustered out.

Total disappeared or deserted after Companies A, B, C, and D arrived at Fort Laramie: 53, or 13.8 percent.
From Companies E, F, G, and H: 111, or 19.8 percent.
From Companies I and K: 7, or 3.7 percent.
From Company L: 1, or 1.11 percent.

About 20 percent of those who enlisted in 1863 and early 1864 are not accounted for. Of the whole, 14 percent are not accounted for. Companies I and K, largely made up of "Galvanized Yankees," had the fewest who disappeared or deserted, except for Company L, composed largely of transfers from other regiments.

Bibliographic Notes

In addition to the *War of the Rebellion: A Compilation of the Official Records of the Union and Confederate Armies*, cited as *O.R.* [*Official Records*] in the text, volume XI of the *Official Roster of the Soldiers of the State of Ohio in the War of the Rebellion, 1861–1866,* proved most useful. Richard N. Ellis conveniently provided "General Pope's Report on the West, 1866," which fell outside the scope of the *Official Records.*

The *William Oliver Collins Family Papers, 1862–1865,* located in the Denver Public Library's Western History Collection, contributed a great deal of value. The *Papers* included some items from 1861 as well as some after 1865. These are the papers of Lieutenant Colonel William O. Collins, who commanded the battalion of Ohio cavalry that in 1863 expanded to become the 11th Ohio Volunteer Cavalry regiment. The papers include manuscript letters of his son, Caspar Collins, who journeyed west with his father and the battalion as a civilian in 1862, then enlisted as a second lieutenant in 1863. Included also are letters of Colonel Collins's wife and a few other individuals connected with his military service. Agnes Wright Spring used these papers as a basis for her biography of Caspar Collins, as well as an article, "An Army Wife Comes West." There she reprinted letters of Catherine, but also added material in the introduction and footnotes not otherwise easily available. Some of Spring's notes are in the Collins papers as well. Alex Service's

The Life and Letters of Caspar W. Collins printed Caspar's letters from the originals in the *Collins Family Papers*, and also provided prints of some letters to demonstrate how Caspar interspersed drawings in them.

Ben Arnold's *Rekindling Camp Fires* is an edition of his diary as a private in Company E, 11th Ohio. His real name was Benjamin J. Connor. As Connor, he deserted from the 39th Ohio Infantry in 1862, then as Benjamin Munroe (Ohio records spelled it Monroe) he enlisted in the 11th Ohio in July 1863 and deserted from it nearly a year later. He used the alias Ben Arnold the rest of his life. He never returned to Ohio. Ed Lemmon, *Boss Cowman*, knew Arnold in later years in the West, and draws quite a fanciful picture of him.

The letters of Hervey Johnson, Company G, 11th Ohio, are reprinted in *Tending the Talking Wire*, edited by William E. Unrau. Johnson enlisted in July 1863, made corporal a year later, and was mustered out with his company in 1866. He hated military discipline and disliked officers. Lewis B. Hull's "Soldering on the High Plains" is an edition of his diary as a member of Company K, 11th Ohio, from February 1864 to July 1866. A veteran of the 60th Ohio Infantry, he quickly made sergeant. Along with Johnson, Colonel Collins, and Caspar, he came from Highland County, Ohio.

When Dee Brown wrote *The Galvanized Yankees,* he included not just the six regiments enlisted from among Confederate prisoners of war in Union prison camps, but also those found in the 11th Ohio. Ohio records failed to identify them. Most used names other than their own.

The *Life of George Bent: Written from his Letters* that George E. Hyde collected, and was subsequently edited by Savoie Lottinville (longtime editor of the University of Oklahoma Press), is in fact Bent's autobiography. George Bent was a son of trader William Bent and his Cheyenne wife. George served briefly in the Confederate army, then after his capture and parole joined his mother's people and fought against white troops in the West, including both Colonel Collins and Lieutenant Collins, as well as others of the 11th Ohio.

Henry E. Palmer ("History of the Powder River Expedition of 1865") was a captain in the 11th Kansas Cavalry, served as a staff officer at department headquarters, became acquainted with the 11th Ohio in 1864, and then served with them and others in the Powder River Expedition. Portions of Palmer's diary is quoted in Rogers, *Soldiers of the Overland.* Captain George M. Walker, "Eleventh Kansas Cavalry, 1865," wrote of his experience with that unit, especially concerning the fight at Platte Bridge where young Lieutenant Caspar Collins was killed while leading a patrol of the 11th Kansas.

Portions of Sergeant Isaac B. Pennick's diary is reproduced in volume I of Hebard and Brininstool's *The Bozeman Trail.* Pennick served with the 11th Kansas and was at the battle of Platte Bridge. Bits of Lieutenant William Y. Drew's diary, 11th Kansas, appears in the same volume. Captain Benjamin F. Rockafellow's diary, "6th Michigan," is quoted in Hafen and Hafen's *Powder River Campaigns.*

Eugene F. Ware wrote *The Indian War of 1864*, first published in 1911. A veteran of both Wilson's Creek and Pea Ridge (with the 1st Iowa Infantry, next the 4th Iowa Cavalry), he served with Company F, 7th Iowa Cavalry, on the Oregon road, where he met up with the 11th Ohio. He rose through the ranks to captain. Historian Clyde C. Walton annotated later editions of Ware's volume, adding a good deal of information. John J. Pattison ("With the U. S. Army Along the Oregon Trail") another member of the 7th Iowa, Company B, kept a rather sketchy, but often useful, diary.

Charles H. Springer (*Soldiering in Sioux Country*) left his diary, edited by Benjamin Franklin Cooling III. Springer, a deserter from the 1st U.S. Cavalry and a veteran of Missouri militia cavalry, enlisted in Company B, 12th Missouri Cavalry, and soon became a lieutenant. He served in the Powder River Campaign with Colonel Nelson F. Cole's column and later at Fort Laramie with elements of the 11th Ohio.

John D. McDermott's *Frontier Crossroads* provided a great deal of original research into valuable primary material. McDermott at one time was chief historian of the Fort Laramie National Historic Site and gathered considerable material from several record groups in the National Archives, as well as from Colorado State University and other sources, providing Fort Laramie's library with many useful files.

The letters of James H. Kidd, *One of Custer's Wolverines*, were edited by Eric J. Wittenberg. After a distinguished career fighting in the East, even participating in the Grand Review in Washington after the end of hostilities there, Colonel Kidd's 6th Michigan went west to join briefly in the Powder River Expedition and made contact with portions of the 11th Ohio.

William Smedley ventured *Across the Plains* in 1862, not really an emigrant so much as an adventurer. He encountered the 11th Ohio on the Oregon road that year.

Bibliography

Alter, J. Cecil. *Jim Bridger*. Norman: University of Oklahoma Press, 1962.

Arnold, Ben. *Rekindling Camp Fires: The exploits of Ben Arnold (Connor)*. Lewis F. Crawford, ed. Bismarck, N.D.: Capital Book Company, 1926.

Ayres, Elsie Johnson. *The Hills of Highland*. Springfield, Ohio: H. K. Skinner and Son, 1971.

Bain, David Howard. *Empire Express: Building the First Transcontinental Railroad*. New York: Viking Penguin, 1999.

Basler, Roy P., ed. *The Collected Works of Abraham Lincoln*. 8 vols. New Brunswick: Rutgers University Press, 1953–55.

Becher, Ronald. *Massacre Along the Medicine Road: A Social History of the Indian War of 1864 in Nebraska Territory.* Caldwell, Idaho: Caxton Press, 1999.

Biographical Dictionary of the Union: Northern Leaders of the Civil War. John T. Hubbell and James W. Geary, eds., Westport, Conn.: Greenwood Press, 1995.

Brown, Dee. *Bury My Heart at Wounded Knee: An Indian History of the American West.* New York: Holt, Rinehart & Winston, 1970.

———. *The Galvanized Yankees.* Lincoln: University of Nebraska Press, 1986.

———. *Wondrous Times on the Frontier.* New York: HarperPerennial, 1992.

Colton, Ray C. *The Civil War in the Western Territories: Arizona, Colorado, New Mexico, and Utah.* Norman: The University of Oklahoma Press, 1959.

Cozzens, Peter. *General John Pope: A Life for the Nation.* Urbana: University of Illinois Press, 2000.

Crawford, Lewis F., ed. *Rekindling Camp Fires: The Exploits of Ben Arnold (Connor).* Bismarck, N.D.: Capital Book Company, 1926.

Czaplewski, Russ. *Captive of the Cheyenne: The Story of Nancy Jane Morton and the Plum Creek Massacre.* Kearney, Nebraska: The Dawson County Historical Society, 1993.

Edwards, William B. *Civil War Guns: The Complete Story of Federal and Confederate Small Arms, Design, Manufacture, Identification, Procurement, Issue, Employment, Effectiveness, and Postwar Disposal.* Harrisburg, Penn.: The Stackpole Company, 1962.

Ellenbecker, John G. *Tragedy at the Little Blue: The Oak Grove Massacre and the Captivity of Lucinda Eubank and Laura Roper.* Revised 2nd editon, Niwot, Colo.: Prairie Lark Publications, 1993.

Ellis, Richard N. "Civilians, The Army and the Indian Problem on the Northern Plains, 1862–1866." *North Dakota History* 37, no. 1 (Winter 1970).

———. "General Pope's Report on the West, 1866." *The Kansas Historical Quarterly* 35, no. 4 (Winter 1969).

Fort Laramie National Historic Site, Library, photocopied files from National Archives Record Groups 94 and 98, in folders MCOR (Military Correspondence), MREP (Military Reports). MMP (Military Personnel), MREC (Military Regiments and Companies), MDIA (Military Diaries), and one roll of microfilm from the Ohio Historical Society (manuscript muster rolls of the 11th Ohio), and copies of 11th Ohio letter books (originals in the Colorado State University archives).

Fort Sedgwick Historical Society. "Fort Sedgwick, Colorado Territory," FSH Society Documentation Project, 1996. Brochure.

Franzwa, Gregory M. *Maps of the Oregon Trail.* St. Louis: The Patrice Press, 1990.

Grinnell, George Bird. *The Fighting Cheyennes.* Norman: University of Oklahoma Press, 1956.

Guenther, Todd. "Pioneers Extraordinaire: A Most Unusual Wagon Train." *Overland Journal* 18, no. 4 (Winter 2000/2001).

Hafen, LeRoy R. *The Overland Mail, 1849–1869.* Cleveland, Ohio: The Arthur H. Clark Company, 1926.

———, and Ann W. Hafen. *Powder River Campaigns and Sawyers Expedition of 1865.* Glendale, Calif.: The Arthur H. Clark Company, 1961.

———, and Francis Marion Young. *Fort Laramie and the Pageant of the West, 1834–1890.* Lincoln: University of Nebraska Press, 1984.

Hampton, H. D. "The Powder River Expedition of 1865." *Montana: The Magazine of Western History* 14, no. 4 (October 1964).

Hebard, Grace Raymond, and E. A. Brininstool. *The Bozeman Trail: Historical Accounts of the Blazing of the Overland Routes into the Northwest, and the Fights with Red Cloud's Warriors.* 2 vols., Cleveland, Ohio: The Arthur H. Clark Company, 1922.

Hubbell, James T., and James S. Geary, eds. *Biographical Dictionary of the Union: Northern Leaders of the Civil War.* Westport, Conn.: Greenwood Press, 1995.

Hull, Lewis Byram. "Soldiering on the High Plains: The Diary of Lewis Byram Hull, 1864–1866." Myra E. Hull, ed., *Kansas Historical Quarterly* 7, no. 1 (February 1938).

Hyde, George E. *Life of George Bent: Written from his Letters*. Savoie Lottinville, ed. Norman: University of Oklahoma Press, 1968.

Jackson, W. Turrentine. *Wagon Roads West: A Study of Federal Road Surveys and Construction in the Trans-Mississippi West, 1846–1869*. Lincoln: University of Nebraska Press, 1979.

Johnson, Dorothy M. *The Bloody Bozeman: The Perilous Trail to Montana's Gold*. Missoula, Mont.: Mountain Press Publishing Company, 1983.

Jones, Robert H. "Whitelaw Reid," in Kenneth Wheeler, ed., *For the Union: Ohio Leaders in the Civil War*. Columbus: Ohio State University Press, 1968.

———. *The Civil War in the Northwest: Nebraska, Wisconsin, Iowa, Minnesota, and the Dakotas*. Norman: University of Oklahoma Press, 1960.

Josephy, Alvin M. Jr. *The Civil War in the American West*. New York: Alfred A. Knopf, 1991.

Kidd, James H. *One of Custer's Wolverines: The Civil War Letters of Brevet Brigadier General James H. Kidd, 6th Michigan Cavalry*. Eric J. Wittenberg, ed. Kent, Ohio: Kent State University Press, 2000.

Klement, Frank L. "Clement L. Vallandigham," in Kenneth W. Wheeler, ed., *For the Union: Ohio Leaders in the Civil War*. Columbus: Ohio State University Press, 1968.

Larsen, Robert W. "Red Cloud, Part I: The Warrior Years." *Montana: The Magazine of Western History* 47, no. 1 (Spring 1977).

Lass, William E. *From Missouri to the Great Salt Lake: An Account of Overland Freighting*. Nebraska State Historical Society, *Publications*, vol. 26, 1972.

Lemmon, Ed. *Boss Cowman: The Recollections of Ed Lemmon, 1857–1946*. Nellie Snyder Yost, ed. Lincoln: University of Nebraska Press, 1969.

Long, E. B. *The Saints and the Union: Utah Territory during the Civil War*. Urbana: The University of Illinois Press, 1981.

Lowe, James A. *The Bridger Trail: a viable alternative route to the gold fields of Montana Territory in 1864*. Spokane, Wash.: The Arthur H. Clark Company, 1999.

Madsen, Brigham D. *Glory Hunter: A Biography of Patrick Edward Connor*. Salt Lake City: University of Utah Press, 1990.

Mattes, Merrill J. *The Great Platte River Road: The Covered Wagon Mainline via Fort Kearny to Fort Laramie*. Lincoln: University of Nebraska Press, 1979.

McDermott, John D. *Frontier Crossroads: The History of Fort Caspar and the Upper Platte Crossing*. Casper, Wyo.: The City of Casper, 1997.

Merrill, Julius. *Bound for Idaho: The 1864 Trail Journal of Julius Merrill*. Irving R. Merrill, ed. Moscow, Idaho: The University of Idaho Press, 1988.

Mokler, Alfred James. *Fort Caspar (Platte Bridge Station)*. Casper, Wyo.: The Prairie Publishing Company, 1939.

Nadeau, Remi. *Fort Laramie and the Sioux*. Englewood Cliffs, N.J.: Prentice-Hall, Inc., 1967.

National Archives and Records Administration. Record Groups 94 and 98: 11th Ohio Volunteer Cavalry. Orders, General and Special, Company Order Books, Letters Sent, etc., dates vary, 1861–66. [In files at the Fort Laramie National Historic Site Library.]

Nichols, Jeannette P. "John Sherman," in Kenneth W. Wheeler, ed., *For the Union: Ohio Leaders in the Civil War*. Columbus: Ohio State University Press, 1968.

Official Roster of the Soldiers of the State of Ohio in the War of the Rebellion, 1861–1866. Published by the Authority of the General Assembly, Akron, Ohio: Werner Ptg. & Litho. Co., 1891. Vol. XI.

Ohio Historical Society. Microfilm of manuscript muster rolls of the 11th Ohio Volunteer Infantry. [In Fort Laramie National Historic Site Library. Original cannot be found in the Ohio Historical Society Archives at Columbus, Ohio.]

Olson, James C. *Red Cloud and the Sioux Problem*. Lincoln: University of Nebraska Press, 1965.

Palmer, Henry E. "History of the Powder River Expedition of 1865." *Transactions and Reports of the Nebraska State Historical Society*. Vol. 2, 1887.

Pattison, John J. "With the U. S. Army Along the Oregon Trail, 1863–66." *Nebraska History Magazine* 15 (1934).

Perkins, J. R. *Trails, Rails, and War: The Life of General G. M. Dodge*. Indianapolis, Indiana: The Bobbs-Merrill Company, 1929.

Ramage, James A. *Rebel Raider: The Life of General John Hunt Morgan*. Lexington, Ky.: The University Press of Kentucky, 1986.

Reid, Whitelaw. *Ohio in the War: Her Statesmen, her Generals, and her Soldiers*. 2 vols., Cincinnati: Moore, Wilstach, & Baldwin, Publishers, 1868.

Robrock, David B. "The Eleventh Ohio Volunteer Cavalry on the Central Plains, 1862–1866." *Arizona and the West* 25, no. 1 (Spring 1983).

Rogers, Fred B. *Soldiers of the Overland: Being Some Account of the Services of General Patrick Edward Connor and his Volunteers in the Old West*. San Francisco, Calif.: The Grabhorn Press, 1938.

Service, Alex. *The Life and Letters of Caspar W. Collins*. Casper, Wyo.: The City of Casper, 2000.

Shannon, Fred A. *The Organization and Administration of the Union Army, 1861–1865*. 2 vols., Gloucester, Mass.: Peter Smith, 1965.

Smedley, William. *Across the Plains: An 1862 Journey from Omaha to Oregon*. Boulder, Colo.: Johnson Books, 1994.

Spring, Agnes Wright, ed. "An Army Wife Comes West." *The Colorado Magazine* 31, no. 4 (October 1954).

———. *Caspar Collins*. Lincoln: University of Nebraska Press, 1969.

———. "Old Letterbook Discloses Economic History of Fort Laramie, 1858–1871." *Annals of Wyoming* 13, no. 4 (October 1941).

Springer, Charles H. *Soldering in Sioux Country: 1865*. Benjamin Franklin Cooling III, ed. San Diego, Calif.: Frontier Heritage Press, 1971.

Tate, Michael L. "From Cooperation to Conflict: Sioux Relations with the Overland Emigrants, 1845–1865." *Overland Journal* 18, no. 4 (Winter 2000/2001).

Unrau, William E., ed. *Tending the Talking Wire: A Buck Soldier's View of Indian Country, 1863–1866.* Salt Lake City: University of Utah Press, 1979.

Unruh, John D. Jr. *The Plains Across: Overland Emigrants and the Trans-Mississippi West.* Urbana: University of Illinois Press, 1993.

Utley, Robert M. *Frontiersmen in Blue: The United States Army and the Indian, 1848–1865.* New York: The Macmillian Company, 1967.

Varley, James F. *Brigham and the Brigadier: General Patrick Connor and His California Volunteers in Utah and Along the Overland Trail.* Tucson, Ariz.: Westernlore Press, 1989.

Vaughn, J. W. *The Battle of Platte Bridge.* Norman: University of Oklahoma Press, 1963.

Walker, George M. "Eleventh Kansas Cavalry, 1865, and Battle of Platte Bridge." *Collections of the Kansas State Historical Society, 1915–1918*, vol. 14.

War of the Rebellion: A Compilation of the Official Records of the Union and Confederate Armies. 130 vols., Washington, D.C.: Government Printing Office, 1880–1901.

Ware, Eugene F. *The Indian War of 1864.* Lincoln: The University of Nebraska Press, 1994.

West, Elliot. *The Contested Plains: Indians, Goldseekers, and the Rush to Colorado.* Lawrence: The University Press of Kansas, 1998.

Westbrook, Robert B., and P. Richard Metcalf. "William Selby Harney," in Howard L. Lamar, ed., *The Reader's Encyclopedia of the American West.* New York: Harper and Row, 1977.

Western Emigrant Trails: 1820–1870. [Map] Omaha, Nebraska: Western Emigrant Trails Research Center, 1999.

Wheeler, Kenneth W., ed., *For the Union: Ohio Leaders in the Civil War.* Columbus: Ohio State University Press, 1968.

White, David, comp. *News of the Plains and Rockies, 1803–1865*, vol. 4. Spokane, Wash.: The Arthur H. Clark Company, 1988.

William Oliver Collins Family Papers, 1862–1865. Western History Collection, Denver Public Library, Denver, Colorado.

Index

Guarding the Overland Trails:
The Eleventh Ohio Cavalry in the Civil War
by Robert Huhn Jones
has been produced in an edition of 750 copies.

The typeface used is Caslon.
Design by Ariane C. Smith.
Printing by Sheridan Books, Inc.,
of Ann Arbor, Michigan.